PUBLIC ATTITUDES TO SENTENCING

CAMBRIDGE STUDIES IN CRIMINOLOGY

XXII. *Crime in England and Wales,* F. H. McClintock and N. H. Avison
XXIII. *Delinquency in Girls,* J. Cowie, V. Cowie and E. Slater
XXIV. *The Police: A Study in Manpower,* J. Martin and Gail Wilson
XXV. *Present Conduct and Future Delinquency,* D. J. West
XXVI. *Crime, Law and the Scholars,* G. O. Mueller
XXVIII. *The Social Consequences of Conviction,* J. Martin and D. Webster
XXIX. *Suspended Sentence,* M. Ancel
XXX. *Local Prisons: The Crisis in the English Penal System,* R. F. Sparks
XXXI. *Sentencing the Motoring Offender,* R. Hood
XXXII. *Criminals Coming of Age,* A. E. Bottoms and F. H. McClintock
XXXIII. *Drivers After Sentence,* T. C. Willett
XXXIV. *Who Becomes Delinquent?* D. J. West and D.P. Farrington
XXXVII. *The Social Organization of Juvenile Justice,* Aaron Cicourel
XXXVIII. *Alibi,* R. N. Gooderson
XXXIX. *Juvenile Justice?* A. Morris and M. McIsaac
XLII. *Community Service Orders,* Warren Young
XLIV. *The Phantom Capitalists: The Organization and Control of Long-Term Fraud,* Michael Levi
XLVI. *Crime, Justice and Underdevelopment,* Colin Sumner (ed.)
XLVII. *Dangerousness and Criminal Justice,* Jean Floud and Warren Young
XLVIII. *The Home Office 1848–1914: From Clerks to Bureaucrats,* Jill Pellew
XLIX. *Burglary in a Dwelling,* Mike Maguire and Trevor Bennett
LI. *Consumerist Criminology,* Leslie T. Wilkins
LIII. *Victims in the Criminal Justice System,* Joanna Shapland, Jon Willmore and Peter Duff
LIV. *A Guide to United Nations Criminal Policy* Manuel López-Rey
LV. *Transcarceration: Essays in the Sociology of Social Control,* John Lowman, Robert J. Menzies and T. S. Palys (eds)
LVI. *The Effects of Crime and the Work of Victims Support Schemes* Mike Maguire and Claire Corbett
LVII. *Sexual Crimes and Confrontations,* D. J. West
LVIII. *Problems of Long-Term Imprisonment,* Anthony E. Bottoms and Roy Light (eds)
LIX. *Public Attitudes to Sentencing,* Nigel Walker and Mike Hough (eds)

Public Attitudes to Sentencing

Surveys from Five Countries

Edited by
Nigel Walker
and
Mike Hough

Series Editor: A. E. Bottoms

Gower
Aldershot · Brookfield USA · Hong Kong · Singapore · Sydney

Published by
Gower Publishing Company Limited
Gower House
Croft Road
Aldershot
Hants GU11 3HR
England

Gower Publishing Company
Old Post Road
Brookfield
Vermont 05036
USA

British Library Cataloguing in Publication Data

Public attitudes to sentencing:
surveys from five countries.—(Cambridge
studies in criminology).
1. Sentences (Criminal procedures)—
Public opinion
I. Walker, Nigel, 1917– II. Hough, Mike
III. Series
342.5′772 K5121

Library of Congress Cataloguing-in-Publication Data

Public attitudes to sentencing:
surveys from five countries/edited by Nigel Walker and Mike Hough
p. cm. — (Cambridge studies in criminology; 59)
Includes bibliographies and index
1. Sentences (Criminal procedure)—Public opinion —Cross-cultural studies. 2. Punishment—Public opinion—Cross-cultural studies.
3. Public opinion—Cross-cultural studies. I. Walker, Nigel.
II. Hough, J. M. III. Series.
HV8708.P8 1988 364.6—dc19 87-33257 CIP

ISBN 0566 05545 7

Typeset in Great Britain by
Guildford Graphics Limited, Petworth, West Sussex.
Printed and bound in Great Britain by
Biddles Limited, Guildford and King's Lynn

Contents

Acknowledgements

We acknowledge with gratitude a contribution from an emeritus fellowship award from the Leverhulme Trust to Nigel Walker towards the cost of compiling this collection.

Nigel Walker
Mike Hough

November 1987

Notes on contributors

Yves Brillon received his BA degree in sociology at the University of Geneva, his Master's degree in criminology at the University of Lausanne, and his Doctorate in criminology at the University of Montreal. He has since been in charge of Group Research on Attitudes Towards Crime (GRAC) at the Centre Internationale de Criminologie Comparée of the Université de Montreal. He has been awarded the Beccaria Award of the Quebec Society of Criminology, and the Denis Carroll Award of the International Society of Criminology.

Mark Collins is Lecturer in the Department of Mathematics, Australian Defence Force Academy, in Canberra. His interests lie particularly in the statistical theories of permutation tests and robust methods. Recent publications include 'A Permutation Test for Planar Regression' in the *Australian Journal of Statistics*, and 'Distribution-free Tests of Sub-hypotheses' in the *Bulletin of the Australian Mathematical Society*.

Jan van Dijk is Director of the Research and Documentation Centre, Ministry of Justice, the Netherlands, where he has worked since 1976. Dr van Dijk has been a member of several committees of experts of the European Committee on Crime Problems of the Council of Europe. He is presently a member of the Select Committee of experts on the Victim and Criminal and Social Policy. He is a member of the Editorial Board of the Dutch *Journal of Criminology* and the International Advisory Board of the *British Journal of Criminology*.

Anthony N. Doob is Professor of Criminology and Psychology and Director of the Centre for Criminology, University of Toronto. He was a member of the Canadian Sentencing Commission. He has collaborated with Julian V. Roberts in research on public attitudes to crime, the criminal justice system and sentencing since 1982. His other research areas include work on various aspects of the juvenile justice system and on providing easily accessible sentencing information to judges with the aid of micro-computers.

Stephen G. Gottfredson is Chairman of the Department of Criminal Justice at Temple University, Philadelphia. Previously the Executive Director of the Maryland Criminal Justice Co-ordinating Council and the Associate Director for Research at the Johns Hopkins University's Center for Metropolitan Planning and Research, he is now completing (with Don Gottfredson) a book entitled *Behavioural Prediction in Criminal Justice* to be published by Springer Verlag.

Mike Hough is a Principal Research Officer at the Home Office Research and Planning Unit. He was one of the research team responsible for the unit's programme of work on situational crime prevention in the 1970s, and has also published extensively on policing (police effectiveness in particular). Since 1981 he has been one of the key researchers on the *British Crime Survey*.

Helen Lewis joined the Home Office Research and Planning Unit as a Research Officer in 1985. She has carried out analysis of the *British Crime Survey* and has worked on a number of policing projects.

Catherine Marsh is a lecturer at the Cambridge Social and Political Sciences Committee Cambridge University, and a Fellow of Newnham College. She is an expert on survey methodology and has researched and published extensively on the topic. Her book, *The Survey Method,* was published in 1982.

David Moxon is a Senior Research Officer at the Home Office Research and Planning Unit, where he has worked since 1978. He has carried out research on police interrogation, fine enforcement and sentencing practice in particular, including juvenile courts. He is currently engaged in the first major empirical study of sentencing in the Crown Court. In 1985 he edited a collection of papers published under the title *Managing Criminal Justice* which had as its theme the interdependence of the criminal justice system.

Simon Orton is a director of the British Market Research Bureau Limited, where he has worked for 15 years. He has published and presented papers through the UK Market Research Society and the European Society for Opinion and Marketing Research, on social survey results and techniques.

Julian V. Roberts is Senior Criminologist, Department of Justice, Canada. He was a research analyst for the Canadian Sentencing

Commission. He has collaborated with Anthony Doob in research on public attitudes to crime, the criminal justice system and sentencing since 1982. His other research interests include work on selective memory and on public understanding and acceptance of various principles of criminal law.

Carl Steinmetz is a Senior Research Fellow at the Research and Documentation Centre, Ministry of Justice, the Netherlands, where he has worked since 1978. He has published extensively, covering, amongst other things, the Dutch crime surveys, analysis of crime risks and the evaluation of crime prevention strategies in Holland. He has also researched in the fields of psychometrics and absence from work through illness.

Ralph B. Taylor is Associate Professor of Criminal Justice at Temple University, Philadelphia. Previously the Director of the Criminal Justice Studies Program at the Johns Hopkins University's Center for Metropolitan Planning and Research, his interests are in the areas of community crime prevention and environmental criminology.

Julie Vennard is a Principal Research Officer at the Home Office Research and Planning Unit. She is responsible for research on criminal procedure and sentencing in relation to adults and young offenders and has published a number of reports and articles in this field.

John Walker is a criminologist with the Australian Institute of Criminology in Canberra. He is author of the annual prison census reports (*Australian Prisoners 1982–1987*) and, in 1986, co-ordinated and compiled the results of the first National Census of Community Based Corrections (*Australian Community Based Corrections 1985–86*). His analysis of the demographic characteristics of offenders and of sentencing patterns has led to significant contributions to the problem of forecasting prisoner numbers.

Nigel D. Walker is an Emeritus Professor of Criminology of Cambridge University, and a former Director of its Institute of Criminology. He is the author of four books on sentencing (and of books on psychiatry and the law, civil service morale and the explanation of misbehaviour). He was Chairman of the Home Secretary's Advisory Council on Probation, President of the British Society of Criminology, and a member of several committees concerned with aspects of sentencing.

Barbara D. Warner is a Doctoral Candidate in the Department of Sociology, SUNY — Albany, New York. Previously she was a Research Analyst with the United States Secret Service and with the New York Office of Mental Health. Her interests are in the sociology of deviance.

Paul Wilson is Assistant Director (Research and Statistics) at the Australian Institute of Criminology in Canberra. He is the author of over 20 books and has researched and written widely on Australian crime and criminal justice and other areas including aborigines, the mass media, migrants and immigration, public and private housing, youth and leisure issues, professions in Australia, political sociology and social issues generally.

Foreword

A. E. Bottoms

This book places firmly on the criminological agenda a subject which has been developing for some time, but which most criminologists have hitherto regarded as something of a side-issue: namely, the systematic study of public attitudes towards sentencing and punishment. The book's particular strength is that it considers this subject by bringing together empirical studies from five countries — the kind of exercise that criminologists are always advocating, but which they seldom actually attempt. The book does not, however, simply report empirical findings, but attempts to assess their meaning, and their relevance for policy; and in this connection, the editors' distinction between 'tolerance limits' and 'fine tuning' will be perceived as an important one.

It is a particular pleasure for me to be able to welcome the two editors as contributors to the *Cambridge Studies in Criminology*. Nigel Walker was my predecessor in the Wolfson Chair at Cambridge, and his contribution to British criminology, especially in penal studies, has been enormous. One of his most characteristic hallmarks has been his ability to see an old problem in a new light, and thus to make a distinctive and innovative contribution: that hallmark is seen once again in the present volume. Mike Hough has been, over the last decade, one of the more prolific and interesting of the researchers at the Home Office Research and Planning Unit, and his work on (especially) policing and on the British Crime Survey has won him many admirers. I am delighted that these two researchers have pooled their talents, together with their international collaborators, to produce the present volume, which greatly enriches the *Cambridge Studies*.

1 Introduction: developments in methods and perspectives

Nigel Walker and Mike Hough

This book collects together the results of some British, Dutch, Australian and North American studies dealing with public attitudes towards sentencing. Those which we have selected for inclusion are all recent; they all employ the sample survey method; and individually they are of interest either because of their findings or because of the special techniques which they employ.

Several factors have prompted us to bring the nine studies together as a book. Crime is far more visible politically than it was a decade or so ago, and political arguments about the response to crime are increasingly buttressed by appeals to public opinion. But opinion about punishment is so sketchily charted that it is often invoked to justify quite contradictory positions. This alone seems reason enough to collect together a selection of empirical studies.

At the same time, rather more specific developments within penological theory are lending salience to questions about public attitudes towards punishment. The sentencer who is trying — as most do — to strike a balance between 'individualization' — the selection of a sentence which will reform, deter or control the offender in question — and 'tariff' sentencing cannot altogether disregard public opinion. In theory the severity and proportionality of tariffs are determined by legislatures and judiciaries; but in practice both have an eye on the audience; and in this case, the audience is not the man in the court but the man in the street. Even some preachers of 'just deserts' regard the public as the arbiter of what is just; and any departure from what is deserved in the name of 'individualization' runs the risk of public criticism. Penological theory and debate have for several years now been in retreat from ideals of rehabilitation and special deterrence: the pendulum in swinging from individualized to tariff sentencing. Whether the principles embedded in sentencers' practice have changed much is questionable; but there are signs that at a political level, at any rate, greater importance is now being attached to the congruence of opinion and sentencing practice.

Finally, in the course of our own research it became clear that researchers in different countries were ploughing parallel furrows in isolation. Collecting outstanding examples of their work promised to deepen both knowledge of the subject and appreciation of its complexity. We have ordered the chapters of the book according to the dates of the surveys reported in them.

The development of survey research on attitudes to punishment

Interest in the reaction of the public to sentences or sentencing policy is not new, but the last few years have seen a considerable crop of studies. A little history will set this work in context. In 1961 the *Criminal Law Review* devoted a whole issue to articles about public opinion and criminal law. One of them reported the more interesting findings of two surveys; one by Gallup for the *News Chronicle,* the other by the British Broadcasting Corporation (which wanted to assess the effect of a recent programme on crime: Silvey, 1961). The issue is of historical importance not only because of the views expressed but also as evidence that by the end of the 1950s the importance of public opinion on crime and sentencing was beginning to be recognized by lawyers. It had of course been acknowledged long before that by politicians, but only in the context of the very narrow issues on which public attention had from time to time been focused: capital and corporal punishment. Indeed until both were abolished it was difficult to arouse public interest in any other aspect of sentencing policy. It was not until the suspension of the death penalty in 1965 that such matters as the state of the prisons, the merits of parole and the notion of suspending sentences became topics of wide discussion. Non-custodial measures were a non-subject.

The Gallup polls

Any history of public opinion and sentencing, however, must begin with the Gallup polls. Though several organizations are now active in the field, none, in Britain at least, has so regularly, so systematically and for so long sampled the views of the adult population, and it is worth examining Gallup's contribution in a little detail.

The interests of the Gallup organization in Britain were influenced by its contractual relationship with newspapers: first the *News Chronicle* and later the *Daily Telegraph.* The first Gallup polls were conducted in 1937; and in 1938 the introduction of the Criminal Justice Bill prompted the inclusion of questions on flogging (favoured by 50 per cent) and capital punishment (favoured by 55 per cent). This was the beginning of a long tradition. Except for the war years, when no questions were asked about penal matters,[1] most years' surveys included the occasional question about corporal and/or capital punishment.

Corporal punishment as a court-ordered punishment disappeared from the regular questions in the 1960s; the last question asked about it was put in 1967, and was about corporal punishment by teachers and parents. It was briefly revived in 1982, in a somewhat loaded form: 'What are your views about corporal punishment, that is, birching and flogging? Should we continue to do without the cat, or should we bring it back? [60 per cent bring back] . . . And birching? [62 per cent] and caning [69 per cent]?' Questions about the death penalty, however, continued to be included whenever the subject became topical. From 1977 onwards, they became more elaborate, drawing distinctions between murders of different sorts (by terrorists, of police or prison staff). By the 1980s, percentages in favour of capital punishment usually ran in excess of 70 per cent — in contrast to the pre-war figure of 55 per cent. Gallup were the first to include questions about the aims of a capital sentence (in 1948): 45 per cent chose 'to punish', 43 per cent 'to stop others'.

Salience of crime as a social problem

In 1944 a Gallup survey included a question which was to be repeated — though with important changes in wording — at intervals over the next 40 years, and so provides an interesting index of public interest in criminal justice.[2]

This asked 'which question should be tackled the very first by the government . . .'; later it became 'the most important problem for the government'; and later still 'the most urgent problem for you and your family (or "the country")'. Problems which were named by at least 1 per cent were tabulated, the rest being relegated to 'Other problems'.

At first, 'housing' (39 per cent) topped the list, with 'employment' not far behind (29 per cent), and social security, cost of living and such problems a very long way behind. 'Law and order' either found no choosers or failed to reach the 1 per cent threshold. From 1973, however, 'law and order' occasionally appeared in the league table, with percentages of 1 or 2. When the question was elaborated to include 'and the next most urgent problem' (in 1976) law and order managed to collect 4 per cent of first or second choices, and the percentage fluctuated around this figure until in 1982 it began to rise, at times reaching 18 per cent. In October 1985 it even attained 27 per cent, which placed it second, although far behind 'unemployment' (the first or second choice of 87 per cent).

Law and order was chosen far more often in a series of questions first introduced in 1967, in which respondents were asked to select items from a checklist of 'very serious social problems'. Top of the 1967 list was 'drug-taking' (chosen by 85 per cent), with 'crimes of violence' second (69 per cent) and 'bad housing' third (61 per cent). The use in this question of a checklist contrasts with the series about 'most important problems', where respondents were free to select whatever problems occurred to them; and this probably explains why crime figures so much more in the responses. In common with the first series, however, this question has shown an increase in concern about law and order. By 1972 'crimes of violence' headed the list, and has remained there since, excepting April 1986, when it was temporarily displaced by 'drug-taking', the usual runner-up.

The substantive point to emerge from these questions is that concern about law and order has been on the increase. However, the salience which crime appears to have as a social problem is highly dependent on the form of question. If respondents are offered a list of issues or problems in which 'law and order' or 'crimes of violence' appear, very large percentages will choose them as the most serious; but if asked, without a ready-made list, to name 'the most important' or the 'most urgent' problem not more than one in four or five — and usually much fewer than that — will mention law and order.

Choice of sentence

Capital and corporal punishment apart, the first Gallup question to ask for views about methods for dealing with criminals was put in 1952. 'What method do you think is best for dealing with persons committing crimes of violence: longer term of imprisonment [chosen by 21 per cent], birching [21 per cent], flogging with shorter terms of imprisonment [31 per cent], flogging with longer terms of imprisonment [8 per cent], or some other way [23 per cent]'. In 1956 a question was put about 'the ways we deal with sex offenders' (the Wolfenden Committee was at work; and in the following year respondents were asked for their views on its proposals). In 1960 respondents were asked what should be 'the first concern of the courts in sentencing a criminal':[3] 44 per cent chose 'to punish him for what he has done to others', 25 per cent 'punish him to stop others following his example', and 28 per cent 'to do what they can to reclaim him as a good citizen'. In 1981, the respective figures — 37 per cent, 34 per cent and 20 per cent — show that deterrence had become more popular, at the expense of both retribution and rehabilitation. The 1981 questionnaire included an item about the general adequacy of sentences: 'in your opinion, do the courts give out sentences that are too short or too long to persons convicted of committing crimes?' 64 per cent chose 'too short', 4 per cent 'too long' and 12 per cent 'about right'.

Specialized research

It may be thought remarkable that newspaper reports of Gallup findings in the 1950s did not stimulate academic research workers to probe thoroughly into public beliefs and attitudes on the subject of crime and sentencing. But representative sampling — especially by interviews — is costly. We do not know whether government departments or trusts with funds for research turned down any applications for grants for this purpose. What is certain is that the only published research findings of the 1950s were based on samples which were small, local and drawn from very special groups: for instance Voelcker's interviews with the parents of juveniles who had appeared in court (Voelcker, 1960). Even the first survey commissioned by the Home Office was highly specialized, being concerned with the deterrent effects of teenage males' beliefs about detection and prosecution (Willcock and Stokes, 1968; but based on interviews conducted in the early 1960s). It was followed, however, by a survey of broader scope, commissioned at the request of the ill-fated Royal Commission on the Penal System (Durant *et al.*, 1972), but based on interviews conducted in 1966). Unfortunately the report of the survey was delayed until long after the dissolution of the Royal Commission, was not on sale to the public, and received no publicity until it was the subject of a very short article in the *British Journal of Criminology* by Banks *et al.* (1975). Yet many of its questions were of original and interesting design. It can fairly be said that it was the first survey of the adult public on the subject which did more than merely 'poll' its respondents. Like the Gallup questionnaires it invited respondents to state views and make choices; but it also tried to relate those answers not simply to their age, sex and other demographic variables but also to their experiences and beliefs.

Punitiveness

An aspect of attitudes to sentencing which has received attention from most researchers is 'punitiveness' — indeed this has provided the focus of some surveys. There are several layers of ambiguity to the question whether people are punitive — an ambiguity not usually resolved in the research.

The main layer of the ambiguity lies in the two meanings of 'punitive'.[4] Colloquially, it means 'severe' or at least 'deliberately inflicting hardship or inconvenience'. In this sense some interpreters of surveys have inferred that a majority of the surveyed public is not 'punitive' — that is, not in favour of severe sentencing. Too often the evidence adduced for this is from items about the aims of punishment. For 'punitive' has a narrower meaning for penologists: 'endorsing retributive aims'; and indeed less than half of respondents (usually around 40 per cent) choose retribution or just deserts as the main aim of sentencing. However, when the 'majority' who did *not* choose the retributive aim are examined, substantial percentages are found to have endorsed other aims which justify severity rather than leniency in sentencing. Thus in the Prison Reform Trust's survey, while only 42 per cent chose to 'punish the criminal' as the main aim of imprisonment, another 21 per cent chose to 'keep criminals apart from society' and 12 per cent chose to 'deter would-be criminals' (Shaw, 1982). All three choices are consistent with support for long periods of detention; and when totalled the percentages account for three out of four respondents. Much the same will be found when other questionnaires are examined closely. Yet a NACRO *Briefing* concluded that '. . . public opinion, surveyed with care, is less punitive than is often assumed (NACRO, 1986); and a former Director of the Howard League, in a letter in *The Times* of 4 January 1987 wrote 'It is a myth that the public demands tough punishment . . .; as several surveys have shown, a majority thinks that restorative sanctions . . . make more sense than retributive ones.' Whether people agree with sentencers' aims and whether they agree with the severity of sentences handed out are conceptually and empirically distinct.

Punitiveness and judgements about the adequacy of sentences

Several surveys have examined whether people feel that sentences are punitive enough, in the sense of being adequately severe. Questions pitched at a general level, far from revealing a lenient public, show a clear majority in favour of tougher sentences — both in Britain and elsewhere. Thus, as we have seen in the Gallup polls (Gallup, 1981) two-thirds of respondents felt that prison sentences were too short. Similar findings are to be found in the USA (e.g. Figgie, 1980), France, and Canada (see Chapters 5 and 6).

Several points should qualify these findings. In asking whether sentences are adequate, surveyors are rarely explicit about the criteria against which adequacy is to be judged. We do not know whether respondents understand questions such as Gallup's in terms of deterrence ('Are sentences tough enough *to keep crime in check?*) or in terms of commensurability ('Are sentences tough enough *to fit the crime?*'). Nevertheless, the distinction is an important one:

policy makers may want to attach rather different weight to views about the deterrent effectiveness of sentencing on the one hand, and about its equity or fairness on the other.

Second, though different respondents will probably think of different sorts of crime when they are asked whether sentences are tough enough, evidence from Canada suggests that most people answer with stereotypes of violent and dangerous criminals in mind (see Chapters 5 and 6). Third, the questions often focus — either explicitly or implicitly — on the adequacy of *prison* sentences, which constitute a minority of the total; respondents are not asked to consider whether the right balance is struck between custodial and non-custodial sentences.

Finally, responses to such questions probably depend on the accuracy of respondents' knowledge about crime and sentencing (see Chapters 6 and 11 in particular). For example, people who overestimate the leniency of courts are likely to find them too soft — and the small minority overestimating the severity of courts is likely to find them too tough.

Specificity

These points underscore the value of specificity in eliciting respondents' views on sentences. The Durant survey was probably the first to be specific about the nature of the offence when asking how the offender should be dealt with.[5] It studied the effect of describing the victim ('an old person or child'), of indicating that the offender had previous convictions, or that he had 'planned beforehand'. There is an important difference between a question which asks how 'burglary' should be dealt with and one which asks how a man with previous convictions should be dealt with for the planned burglary of an old person's home. The first sort of question gives the respondent a more or less blank canvas on which he paints his own private picture of burglary: it never seems to be followed by the question 'What sort of burglary were you thinking of?' The second sort of question paints the picture for the respondent. The picture may not correspond to his picture of burglary, so that there is some point in the other kind of question. But the more specific description more closely resembles what respondents are told in real life about burglary, in the stories which they read in newspapers. Newspapers do not simply report 'burglary'; they say that the home of an old lady has been burgled by someone experienced enough to make sure she had gone out, and that the burglar stole £237 worth of money and valuables.

Most of the surveys described in this book have employed specificity in framing questions about court sentences. Overall, specific questions have not shown so consistent a mismatch between opinion and sentencing practice as is implied by general questions asking whether sentences are tough enough or long enough. For most categories of crime — and especially property crime — there appears to be broad agreement between opinion and sentencing practice about the *category* of sentence which is appropriate for different types of offenders, whether in England and Wales (Chapter 7), the Netherlands (Chapter 4) and Australia (Chapter 8). Exceptions however would seem to be crimes of serious violence, such as rape and murder. For them many people want very severe sentences, including capital punishment when this option is offered.

Overall, there may be a fair match between opinion and practice about category of sentence; where prison sentences *are* advocated, however, respondents generally seem to favour longer sentences than are typically meted out. Furthermore, an issue which no survey seems to have tackled adequately concerns the nominal length of sentences and time actually served. As will be seen in Chapter 10, respondents in England show some awareness of remission, but less of parole. When they are assessing or advocating a sentence of six months, for example, or two years, or a life sentence, we simply do not know how many have an accurate idea of the time actually served — though it could well be a minority.

It is usually assumed that specificity in describing the offence cannot be achieved in sample surveys without sacrificing another important feature: examining an adequate variety of offences. But sub-samples can be presented with descriptions of, say, burglaries that differ in their details — as described in Chapter 10. This refinement has been carried even further by Rossi et al. (1985). Instead of using a *standard* set of vignettes with variations introduced systematically for a limited number of sub-samples, they showed each respondent a *unique* set of vignettes (randomly generated by computer), and used multivariate analysis to assess the effect of varying the details about offender and offence. Amongst the important payoffs is the possibility of measuring with considerable sensitivity the contribution of each variable to respondents' responses.

'Cynicism'

Specificity is important, then, if people's views are to be elicited about the appropriateness of sentences; but this does not entitle us to ignore the results of unspecific questions about sentencing policy. They may be measuring something which specific questions do not: a generalized satisfaction or — more often — dissatisfaction with what respondents vaguely believe to be official sentencing policy. Most discussions of this issue have assumed that those who are dissatisfied believe that sentences are uniformly too severe or too lenient. This ignores a third, and equally likely source of dissatisfaction — the belief that courts impose severe sentences when leniency is called for, and are too lenient when tough sentences are called for. For want of any other term of art Walker and Marsh called this 'cynicism', and measured it by comparing the severity of the sentences which their respondents thought right for the offences described in their newspaper cuttings with the sentences which they expected courts to award (see Chapter 3). It is arguable, however, that less specific descriptions of offences are a better basis for measuring cynicism about sentencing policy.

Information

Cynicism is likely to be a product of at least two factors (and probably several others which have not been identified). The more obvious is the line taken by the news media in discussions of sentencing policy (a theme taken up in Chapters 6 and 10). The less obvious one is the inaccuracy of popular beliefs about the severity or leniency of sentences. It is only recently, in the 1980s, that surveys have questioned respondents about this. Durant *et al.* tested respondents' knowledge of criminal procedure, for example by asking whether previous convictions were disclosed in courts; and about the extent of increases in the volume of crime; but not about the use of penalties. In 1981 Gallup, as we have seen, included a very general question as to whether courts' sentences were 'too short' or 'too long': a question which measured cynicism rather than knowledge. The *British Crime Survey* of 1984 asked respondents 'what proportion of people aged 21 or over who are convicted of burglary do you think get sent to prison?'; and a similar question was asked in the 1986 survey by Walker, Hough and Lewis (see Chapters 10 and 11). Not many of the public made good estimates. This is hardly surprising when one considers that the relevant figures are buried deep in the expensive *Criminal Statistics, England and Wales*. On this aspect of sentencing the public mind is a *tabula rasa* upon which the news media and penal reformers can draw almost any picture that suits them.

Information about individual cases

With one exception we know of no studies of the relationship between the extent of an individual's knowledge about sentencing decisions and his or her attitudes towards these sentences. The exception is the series of studies by Doob and Roberts which are reported in Chapter 6. These are concerned with a very special — but important — aspect of the subject: the effect of providing respondents with more information about sentencers' reasoning in individual cases than is usually to be found in the news media. The findings suggest that the more information respondents are given, the more likely they are to accept the sentence as appropriate. It follows that the more explicit judges and magistrates can be about the considerations in their minds the better. Unfortunately there are limitations. One is the selectivity with which the news media are apt to report what the sentencer says. Expressions of judicial disapproval seem more likely to be reported than remarks about blameless records. Equally important is the fact that some of the considerations which sentencers rightly take into account are properly treated by them as confidential: examples are psychiatric diagnoses and intimate domestic complications. In consequence the public's beliefs about sentencing policy are almost unavoidably based on incomplete reports about cases in which the sentences appear unusually severe or lenient.

Victims' and offenders' views

Victims of crime comprise an important sub-group of the general public. Some have argued that the courts should place greater emphasis on redressing the harm done to victims, and that sentences should thus attach special weight to their views; and in North America at least it is becoming increasingly common for courts to give victims an opportunity to state their preferences before sentence is passed. On the other hand, one of the purposes of justice is to stand between offenders and the capricious vengeance of their victims. A few studies have examined victims' attitudes to the sentencing of 'their' offender (e.g. Shapland, 1981; Maguire, 1982) and findings from the *British Crime Survey (BCS)* on victims are included in Chapter 7 of this book. Rather surprisingly, the message to emerge from these studies is that the first-hand experience of crime as a victim does not in general fuel a desire for heavy sentences. It should be remembered that victims are well-informed about most aspects of their crime, except — very often — the identity of the offender.

There is another special group which is rarely sampled: people who have received, or are likely to receive, the penalties in question. Few researchers have set out to question identified offenders about sentencing, odd though this may seem, and where they have, consideration has usually been given to the more 'professional' criminals (e.g. Maguire, 1982; Bennett and Wright, 1984). This means that the survey by Orton and Vennard described in Chapter 9 is doubly unusual, being concerned not with indictable offences, but with regulatory ones of a kind which most respondents will have contemplated, and many committed.

Sentencers' and legislators' beliefs

Sentencers' beliefs about public reactions to their sentences are equally important, but seldom studied systematically. An interesting example is the belief of English judges — expressed long before Durkheim — that the public's moral attitudes to crimes are improved by the knowledge that they are severely punished (see Walker, 1981, for a short history of the notion). In 1974 the Court of Appeal (Criminal Division) made it clear in the case of *Sargeant* that this was their view. Walker and Marsh devised an experimental test of this assumption, using a technique originally suggested by Argyle (see Argyle and Walker, 1964). Their findings are reported in Chapter 3, and throw considerable doubt on what they call 'the Sargeant effect'.

That sentencers and legislators should have an accurate feel for the tenor of public opinion is, of course, one of the main justifications of most of the survey work in this area. However only one study has set out to research this particular question, by Gottfredson, Warner and Taylor, reported in Chapter 2. They found quite widespread agreement about the nature of prison reform needed in Maryland, but 'pluralistic ignorance' of this convergence of views: policy makers misperceived public opinion as being punitive and hostile to reform. This chapter should be of interest to 'conflict' and 'consensus' theorists.

Factors underlying attitudes to sentencing

Although the Gallup surveys usually recorded variables such as sex, age, occupational group and — less often — voting preferences, breakdowns on these lines were not usually published in the Political Index, and can be studied only by access to the organization's printouts. Some of Durant et al.'s tables distinguished sex, age and — more rarely — socio-economic group or level of education. The Prison Reform Trust's 1982 survey, financed by the *Observer*, recorded age-group, sex, 'class' (i.e. IPA occupational group) and voting preferences. Some of the demographic correlates of attitudes to sentencing seem consistent between countries — age and length of education, for example, and to a lesser extent, gender — as can be seen from Chapters 4, 5, 8 and 11. At least in Canada (Chapter 5), Australia (Chapter 8) and England and Wales (Hough and Lewis, 1986) there is evidence that rural dwellers favour tougher sentences than others — except those who live in high-crime areas.

Demographic factors may identify those with distinctive attitudes towards sentencing, but only go a little way towards explaining the difference: other variables must also be examined. In the Netherlands, van Dijk and Steinmetz, whose surveys are reported in Chapter 4, found that preferences for repressive crime control policies were associated more closely with respondents' political ideologies than with demographic characteristics. Similarly, we present findings in Chapter 11 showing that the best single predictor of a scale of punitiveness was respondents' assessment of the need for discipline in other areas of life.

Pseudo-views

We wonder, however, whether the principles of attitude measurement — well-established by methodologists such as Oppenheim (1966) and Moser and Kalton (1971) — too often get forgotten in practice. Our point is not merely that a question may be drafted in loaded terms (for example. 'Can we afford to do without the cat?') or that respondents may be offered too limited a range of responses (for example, 'Agree/Disagree'). Equally, if not more, important is the possibility of eliciting a view from someone who does not really have one. Where people's attitudes are likely to be latent, to use the terminology of the survey literature, surveyors should be more ready to allow respondents to express their lack of opinion.

There are several strategies for doing this. Filter questions can be used, to ask respondents whether they have thought about, or have any interest in, a topic, before they are asked for their views on it. And the 'don't know' option can be made more accessible to respondents: some organizations train their interviewers to 'squeeze' respondents — not to offer 'don't know' as a response, and to accept it only as a last resort; and in any case, respondents can feel stigmatized by the implied ignorance behind a confession of 'don't know'. Given the limited amount of information available to most people about the sentencing process, there must be a presumption in favour of allowing respondents the option of respectable agnosticism on the topic, with wording couched in value-free terms such as 'not enough information to say'.[6]

Tolerance

Even when respondents express genuine disagreement with a view or a course of action, distinctions need to be made. The obvious one is between those who merely choose 'disagree' and those who choose 'strongly disagree'. It is not difficult to design questions on such matters as sentencing which will offer respondents such options. Clearly policy makers and sentencers should take note of percentages of respondents who consider such and such a sentence to be '*much* too tough' or '*much* too soft'. But what about those who merely rate it 'a *little* too tough (or soft)?' How critical are their feelings? Walker, Hough and Lewis experimented in their 1986 survey with an operational measure of 'tolerance' which seems to discriminate fairly well between respondents who are expressing mere 'armchair criticism' and those who feel strongly enough to want something drastic done about the sentence or the sentencer (see Chapter 10).

This leads to an important point. Both politicians and sentencers — at least in England and the USA — have by now acquiesced in at least one of the doctrines of penal reformers: that they must pay attention to public reactions to their sentencing policies, however vague or inaccurate may be the public's knowledge of what those policies are. There is a difference, however, between a policy of 'fine-tuning' sentences so as to accord precisely with the responses to survey questions given by (not very knowledgeable) respondents, and a policy of taking account of what the public will tolerate. The first allows no freedom for the exercise of professional judgement, based on a deeper knowledge and experience of the practical and ethical implications of sentencing decisions. The second does, since it merely warns politicians and sentencers not to overstep certain limits of public tolerance. Given the extent to which the public's views about the 'right' sentence for crimes of various kinds can be temporarily swayed by the news media, the 'tolerance' approach seems the most sensible.

Notes

1. A question was asked in 1942 about the Home Secretary's power to imprison without trial; but that was outside the scope of the criminal justice system.
2. At first it was used only once a year; but in the later 1970s nearly every monthly survey included it.
3. As we have seen, a question of this sort had been asked about capital punishment in 1948.
4. A second layer of ambiguity arises because punishment can mean both penalty and retribution. To impose punishment, in the sense of penalties, is tautologously the aim of sentencing; arguably, this encourages respondents to select 'punishment' from a menu of sentencing objectives regardless of their penal philosophy (or lack of philosophy). Walker, Hough and Lewis (Chapter 10) have tried to surmount this problem by wording the retributive option very simply, with no reference to punishment: 'Give what offender deserves'; nor were respondents forced to choose a single 'main aim' — a highly artificial exercise.
5. Willcock and Stokes' (1968) survey of male teenagers' attitudes to deterrents was less obviously specific.
6. The survey we describe in Chapters 10 and 11 provides some interesting examples of variations in 'don't knows'. A multiple question was included of the kind which measures authoritarianism and 'liberality'. Respondents were faced with

propositions such as 'A good employer should be strict with his employees', and offered as choices 'Agree strongly', 'Agree', 'Disagree', 'Disagree strongly', but also 'Neither agree nor disagree'. The interviewers recorded very small percentages as 'Don't knows': 0.8 per cent in the case of this proposition. When faced, however, with a statement that must have been quite unfamiliar to most respondents — 'Soldiers should refuse to obey orders that they feel are morally wrong' — as many as 5 per cent didn't know. More important, the percentages who chose 'Neither agree or disagree' were by no means negligible: 14 per cent for the 'soldier' statement and close on 14 per cent for the 'employer' statement. The only statement which elicited either agreement or disagreement from 95 per cent of respondents was on a subject about which most respondents must have thought: 'school children should be given plenty of discipline'. The inclusion of 'Neither agree nor disagree' demonstrated the danger of eliciting pseudo-views if an option of this kind is not explicitly offered.

References

Argyle, M. and Walker, N. (1964), 'Does the Law affect moral judgements?', *British Journal of Criminology*, 570–581.

Banks, C., Maloney, E. and Willcock, H. D. (1975), 'Public Attitudes to Crime and the Penal System', *British Journal of Criminology*, **15(3),** 228–240.

Bennett, T. and Wright, R. (1984), *Burglars on Burglary*, Aldershot: Gower.

Brillon, Y., Guerin, C.L. and Lamarche, M.C. (1982), *Les Attitudes du Public Canadien envers les Politiques Criminelles, Phase II*, Montréal: Centre International de Criminologie Comparée, Université de Montréal.

Durant, M. et al. (1972), *Crime, Criminals and the Law: a study of public attitudes and knowledge*, London: OPCS.

Figgie (1980), *The Figgie Report on Fear of Crime: America Afraid, Part I*, New York: Research and Forecasts Inc.

Gallup, G. (ed.) (1976), *The Gallup International Public Opinion Polls: Great Britain 1937–1975*, (2 vols), New York: Random House.

Gallup (1981), *Gallup Political Index, No. 252, August 1981*, London: Social Surveys (Gallup Poll) Ltd.

Gallup (1982), *Gallup Political Index, No. 260, April 1982*, London: Social Surveys (Gallup Poll) Ltd.

Hough, M. and Lewis, H (1986), 'Penal hawks and penal doves: attitudes to punishment in the British Crime Survey', *RPU Bulletin No. 21*, London: Home Office Research and Planning Unit.

Maguire, M. (1982), *Burglary in a Dwelling*, London: Heinemann.

Moser, C. A. and Kalton, G.(1971), *Survey Methods in Social Investigation*, London: Heinemann.

NACRO (1986), *Public Opinion and Sentencing*, (in the series of NACRO Briefing Papers), London: National Association for the Care and Resettlement of Offenders.

Oppenheim, A. N. (1966), *Questionnaire Design and Attitude Measurement*, London: Heinemann.

Rossi, P. H., Simpson, J. E. and Miller, J. L. (1985), 'Beyond crime seriousness: fitting the punishment to the crime', *Journal of Quantitative Criminology*, **1** (1), 59–90.

Shapland, J. with Willmore, J. and Duff, P. (1981), *The Victim in the Criminal Justice System*, Oxford: Centre for Criminological Research.

Shaw, S. (1982), *The People's Justice: a major poll of public attitudes to crime and punishment*, London: HMSO.

Silvey, J. (1961) 'The Criminal Law and Public Opinion', *British Journal of Criminology*, 349–358.

Social Surveys (Gallup Poll Limited) (1960), *Capital Punishment and Corporal Punishment: a Gallup poll conducted for the News Chronicle.*

Voelcker, P. (1960), 'Juvenile Courts: the parents' point of view', *British Journal of Criminology*, *1*, 154–166.
Walker, N. (1981), 'The Ultimate Justification', in C. Tapper (ed.), *Crime, Proof and Punishment*.
Walker, N. and Marsh, C. (1984), 'Do sentences affect public disapproval?', *British Journal of Criminology*, **24** (1), 27–48.
Willcock, H. and Stokes, J. (1968), *Deterrents to Crime among Youths aged 15–21*, (unpublished).
Willcock, H. and Stokes, J. (1974), *Deterrents and Incentives to Crime among Boys and Young Men aged 15–21 years: an enquiry undertaken for the Home Office in 1963*, (unpublished).

2 Conflict and consensus about criminal justice in Maryland

Stephen D. Gottfredson, Barbara D. Warner and Ralph B. Taylor

Conflict theorists have argued that the criminal justice system primarily reflects the values or the interests of one group in society; that which has social power over other groups (Vold, 1958; Dahrendorf, 1959; Quinney, 1970). This theory has been used within criminal justice to deal with issues such as law formation, law enforcement and sentencing practices. One of the perspectives' major weaknesses, however, has been a lack of attention to the actual processes involved in the differential imposition of values. That is, how is it that certain groups are able to have their views imposed, while others are not?

Although attempts to address questions of process have recently been made, most have been based on indirect evidence. For example, within the area of legal decision making (arrest, court referral, institutionalization), social class and racial differences among juveniles have received much attention, and some of these studies have suggested support for the conflict perspective (e.g., McCarthy and Smith, 1986). But in trying to place findings from a review of seventeen studies in this area within a consistent theoretical framework, Liska and Tausig (1979) point out that the studies

> provide few explicit tests of the conflict interpretation of social differentials. Rather than studying processes of power at different decision-making levels, conflict theorists have focused on structural sources of such processes. In effect, social class and race have frequently been used to operationalize power so a relationship between social class, race and legal decision-making has been used as evidence to support the conflict perspective. Yet, because such a relationship is equally consistent with other theoretical perspectives, it cannot be used as a crucial test of the conflict interpretation. The explanatory or mediating processes must be identified and studied. (p. 205).

In the area of law enforcement, the relation between racial and cultural dissimilarity and size of police force has been examined. Liska, Lawrence and Benson (1981) attempt to explain an observed race effect on police force size through an examination of fear of crime. Their findings suggest that race (more precisely, the percentage of non-whites) affects fear of crime, which then influences police force size. The implicit argument is that the 'powerful' group (whites, in this case) is able to translate the threat it perceives into public policy, thereby influencing the size of the police force. Although this is one of the most sophisticated studies of police force size that has used conflict theory, we are still left wondering why increased police force size is seen as a result of the will and power of whites. Blacks are more threatened by crime, and are more fearful as well; therefore they may be just as likely to press for police protection. Neither has it been shown that some mechanism exists through which whites can make their fears realized in policy, and blacks cannot.

In attempting to explain the relation between unemployment, imprisonment rates and sentence lengths, Box and Hale (1982) argue that the judiciary is the controlling mechanism. They suggest that most judges accept the notion that unemployment leads to crime, and, for purposes of deterrence and incapacitation, they increase the number and length of prison sentences. In this sense the judiciary is viewed as a 'barometer of anxiety levels felt by the superordinate class' (p. 22). Unfortunately, the only independent variable in this argument that actually is measured is unemployment.

In the area of law formation, one of the more sophisticated conflict models of the legal order is that of Chambliss and Seidman (1982), who suggest that the legal order is best depicted by combining a conflict model with a choice model. According to them, underlying economic relations and political organization shape, but do not determine, people's behaviour. Ultimately, people make choices. Chambliss and Seidman argue that due to differences in social background, experiences, and social acquaintances, there is no consensus among law makers, law enforcers and addressees of the law. The choices that those in power make will not be the choices of those being ruled:

> Our model, therefore, suggests that demands come from various segments of the population and that the state through legal order exercises its power to induce or coerce certain desired behavior by some set of role-occupants. In the nature of things demands of this sort respond to the interest of those making the demands. They call for the exercise of state power to induce or coerce the desired activity. The legal order, thus defined, becomes a system by which one part of the population uses state power to coerce another segment (p. 22).

> The model depicts a deeply authoritarian legal order . . . It assumes that the governors remain distinct from the masses of the people (p. 80).

For Chambliss and Seidman, the mechanism by which those in

power maintain their interests is simply the choices that individuals in power make. That is, the interests of those in power are maintained through the choices that those in power make. Of course, this is inevitably tautological in that one always can suggest that whatever choices are made can be argued to be in the interests of the ruling group since those were the choices that they made. However, the hypothesis that the attitude and choices of those in power are different from those of the people being ruled certainly is testable. To the extent that this is true, more credence is given to this model.

Consensus theory also remains vague on the issue of process. Consensus theory views society as being held together by a shared set of values and beliefs. In his discussion of the legislation of morals, Devlin (1965) argues that without a consensus of values there would be no society. It is the shared values which define a society, and they are thus necessary for its continued existence. Hence, the existence of a society necessitates consensus of values.

> What makes a society of any sort is community of ideas, not only political ideas but also ideas about the way its members should behave and govern their lives; these latter ideas are its morals (p. 9)... Without shared ideas on politics, morals and ethics no society can exist (p. 10).

Devlin also points out that those morals which the law will be used to preserve are those which are 'already accepted by the society'.

> [T]he work of the courts is to be the guardian of a heritage and not the creation of a system (p. 89)... The morals which the [lawmaker] enforces are those ideas about right and wrong which are already accepted by the society for which he is legislating and which are necessary to preserve its integrity (p. 90).

This perspective has been used to dismiss sub-cultural and conflict theories of crime by maintaining that across diverse classes and ethnic groups the values which parents attempt to instil in their children are the same, and thus criminal behaviour is not a result of different value orientations (Kornhauser, 1978).

Support for consensus theory among criminologists has arisen mainly from research concerned with attitudes toward, and the seriousness of, criminal behaviour. Studies of attitudes toward law-violating behaviour among different socio-economic areas or areas which differ in crime rates, have shown very few differences in attitudes or values (Macoby, Johnson and Church, 1958; Conklin, 1971). In addition, studies of seriousness of crimes have indicated considerable agreement in rank orderings of seriousness of crimes across divergent groups (Sellin and Wolfgang, 1964; Rossi, Waite, Bose and Berk, 1974; Levi and Jones, 1985, although for further discussions of the methodological and substantive interpretations of seriousness ratings see Gottfredson, Young and Laufer, 1980; Rossi and Henry, 1980; Miethe, 1982; and Cullen, Link, Travis and Wozniak, 1985).

According to this model, there are no differences in values or interests between those who rule and those who are ruled, and the state is viewed as value-neutral — it simply carries out the values of the society. It seems, therefore, that the mechanism or process in this model assumes that those who rule are aware of the community's attitudes, share them, and implement them through legislation. Support for this seems limited and mixed.

Levi and Jones (1985) examined the perceived seriousness of fourteen items for a sample of the general population as well as a sample of police officers. They found a high degree of consistency between these two groups in terms of the overall rank order of seriousness of offences (r = .90), but they also found quite a bit of disparity on mean ratings of each of the fourteen items between the two samples. Although the police rated all violent offences as more serious than did the public, they rated 9 of the 14 items as less serious than the public did. This suggests that there may not be consensus between the 'ruled' and the 'rulers', yet it certainly does not support a conflict model of the rulers oppressing the ruled, either. As to the extent of awareness and shared beliefs on the part of policy makers, we know of few studies which explicitly address this point (the work of Riley and Rose, 1980, to be discussed below, is an exception).

This chapter addresses the conflict/consensus controversy through examination of two sets of studies. First, we present a novel approach to the measurement of judged offence seriousness, and demonstrate that this approach allows an exploration of group differences not possible in prior work. Second, we focus directly on the issue of consensus between the general public and those in criminal justice policy-making authority.

Offence seriousness

As suggested by Rossi *et al.* (1974: p. 224), 'the seriousness of criminal acts represents a conceptual dimension of criminality that is indispensable in common, everyday discourse, in legal theory and practice, and in sociological work'. In effect, this asserts that (a) there exists for each of us a subjective ordering of acts or offences in terms of seriousness, and (b) there exists (or should exist) some fair degree of consensus among the populace and among specific relevant groups concerning the placement or positioning of specific acts relative to that dimension. The problem of demonstrating consensus or agreement, however, is a difficult one. Summarizing the methods employed in several major studies involving the measurement of consensus, Rossi et al. (1974, p. 225) find that 'the methods of ascertaining agreement among subgroups and between samples range from visual inspection of data arrays to regression coefficients'. Rossi et al. (1974, p. 227) essentially opt for the latter (treating the problem as one of reliability, i.e., substantial correlations among subgroups or samples are taken as reflective of consensus), while noting that 'It is easier to *assert* that there should be consensus than it is to devise a suitable standard against which a given degree of consensus should be measured'.[1]

It is our position that issues of consensus concerning the judged seriousness of criminal and delinquent acts may be confounded with, or clouded by, issues of measurement concerning the concept itself. In particular, we feel that a dimensional approach may provide some clarification.

Dimensions of offence seriouness?

> Is one homicide to be equated with ten petty thefts? 100? 1000? We may sense that these are incommensurables and so *feel* that the question of comparing their magnitude is a nonsense question. Yet this feeling is only a prelude to recognition of the more general fact that we have no strict common denominator for social problems and so have no workable procedures for comparing the scale of different problems, even when the task is simplified by dealing with two kinds of criminal acts. (Merton, 1961, p. 703).

The problem of the commensurability of the apparently incommensurable is old, and has received a great deal of attention from philosophers, legal theorists, and social scientists. In sentencing, judges are commonly confronted with this problem. Consider, for example, the *lex talionis* (an eye for an eye, a tooth for a tooth). The concept is clear: punishment should fit — be commensurate with — the crime (and, of course, the criminal). But in application, the concept quickly becomes complex. As Kleinig (1973, p. 120) notes:

> a literal interpretation lands one in insuperable difficulties: what penalty would you inflict on a rapist, a blackmailer, a forger, a dope peddler, a multiple murderer, a smuggler, or a toothless fiend who has knocked somebody else's teeth out?

Moving from a literal interpretation resolves some obvious problems, but raises others. For example, the US Supreme Court recently ruled that a sentence of life imprisonment is not incommensurate with a history of three property offences occurring over a period of several years, and which resulted in a total amount of property loss of under $500 (*Rummel* v. *Estell,* 100 S.CT. 1133, 1980). At the same time, some murderers and rapists are returned to the streets after relatively short periods of confinement. Although this example is extreme, and our presentation ignores the complexities surrounding the issue, the point is clear: even with a common metric (time spent in prison) commensurability may be difficult to achieve.[2] Thus, current sentencing controversies (cf. Dershowitz, 1976; Morris, 1974; von Hirsch, 1976) are intimately involved with the commensurability issue.

Sentencing typically requires a notion of commensurability between crimes and sanctions. But as pointed out by Merton (1961), Kleinig (1973), and others there is also the difficult problem of commensurability *within* crimes and sanctions. How many burglaries equal a robbery? Can we equate homicides and thefts?

One starting point for any measurement study designed to address the 'commensurability of the (apparently) incommensurable' may be an attempt to determine a common metric — what Blair (1956) calls the 'principle of dimensional homogeneity'. While there are a number of ways in which one can seek to achieve a common metric (see Blair, 1956; Sellin and Wolfgang, 1964, p. 336–338), the fundamental principle is that of homogeneity.

In *The Measurement of Delinquency*, Sellin and Wolfgang (1964: 338) took the position that

> judged seriousness of delinquency is the homogeneous dimension which can allow for quantitative measurement of this phenomenon [crime] and that there are ways of ascribing values to the magnitudes in this common medium of seriousness.

Major attempts at scaling the judged seriousness of criminal or delinquent acts have all been unidimensional; no systematic investigation of the dimensionality of offence seriousness has yet been undertaken. While a major goal of science is the parsimonious description and explanation of complex events, the assumption of unidimensionality has been questioned profitably in many measurement realms: intelligence, personality, academic achievement, and creativity, to name but a few. Quite often it has been demonstrated that despite the parsimony and simplicity benefits of single-dimension methods, the frequently found power of multidimensional methods cannot be denied for their increases in conceptual utility, explanatory power, and predictive utility.

The next sections of this chapter explore the concept of dimensions of judged offence seriousness, illustrate the utility of a dimensional approach, and examine issues of consensus concerning such judgements.

Offence descriptions. This investigation was undertaken as part of a larger research project concerned with improving measures of criminal recidivism. Of specific concern to the larger study were offences which are typically regarded as non-serious. Unfortunately, descriptions of such offences have been under-represented in most scaling work (cf. Sellin and Wolfgang, 1964; Rossi et al., 1974). To ensure an adequate representation of the universe of offences likely to be encountered in the larger project, arresting officers' reports (which typically contain some detail of the 'actual offence') were gathered from a medium-sized probation department in New York State. Two examples (randomly selected) of each misdemeanour offence type represented in the probation caseload during a calendar year were gathered.

Since many criminal events are composed of a number of specific acts, it was important that we identify and deal with these discrete acts, rather than with a global 'offence episode'. Accordingly, each arresting officer's report was coded into these specific acts and brief (one or two sentence) summary descriptions of all such discrete acts were prepared. These were then combined with some items used by Sellin and Wolfgang (1964), Rossi et al. (1974) and others, resulting in a list of about 2,500 statements descriptive of criminal or delinquent behaviour.

This item pool was edited for redundancy (which was, of course, substantial), resulting in a list of 162 offence descriptions covering a wide range of apparent seriousness. Since the combination of factors involved in criminal offence episodes is known to be complex (Gottfredson et al., 1980), care was taken to ensure that as few aggravating, mitigating, or extra-legal circumstances as possible appeared in the offence descriptions.[3]

These offence descriptions were then randomly ordered within a questionnaire booklet and subjects were directed to give their judgement of the relative seriousness of each offence description on a 1 to 15 category scale, with 1 reflective of the 'least serious' and 15 reflective of the 'most serious' offence. A category-scaling approach was used because of its simplicity of presentation, its practical utility, and demonstrated success (cf. Rossi et al., 1974; Sparks et al., 1977; Gottfredson et al., 1980). Further, several studies have shown that scales developed using this, as compared with more sophisticated techniques such as magnitude estimation, are monotonically related (cf. Sellin and Wolfgang, 1964; Walker, 1978).

Subjects were 1,154 undergraduate students enrolled in day or evening classes at five different educational institutions in two states and in the District of Columbia. In order to ensure as heterogeneous a sample as possible within the constraints of our research budget, these schools were chosen to reflect wide differences in academic selectivity, ages of the student populations, and ethnic balance. While the sample is undoubtedly not representative of the population at large, it is clearly more heterogeneous than the typical sample of college students. Subjects were directed either to work through the questionnaire from front to back, or back to front, resulting (for all practical purposes) in two 'random' orderings of items.

Of the 1,154 students given the questionnaire, responses from 130 were discarded due to lack of completion, obvious manipulation, or lack of variability in response, resulting in a final subject pool of 1,024 students.

The question of scale value. A basic question addressed in any scaling study is that of the best estimate of the value of each stimulus (offence, in our case). Typically, the arithmetic mean is taken as the measure of choice because of its relative stability. However, characteristics of item distributions must be examined to ensure that this is indeed the appropriate measure to use.

Since inspection of individual response distributions suggested modest end effects (Torgerson, 1958), data were rescaled following the method of successive intervals (Torgerson, 1958; Diederich et al., 1957) to minimize any displacement of item means. This manipulation had both the anticipated and desired effect, resulting in a near-normal distribution of item means.[4] The ordering of offences is intuitively appealing and generally consonant with expectation (i.e., the 'most serious' offence description was 'a person impulsively kills a stranger', and the 'least serious' offence read 'two people willingly engage in a homosexual act').

Comparisons with other scaling studies. As mentioned earlier, we included in the pool of offence descriptions items which were used by Sellin and Wolfgang (1964) and/or Rossi et al. (1974), as well as some items used in a large scaling study employing a representative national sample of the US population (Figlio, 1979). While the number of items used from each study varies, some comparisons are possible.

Table 2.1 gives the correlations between scale scores observed in the current study and those presented by previous investigators. In all cases, the joint distributions of scale values were inspected, revealing a few outliers in two cases.

The first row of Table 2.1 presents the relation between this study and that of Sellin and Wolfgang (1964). The correlation across the 29 offences common to both studies is modest at best (r = .57). Examination of outliers, however, demonstrates that two phenomena probably account for much of the apparent disparity. Three

Table 2.1 *Comparisons of scale values with scale values observed in previous studies*

Study	Number of items in common	Correlations coefficient
Sellin & Wolfgang (1964)	29	.57
Sellin & Wolfgang (1964)	25	.83
Rossi et al. (1974)	46	.84
Rossi et al. (1974)	43	.90
Figlio (1979)	38	.87

Note: Outliers have been omitted in rows two and four. See text for explanation.

offences — involving the use, possession, or sale of marijuana — were judged as quite serious in Sellin and Wolfgang's original work, but were perceived as quite non-serious in the current study. Given that approximately two decades elapsed between the two investigations, and given current interest in the decriminalization of marijuana, it would seem quite reasonable to ascribe these differences to changes in attitudes rather than to disparity due to scaling approaches. One additional item (having to do with truancy) was also judged quite differently in the two studies. Inspection revealed that a likely explanatory hypothesis lies in the differences in wordings between the two items.[5] When these four items are excluded from consideration (row two, Table 2.1), the correlation increases to .83, suggesting substantial relation between the two scales.

The third row of the table gives the relation observed with the study conducted in Rossi et al. (1974). While the same general method of scaling was used in both works, this comparison is of considerable interest since the Rossi et al. study employed a representative sample of the population from a large urban environment. Again, substantial correlation is observed (r = .84), but again some outliers are apparent. Examination demonstrates that all three apparent outliers involve the sale or use of drugs, with the most disparate having to do with the sale of marijuana. Again, a plausible hypothesis is that drug offences have been perceived differently over time (in this case, approximately a decade), although the rival hypothesis of differences in subject populations is also plausible. Controlling for these outliers, the correlation increases to .9 (row 4, Table 2.1).

The bottom row of Table 2.1 gives the relation with items in common with the recent replication of Sellin and Wolfgang's scaling procedure based on a representative national sample (Figlio, 1979). The relation between the logarithm of the ratio scores observed in that study and the scale values we observed is .87.

It should be noted that the particular items in common with each study vary and that few items are common to all subsets. While all observed relations are quite high — and would appear to be more than respectable if considered as reliability coefficients — they are not perfect. That the relation is marginally better for the study which used a method closer to our own suggests that some of the unexplained variability perhaps can be attributed to differences in methods. It is also likely the case, however, that some of the remaining variability can be attributed to differences in subject populations as well. Nonetheless, it is clear that substantive conclusions are not likely to be affected simply by choice of scaling procedures.

The question of dimensionality

As the object of these analyses is to represent as much of the information contained in the n-variable matrix as possible with as few composites as possible, a principal components approach is appropriate.

Split-sample investigations. The replicability of factor structures is an important (but often ignored) issue. In general, it is usually observed that beyond the first few components — which typically are large relative to the remainder — structures fail to replicate. Since our sample of subjects is relatively large, we are in a position to examine the replicability of these structures. Accordingly, the subject sample was randomly halved, resulting in two independent samples of sizes 505 and 519.[6,7]

A principal components analysis of the $n = 505$ sub-sample resulted (after Varimax rotation) in a readily interpretable six-component solution which accounted for 45 per cent of the variance. Components are well-defined, and few items load on more than one component. The six-component solution of the remaining sub-sample ($n = 519$) was also computed. While the ordering of dimensions was (trivially) different, it was clear from inspection alone that the structures are substantively identical.

In general, there are two empirical approaches to the question of the 'fit' of factor (or other) matrices. One involves rotating matrices to maximal fit or similarity, and then assessing that similarity using a 'congruence' coefficient. The other, and more conservative, approach involves no further rotation, and compares specific dimensions, rather than the entire matrix. We followed the latter approach.

Table 2.2 Coefficients of factorial similarity between corresponding components

Seriousness component		Coefficient of factorial similarity
I	Victimless/vice-type offences	.97
II	Bodily harm/interpersonal confrontation	.95
III	Property loss/damage	.98
IV	Tertiary victimization	.97
V	Serious drug offences	.87
VI	Fraud, deception	.87

Note: See Table 2.4 for descriptions of seriousness components.

Table 2.2 gives the coefficients of factorial similarity observed (Harmon, 1967). Four dimensions clearly replicate very well — all cofficients are above .95. The two smaller dimensions also replicate well, but somewhat less powerfully — coefficients are both larger than .86. Clearly, then, our investigation of dimensionality has borne fruit. At least six clearly defined and readily interpretable dimensions appear to underlie people's judgements of the seriousness of crime.

Full-sample analyses. The analyses just discussed are conservative since the *n*/variable ratio is somewhat low. Accordingly, the full sample of 1,024 subjects was also analysed, since the resulting structure should be substantially more robust (having essentially doubled the *n*/variable ratio). Results of these analyses are summarized in Table 2.3.[8]

These results of course confirm those of the sub-sample analyses, and the interpretation of components does not change. The structure accounts for 44 per cent of the total variance with six dimensions. Remaining discussion focuses on this solution.

The first component, which represents 11 per cent of the variance after rotation, can be interpreted in a number of ways. Many of the offences which load heavily on this component are 'vice-type' crimes: prostitution, gambling, use and possession of marijuana, adultery, homosexual acts, exposures, etc. A second possible interpretation rests on the fact that many of these offences would fall under the general rubric of 'victimless crimes'. Whether victimless crimes or vice-type crimes, it is clear from an inspection of

Table 2.3 Summary of principal components solution of 162 offence descriptions (n = 1,024)

Unrotated solution Component	I	II	III	IV	V	VI
Eigenvalue	43.97	10.47	5.69	4.82	3.47	3.33
Cumulative percent of variance	32.34	33.60	37.11	40.09	42.23	44.29
Varimax rotated solution Component	**I**	**II**	**III**	**IV**	**V**	**VI**
Eigenvalue	17.45	10.45	19.39	10.12	7.08	7.26
Cumulative percent of variance	10.77	17.22	29.19	35.44	39.81	44.29

standardized item means that in general people view crimes which loaded on this dimension as relatively non-serious.

The second component (17 per cent of the variance after rotation) clearly involves physical assault, personal harm, and interpersonal confrontation. The third component (12 per cent of the variance after rotation) equally clearly represents theft, property damage or loss, and property crimes in general.

The fourth dimension, which also accounts for a reasonable portion of the variance after rotation (6 per cent), seems to represent crimes against the social order. In general, these are either crimes which are committed by an agent or agency in power (an employer, a real estate agent, a police officer, a manufacturer, a producer, a doctor, a public official), or social crimes (i.e., against groups: racism, the pollution of a water supply, the marketing of contaminated products, price fixing, false advertising), or both. Interestingly, two offences involving juveniles ('a juvenile repeatedly runs away from home', and 'a juvenile is beyond parental control') load on this dimension. At first glance, they are anomalous, but their interpretation is clarified if one assumes that (in some sense, at least) subjects were in effect judging the actions of *parents,* rather than that of the juveniles. This interpretation is at least consistent with the overall pattern of this dimension.

The fifth and sixth dimensions, while relatively small (4 per cent and 5 per cent, respectively, of the variance after rotation) and defined by relatively few items, are nonetheless readily interpretable.[9]

Table 2.4 Ranges of scale values for offences by dimension

Seriousness dimension	Minimum value	Maximum value
Victimless/vice-type offences	−1.2362	0.3239
Bodily harm/interpersonal confrontation	0.6716	1.4980
Property loss/damage	−0.7023	1.0552
Tertiary victimization	−0.5029	1.2254
Fraud, deception	−0.5974	0.5427
Serious drug offences	0.2681	0.9836

Note: Based on standardized scores.

Offences loading on the fifth dimension (with two exceptions) all involve serious drug offences: the sale or manufacture of heroin, hallucinogens, or barbiturates and amphetamines. Offences loading on the sixth (and final) dimension by and large involve fraud or deception.

While we have discovered a clean and clear-cut six-dimensional structure which may underlie people's judgements of offence seriousness, that structure quickly loses some of its conceptual utility if in fact the dimensions merely represent 'ranges' along a single underlying dimension. That is, it is clearly of little interest simply to know (for example) that people judge victimless, vice-type offences as less serious than assaultive confrontational offences, and that factor-analytic techniques can demonstrate this fact. In order for a dimensional structure to be theoretically and conceptually heuristic, we would like the distinction among factors or dimensions not simply to be one of relative magnitude. The question, then, is the extent to which these dimensions overlap one another along the 'first-order dimension' of overall judged seriousness.

Table 2.4 provides illustration of this overlap in terms of ranges of the offence means for offences loading on each of the dimensions. Clearly, overlap is substantial. Thus, the orthogonal dimensions obtain within roughly the same ranges of judged 'overall' seriousness, and the second-order dimensions are conceptually meaningful. What this illustration suggests is that two (or more) offences may be judged as roughly (or completely) equivalent in terms of seriousness, but that they may be so judged for different reasons.

Issues of consensus

We now turn attention to the issue of whether our dimensional

Table 2.5 Reliabilities of offence seriousness scales

Scale based on:	Reliability coefficient (a)	*N* (b)	Number of items
Victimless/vice-type offences	.959	910	32
Bodily harm/interpersonal confrontation	.888	934	22
Property loss/damage	.967	899	38
Tertiary victimization	.915	922	21
Fraud, deception	.809	996	8
Serious drug offences	.921	939	6

Notes: (a) Cronbach's alpha.
(b) *N*s vary due to incomplete response.

approach to the study of offence seriousness can add to our understanding of the ways in which members of different groups — whose attitudes may be expected to be important to the functioning of the criminal justice system — may use the concept.

A set of six scales representing the six dimensions described in the above study was constructed by simply adding together scores for single items which fell on a given dimension, thus resulting in a 'total score' for a dimension.[10] Thus far, we have assumed that items falling on the same component are somehow tapping a common underlying dimension of judged seriousness. If we are to use these results meaningfully, and for the scales to be conceptually useful, it is necessary that they be reliable, and that they in fact represent separable dimensions of seriousness.

Table 2.5 gives the internal consistency reliability coefficients observed for the full sample of 1,024 students discussed above. Clearly, all scales have high reliability: homogeneity coefficients all are above .80.

Table 2.6 shows that the scales are not completely orthogonal, which is to be expected, since all reflect, to some extent, the concept of seriousness. Still, in no instance can even half of the variance in one scale be accounted for given knowledge of another. It appears, therefore, that our criteria of conceptual utility have been met.

Several groups of subjects voluntarily participated in this stage of our study:

1. *Students.* A 10 per cent ($n = 112$) random sample of students who participated in the earlier study was generated for use here.

Table 2.6 Intercorrelations of offence seriousness scales

Scale:	Victimless/ vice	Bodily harm	Property loss	Tertiary victimization	Fraud	Serious drug
Victimless/vice	—	.263 (N = 857)	.584 (N = 873)	.526 (N = 891)	.640 (N = 893)	.700 (N = 902)
Bodily harm/ interpersonal confrontation		—	.592 (N = 885)	.516 (N = 906)	.305 (N = 911)	.329 (N = 919)
Property loss/damage			—	.644 (N = 878)	.564 (N = 880)	.433 (N = 888)
Tertiary victimization				—	.538 (N = 904)	.454 (N = 912)
Fraud, deception					—	.501 (N = 923)
Serious drug offences						—

2. *Police officers.* Seventy-four State Troopers from across the State of Maryland participated.
3. *Correctional officers.* One hundred and twenty guards from Maryland correctional institutions completed our forms.
4. *Parole and probation officers.* A total of 87 officers from several Maryland jurisdictions participated.
5. *Judges and criminal attorneys.* Twenty-three members of the Council of Juvenile Court Judges participated, as did 41 defence and prosecuting attorneys from Maryland. These groups were too small to analyse separately, and were combined in all analyses.
6. *Inmates.* Seventy-four felons confined in Maryland correctional institutions voluntarily completed the forms. Inmates were contacted at the Reception, Diagnostic and Classification Center (an intake facility), and hence can be considered representative of the State's confinement population.

Each respondent in the samples described above was scored on each of six scales constructed from items loading on the six components of seriousness. Scale scores were entered as discriminating variables in a multiple discriminant function analysis (with sample membership as the variable to be distinguished), to determine whether members of the respective groups differ in their treatment of these scales. Analyses were performed without regard to prior knowledge of group size. Since all six scales are presumed to be meaningful, all six were used in the calculations of the functions.

Results

The hypothesis that sample members differ with respect to their treatment of the six scales was confirmed. The original value of Wilk's lambda, which assesses potential discriminability based on the scale scores, is .476,[11] which suggests considerable discrimination. The canonical correlation between the first discriminant function and the group membership variable is .590, and the function is of the form

$$\begin{aligned} Y = \; & .63 \text{ (Victimless/vice scale)} \\ & -.42 \text{ (Personal harm scale)} \\ & -.69 \text{ (Property loss scale)} \\ & +.99 \text{ (Tertiary victimization scale)} \\ & -.17 \text{ (Fraud scale)} \\ & -.48 \text{ (Major drug scale)}, \end{aligned}$$

where Y equals predicted group membership.

After removing the effect of the first discriminant function, lambda increases to .73,[12] which suggests significant remaining discriminability. The canonical correlation between the second linear composite and the group membership variable is .41, and the composite is of the form

$$
\begin{aligned}
Y = & -.38 \text{ (Victimless/vice scale)} \\
& -.61 \text{ (Personal harm scale)} \\
& +.10 \text{ (Property loss scale)} \\
& -.41 \text{ (Tertiary victimization scale)} \\
& -.05 \text{ (Fraud scale)} \\
& +.18 \text{ (Major drug scale)},
\end{aligned}
$$

where Y is as before.

While a third discriminant function was also statistically significant,[13] the canonical correlation is small (.32), and we therefore decided to restrict further discussion to the two-function solution.

Figure 2.1 shows the positions of the group centroids in the reduced space defined by the two functions. Using the functions in a 'predictive' way, we correctly classified 58 per cent of the students, 60 per cent of the inmates, and 50 per cent of the judges and criminal attorneys. The remaining three groups (police officers, prison guards, and parole/probation officers) were highly confusable — but only among themselves. That is, while guards were often classified as police officers (and vice versa), neither was likely to be classified as an inmate, a student, or a member of the legal profession.

Large differences in the perceived seriousness of different offences were manifest across the groups. For example, inmates perceived property crimes, major drug offences, and offences involving personal injury as being much less serious than did other groups, while the student group perceived all of these as more serious than did the others. Interestingly, the student sample appeared to perceive *all* types of offences as being much more serious than did any of the other groups — perhaps 'familiarity' with crime breeds contempt.

Summary and conclusions: seriousness scaling studies

Torgerson (1958) has stressed the difference between *classification* and *measurement*. Basic to that distinction is the notion that we *classify* objects or events or things; while we measure *attributes* of things. Thus, for example, we cannot measure burglary, other than through the use of specified attributes. (We can, of course, *classify* burglaries. Any number of reasonable classification schemes can be developed: commercial *vs* non-commercial, daytime *vs* night-time burglaries, and so forth.)

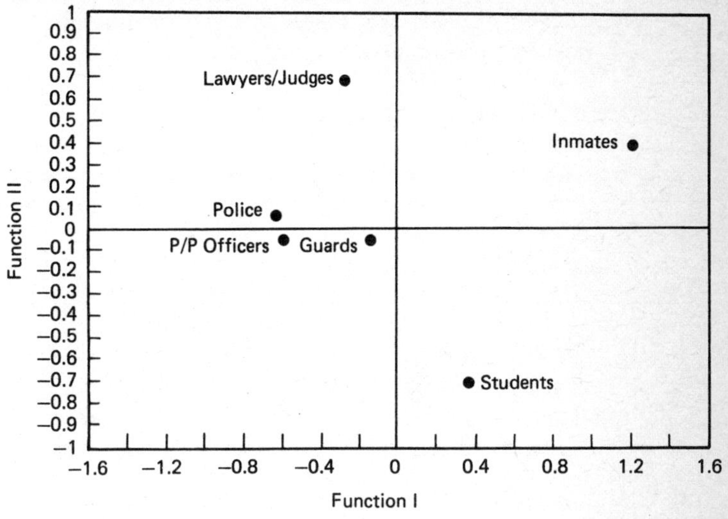

Figure 2.1 *Sample centroids in discriminant space*

To use Torgerson's example, a stick is therefore not measurable — although its length, weight, diameter, hardness, etc. might well be. Likewise, *crime* is not measurable, other than through its attributes. A fundamental problem is to find and utilize a common metric, in this case a common attribute, in the assessment of crime. 'Seriousness' would seem to represent, at first glance, such a metric. And yet, as noted by Merton (1961, p. 703), this metric leaves us dissatisfied.

Our studies cast considerable doubt on the assumption that judged seriousness is in fact a homogenous dimension. Consider again Torgerson's 'stick' example. Suppose we have a large pile of sticks, each of which varies along a number of dimensions: length, heaviness, roughness, diameter, and so forth. If we ask people to judge each stick on a scale representing length, we would anticipate very considerable consistency with respect to the scaling of the sticks.

Likewise, people easily could array our sticks along a single dimension representing heaviness.

Suppose, however, we asked people to judge the 'bigness' of the set of sticks. We still might expect to find a fair amount of agreement among our subjects with respect to the placement of the sticks relative to the 'bigness' dimension, but considerable variation might also be expected. Further, a substantial amount of this variability might be expected to be attributable to separate *dimensions* of 'bigness' — such as length, width, diameter, and heaviness.

We might also expect, of course, people to report some discomfort in making a decision such as 'which stick is bigger' when confronted with a short heavy stick and a long, light stick. Likewise, some of us experience considerable discomfort in comparing, for example, an assault and a theft.

What our studies suggest is that the metric or dimension of 'seriousness' can in some ways be considered analogous to the dimension of 'bigness'. Such dimensions are in some respect non-specific or heterogeneous, and we might expect to find that the combined use of a number of more specific dimensions will increase the specificity with which we can assess the events of interest (see von Hirsch, 1973, p. 79–83).

Indeed, we believe that we have demonstrated that a meaningful set of scales can be developed which reflects at least some of the dimensions underlying the concept of offence seriousness. The scales are highly reliable (internally consistent) and are modestly interrelated — a finding to be expected given the method of development employed and the fact that all reflect (to some extent) the concept of seriousness. Also, we have demonstrated that use of this approach has value for understanding issues of consensus among groups with respect to this important concept. The ways in which specified groups of people perceive these dimensions of seriousness differ. Offenders' perceptions of offences differ dramatically from those of other groups. What these studies show, then, is that by considering offence seriousness as a homogeneous dimension, spurious support is found for consensus theory. By treating offence seriousness in this dimensional manner, the weight of support is shifted to the conflict perspective. Finally, it appears that there may be a 'familiarity' effect with respect to judgements of the seriousness of crime: groups having involvement with the criminal justice system *all* judge offences — of all sorts — as less serious than do persons *not* having criminal justice system involvement.

Correctional policy and public opinion

In a separate set of studies we have examined issues of consensus between those who set correctional policy (the governors) and those affected by those policies (the governed). A basic assumption of representative democracy is that public policy should be responsive to the public will. This principle applies to both the legislative and the administrative branches of government — including those branches concerned with criminal justice and corrections. Indeed, Luttbeg (1968) argues that 'linkage between the public and its leaders is the mechanism that allows public leaders to act in accordance with the wants, needs, and demands of their public.'

Political scientists studying linkages between public opinion and policy formulation have offered a number of suggestions concerning the nature of the assumed ties between representatives and their constituencies. For example, Miller and Stokes (1963) have observed that correlations between constituency opinion and congressional representatives' estimates of that opinion vary across issues. In that study, good correspondence was found with respect to civil rights issues, but the representatives were found to be inaccurate in assessing constituency opinion of foreign affairs and social welfare issues. Hedlund and Friesma (1972) have compared Iowa legislators' perceptions of public opinion with voting results in referenda on these same issues, finding that the legislators were more accurate in assessing constituency opinion on major issues than on lesser ones.

Riley and Rose (1980) have summarized various characterizations of the general public's attitudes toward corrections and correctional issues as:

(a) ambivalent
(b) vague
(c) unconcerned
(d) apathetic and uninformed
(e) uncertain and lacking consensus
(f) disinterested
(g) punitive
(h) ignorant, and infrequently,
(i) optimistic

However (and as noted by Riley and Rose), the sources of these sentiments typically provide little, if any, data supportive of their rather gloomy characterizations.

In 1973, Berk and Rossi conducted a study of correctional policy makers in three states (Florida, Illinois, and Washington). Of principal concern was the understanding of policy-makers' attitudes toward correctional goals and proposals for change. The sample of policy makers was defined as 'persons who were potentially instrumental in initiating, approving, and carrying out programs within state corrections systems'. It was also reasonably assumed that these would be 'persons occupying positions of power and influence' (Berk and Rossi, 1977, p. 3). While Berk and Rossi noted important variations in opinions of and receptivity to different change strategies among the members of different groups within the sample, more striking were the differences they observed between the opinions and attitudes of the policy makers and their assessments of the public view on these issues. In general, it appeared that the correctional policy makers held personal views that could be characterized as liberal, reform-oriented, and rehabilitative. In stark contrast, they saw the general public as punitive and generally concerned only with its own protection and safety.

In a study conducted in the State of Maryland, we have observed this same pattern of findings (Gottfredson and Taylor, 1983; 1984; 1987). Our sample of correctional policy makers appeared to hold relatively liberal views of the proper goals for correctional systems: they stressed rehabilitation, they opposed the abolition of parole, and they typically did not favour simple retributive punishment. Also clear was that they perceived the positions of the general public to be very different from their own views — at least their own views as expressed to us when they were guaranteed absolute confidentiality and anonymity of individual expressions of opinion.

This section examines the accuracy of policy-makers' views of public opinion. Berk and Rossi (1977), although clearly concerned with this issue, were unable to examine it with their data. However, in 1975, Riley and Rose conducted a large-sample survey of residents of Washington State, one of the states whose policy makers ($n = 83$) were surveyed by Berk and Rossi in 1973. In the main their findings do indeed suggest correspondence between the views of the policy makers and those of the general public: but also important misperceptions of the public view on the part of the policy makers. As we shall see, our findings confirm those of Riley and Rose.

The correctional policy makers

In the summer of 1980, an interview schedule containing both structured and open-ended items was administered to 80 members of a group we defined as Maryland's correctional policy makers. In keeping with Berk and Rossi's suggestion that such a group should consist not only of those who initiate and approve programmes within state corrections systems, but also of those charged with carrying out those programmes, our sample included both those who make policy decisions (elected officials, judges, corrections administrators) and those who implement these decisions (institution supervisors, sheriffs and chiefs of police, prosecutors). The sample was chosen to reflect the major components of the criminal justice system and included correctional administrators, planners, and other officials (both elected and appointed) representing the state ($n = 16$); correctional administrators, planners and other officials representing local jurisdictions ($n = 13$); local-level elected officials (mayors, county executives, state legislators) ($n = 14$); supervision officials (wardens, superintendents) ($n = 15$); law enforcement officials (sheriffs, chiefs of police) ($n = 11$); and representatives of the legal system (judges, prosecuting and defence officials) ($n = 11$). Interviews were completed with 91 per cent of the 88 persons contacted.

It should be noted that those interviewed as part of this policy-making sample were not selected so as to be representative of the groups listed. Rather, this is a carefully selected and biased sample, generated from historical/archival sources and discussions with persons intimately concerned with corrections. Thus, it consists of persons who can be presumed to be extremely knowledgeable and concerned about correctional issues.[14] Thus the following discussion of attitudes and perceptions should not be generalized to the larger groups (for example, judges or law enforcement officials) from which our policy-maker sample was drawn. We did conduct a comprehensive survey of these broader groups, and discussion of these findings is given elsewhere (Gottfredson and Taylor, 1983). The present discussion pertains specifically and only to correctional policy makers as defined here.

The interview schedule was designed to be administered in person, and contained both open and structured questions concerning the problems and assets of Maryland's correctional system; perceptions of a 'crisis' in corrections and the reasons underlying it; short- and long-term solutions to prison crowding problems in both state and local jurisdictions; attitudes toward proposed policy changes; assessments of the attitudes of others concerning proposed policy changes; and goals and philosophies for corrections.

The general public

In December of 1980, we conducted a public attitude survey in 13 of Maryland's 24 counties. The counties were selected to sample the constituencies of the policy makers interviewed earlier. A random digit dialling telephone sampling approach was used, and the sample was stratified by sex and restricted to residents, aged 18 or older, of those 13 jurisdictions. Just over 600 interviews were obtained, and the response rate was 64 per cent. The same basic information on attitudes toward correctional goals and proposed policy changes was collected, but using a simpler format.

Subsequent analyses showed that the sampling strategy was

successful, and that the proper proportion of interviews was achieved across jurisdictions. Unsampled jurisdictions, all of which are predominantly rural, account for 12.7 per cent of the entire state population (based on 1980 census counts). While rural jurisdictions are very well represented in our sample, this slight under-representation relative to the entire state population should be considered in the interpretation of statewide findings.[15] Finally, it should be noted that our intent was to sample the constituencies of the policy makers interviewed; and this was achieved.

Assessments of goals

In our face-to-face interviews with policy makers, we were able to obtain rankings of the priorities they assigned (or felt were assigned) to each of four possible correctional goals: incapacitation, punishment, deterrence, and rehabilitation. These were defined as in the Berk and Rossi (1977) study:

1. Incapacitation: protecting the public by removing offenders from the community where they might commit additional crimes.
2. Rehabilitation: rehabilitating offenders so that they might pursue non-criminal lives.
3. Punishment: administering punishment to offenders as retribution for the crimes they have committed.
4. Deterrence: deterring crime by showing potential offenders the serious consequences of committing a criminal offence.

Given the relative complexity of a ranking task, we used a simpler, two-stage rating approach for administration to the general public over the telephone.[16] Thus, while we can obtain mean ranks for the priorities assigned by the policy makers and mean ratings for the priorities assigned by the general public, the two metrics are not the same. Accordingly, we have transformed each to rank-order measures for the analyses that follow, and the policy makers' opinions are here represented by rank-ordered mean ratings. The reader should bear in mind the characteristics of ordinal data when considering our discussion: successive intervals are assumed to be successive in order only — no interpretation of the magnitude of differences between numbers is possible or appropriate. Indeed, in some cases the differences between values in the original metric were small — although in all cases (but for instances in which ranks are presented as tied) they exceeded at least one standard error in magnitude. All analyses are based on slightly different numbers of cases, since not all respondents answered every question we asked.

Figure 2.2 illustrates our findings with respect to the accuracy of our policy makers' perceptions of the value the general public

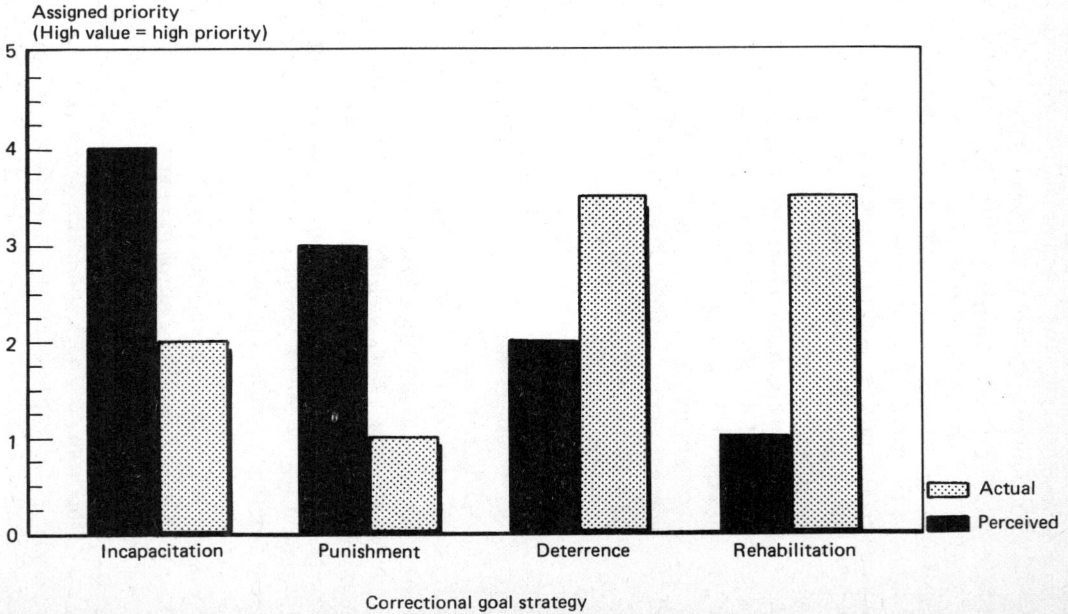

Figure 2.2 *Relation between public opinion of four correctional goals and policy maker perceptions of public opinion*

assigns the goals of corrections. A striking lack of correspondence is apparent from simple inspection: and indeed, the rank-order correlation between the two assessments is large and negative (rho = −.84).[17] While the policy makers feel that the public prefers (in this case, by a wide margin) the goal of incapacitation, this goal is in fact the second lowest priority in the public view. While policy makers likewise feel that the general public strongly supports the goal of retributive punishment (also, in this case, by a wide margin in the original metric), this goal is actually assigned the lowest priority by our sample of the public. It is therefore not surprising that while the policy makers feel that the goal of rehabilitation would be lowest in the public esteem (and by a very wide margin indeed), this goal is in fact tied with that of deterrence for the public's highest priority. Quite clearly, then, there is considerable misperception of the public viewpoint on the part of the correctional policy makers.

What of the correspondence between the policy makers' own views and those of their constituents? Figure 2.3 summarizes these findings. Considerably more agreement is manifest; while moderate, the correlation between the two sets of viewpoints is at least positive (rho = .28). Policy makers and the general public agree that simple retributive punishment is the least desirable goal for a correctional system, and both assign high priority to the goal of rehabilitation or treatment. Such disagreement as exists is over the goals of incapacitation and deterrence.

If we find concordance over goals, what of assessments of the functioning of the correctional system relative to the public's desired goals? Figure 2.4 suggests that the public should be disappointed: the relation between the policy makers' assessments of present correctional system priorities and the priorities desired by the general public is negative (rho = −.27). Indeed, respondents in our survey of the general public reported overwhelmingly that the Maryland corrections system was doing a very poor job at meeting any of its proper goals. When asked about Maryland's attempts to implement these four goals, less than half of the sample responding felt — irrespective of the specific goal — that Maryland was doing a good job at implementation. Further, and again not surprisingly, a very large proportion of the respondents (ranging from 79 per cent for the goal of incapacitation to 70 per cent for the goal of rehabilitation) reported that realistically more could be done to meet these correctional goals.

The picture presented thus far suggests not only that Maryland's policy makers are poor judges of the public's wants, but that the system they are charged with operating is not responsive to the priorities as assigned by the public. Further, since their own views

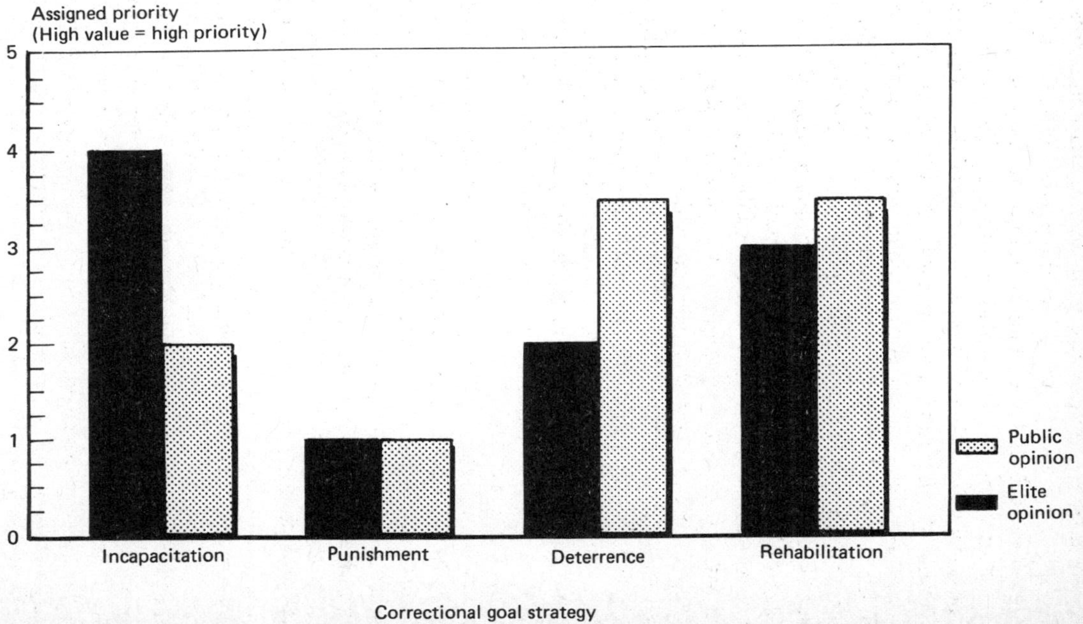

Figure 2.3 *Relation between public and policy maker (élite) opinions of four correctional goal strategies*

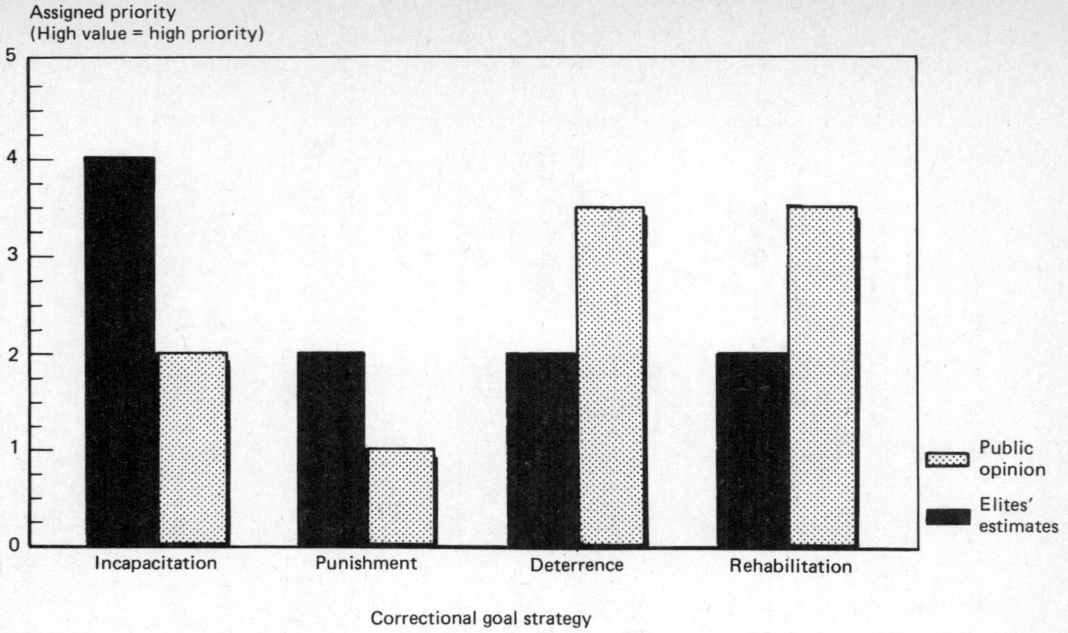

Figure 2.4 *Relation between policy maker (élite) estimates of actual system priorities and priorities desired by public*

are similar to those of the public, the system is also seen as not meeting the goals of the policy makers themselves. This evidence would seem to suggest that with respect to correctional system goals, at any rate, those whom we charge with public responsibility are failing to meet that charge.

But are they? Figure 2.5 illustrates the relation between the policy makers' perceptions of the public will and their perception of how our present correctional system functions. The relation is high and positive (rho = .78), suggesting that correctional policy may indeed be practised in accordance with the public will, as the policy makers perceive that will. While there is little differentiation perceived among most system functions, the overall pattern, given the priority assigned to the goal of incapacitation, is consonant with the perceived public will. This, of course, is the critical point: the extent to which our policy makers misperceive or misunderstand the views of the public may determine the extent to which policy is non-responsive to the public will.

Assessments of change strategies

In our interviews both with correctional policy makers and with the general public, we asked for assessments of several proposals for correctional change that were then prevalent in the correctional policy debate in Maryland. These proposals for reform had figured prominently in public, administrative, and legislative debates over correctional policy for several years. The four proposed change strategies that we studied were:

- a proposal to abolish parole;
- a proposal to incarcerate a larger proportion of the inmate population at the local (as opposed to the state) level;
- a proposal to establish Community Adult Rehabilitation Centers (CARCs) on a widespread basis; and
- a proposal not to build any large new state prison facilities.

In addition to asking policy makers and the general public for their own positions on each of these issues, we asked our policy makers to give their assessments of public support for (or opposition to) each one. Figure 2.6 displays our findings.

On all issues but one (the establishment of CARCs), the policy makers' positions and the positions of the general public are the same. The only statistically significant difference is with respect to the widespread establishment of CARCs; more policy makers support this proposed change than do members of the general public — 93 per cent versus 73 per cent (Chi-squared$_{(1)}$ = 16.60; $p < .01$).

Although policy makers and the general public agree on three out

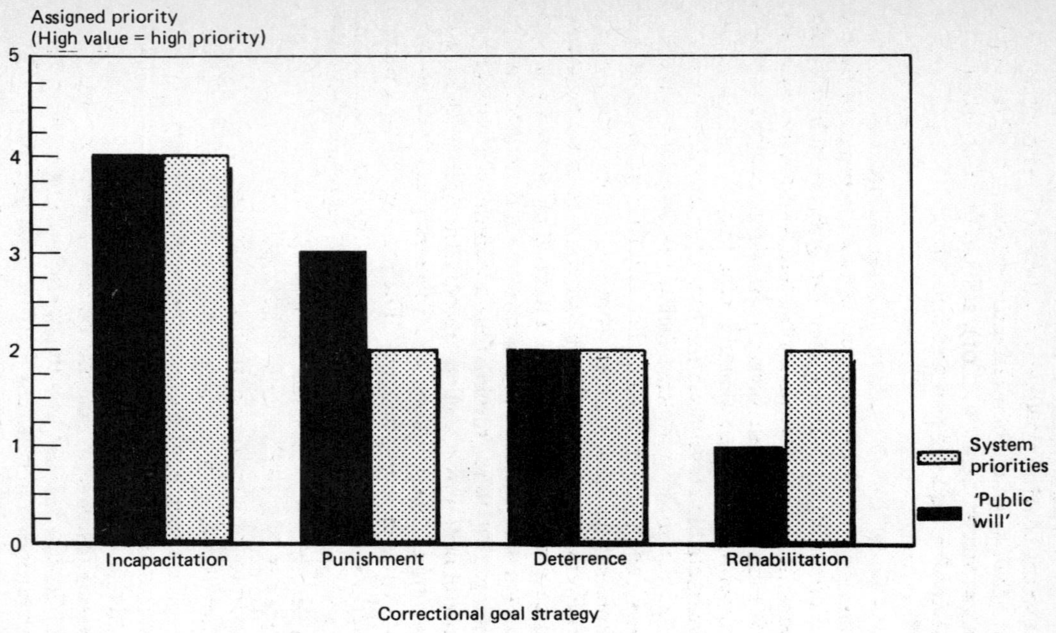

Figure 2.5 *Policy maker estimates of the 'public will' and of the priorities under which the correctional system operates*

of four possible reform strategies, the policy makers' perception of the public view are at variance with the reality on three out of four: only with respect to the building of at least one new state institution do policy makers' perceptions and the actual public view correspond. Substantial and statistically significant differences in perception occur with respect to the abolition of parole (Chi-squared$_{(1)}$ = 38.98; $p < .01$), the movement of inmates to local as opposed to state facilities (Chi-squared$_{(1)}$ = 25.32; $p < .01$), and the widespread establishment of CARCs (Chi-squared$_{(1)}$ = 32.01; $p < .01$).

Summary and conclusions: attitudes of policy makers and the public

It has often been assumed that the general public is not only uninterested in correctional issues, but ignorant of these issues as well. We know from our survey that this is not the case — at least in Maryland. We found that the vast majority of our sample are very interested in corrections and correctional issues. They are quite aware of the major problems facing the state corrections system, and they follow these issues rather regularly in the media. Finally, they hold strong opinions concerning the proper goals of a correctional system. Contrary to general belief, we found the general public not to be especially punitive — rather, they stress more utilitarian goals, such as rehabilitation, deterrence, and incapacitation. These attitudes are reflected in the public's views of the various proposals for correctional reform. The reform strategies that receive most support stress rehabilitation and increasing localization of correctional programmes and facilities. The majority of the general public in Maryland feel that more institutions are needed, but unfortunately it cannot be determined from our data whether this stems from a simple concern over a lack of space, or from knowledge of the conditions in Maryland's present facilities (or both).

Almost without exception, these attitudes are echoed by our sample of policy makers. In no important respect do the attitudes of the policy maker sample differ from the attitudes of the public. In fact, where they do differ, the views of the policy makers would appear more liberal and more reform-oriented.

We also discovered that our policy makers feel that they know the public mood — and that the public's attitude concerning correctional issues is at substantial variance with their own. This chapter has systematically assessed the accuracy of that perception. What we have observed is almost complete congruence between the public and the policy makers with respect to most key corrections issues, but severe misconceptions among policy makers of the public will with respect to these same issues.

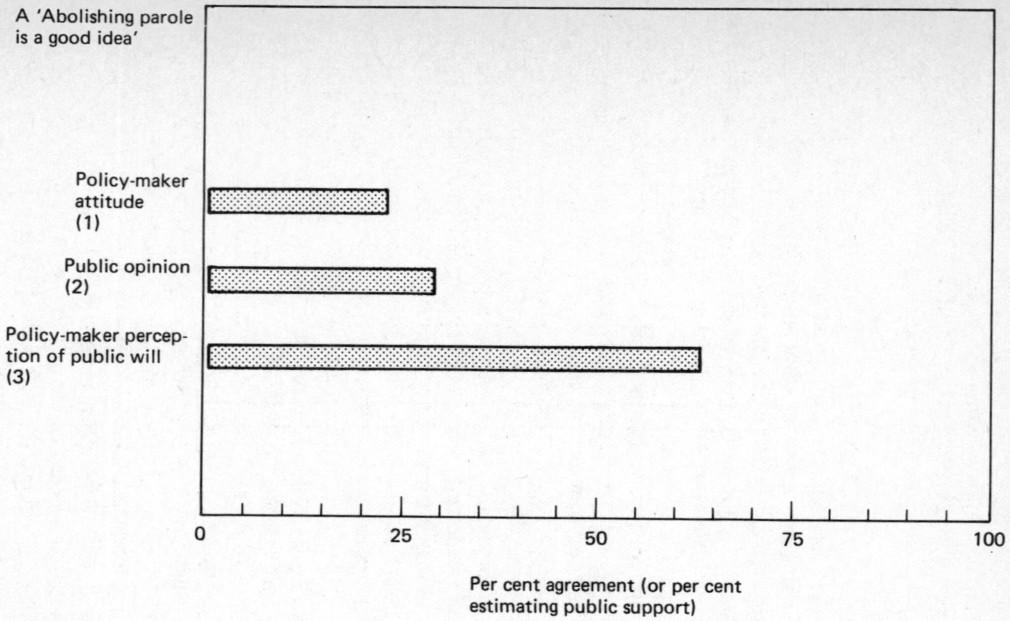

Figure 2.6 *Policy maker attitudes, public opinion, and policy maker perception of public opinion on key correctional issues*

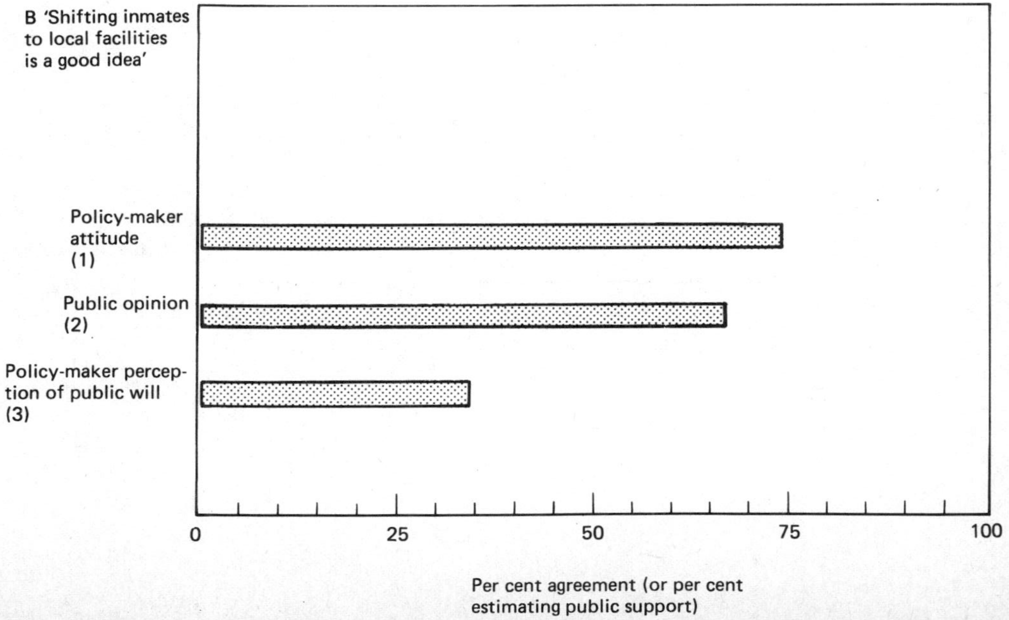

Figure 2.6 *cont.*

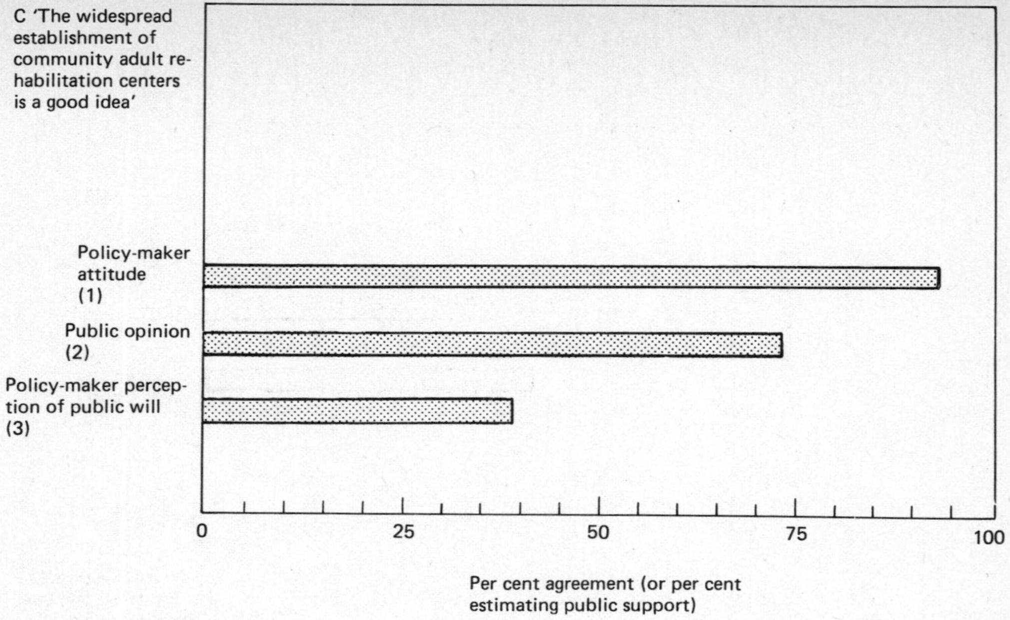

Figure 2.6 *cont.*

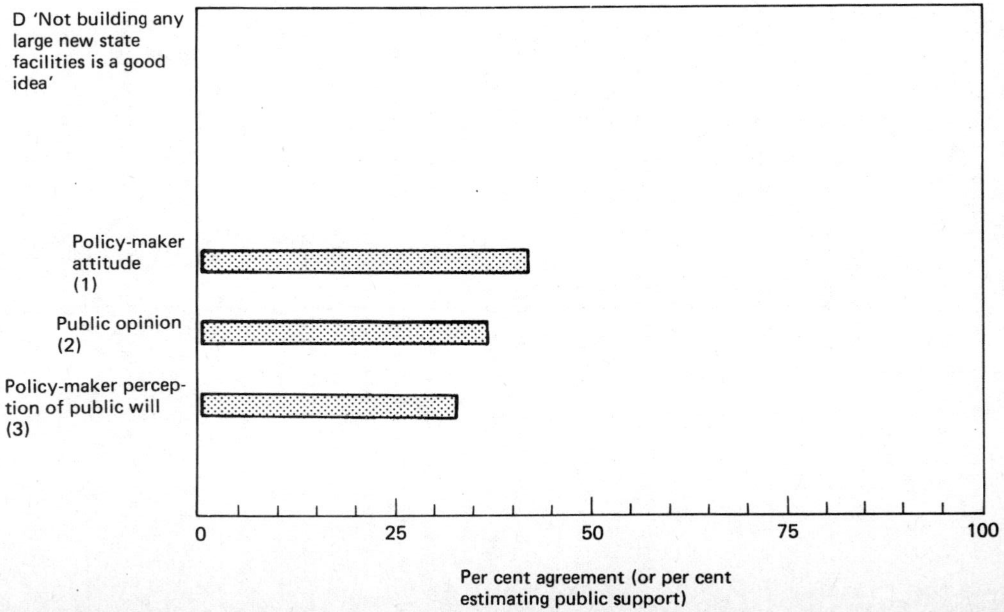

Figure 2.6 *cont.*

Concerning correctional system goals, we find a striking lack of correspondence between the policy-maker group's assessment of public opinion and the reality of that opinion: the correlation (rank order) between the two is large and negative (rho = −.84). While the policy makers report that the general public would strongly support the goal of retributive punishment and would offer only very weak support to the goal of rehabilitation, this is not the case. However, we find relatively good agreement between the policy makers' own goals for corrections and those of the general public (rho = .28). Both groups assign high priorities to the goal of rehabilitation or treatment and agree that simple retributive punishment is the least desirable goal for a correctional system. Thus, both the public and those who are charged with setting and implementing correctional policy appear to support utilitarian, as opposed to retributive, goals.

From the policy-maker sample, we gathered assessments of the priorities that the Maryland corrections system apparently assigns to these goals. When we correlate actual system functioning — as perceived by the policy makers — with the priorities as assigned by the public, we again find a negative relation (rho = −.27). That the public is aware of this lack of correspondence is clear: the general public overwhelmingly responds that Maryland's corrections system is doing a very poor job at meeting any of its proper goals. Fewer than half of the respondents feel — irrespective of the specific goal — that Maryland is doing a good job at implementation. Further, a very large proportion of the sample report that realistically more could be done to meet these intended correctional purposes.

We observed virtually this same pattern in the assessment of various proposals for correctional reform. Virtually no important differences exist between the policy makers' assessment of various change strategies and the public assessment of these same strategies. Yet with the exception of the building issue, the policy makers consistently misperceive the public sentiment. While the attitudes of both the public and the policy makers can be characterized as rather liberal, non-punitive, and reform-oriented, the policy makers attribute almost the reverse to the public.

Several studies concerned wih different policy arenas have observed this same phenomenon (e.g. Miller and Stokes, 1963; Hedlund and Friesma, 1972), and the only other study concerned specifically with correctional policy confirms our findings (Riley and Rose, 1980). We therefore feel it extremely unlikely that our results are spurious or in error.

To what should we attribute the findings? Hedlund and Friesma (1972) have argued that policy makers are better at assessing constituency opinion on major issues than on minor ones. It could readily be argued that the building controversy is the most important, or most visible, of the issues we addressed. If so, our findings support Hedlund and Friesma's argument, since the policy makers' assessments of public opinion on this issue are quite accurate. Harris (1968) has argued that while the public supports the concept of community-based corrections in theory, the public also feels that opposition from neighbours would be so great as to render nil the practical chances that such a programme would succeed. If so, our policy makers may be justified in their lack of faith in public support for this proposal.

Alternatively, one could take the position that the policy-making and implementing groups we studied are failing to meet the responsibilities with which they are charged. A basic assumption of representative democracy is that public policy should be responsive to the public will; and one can argue that this principle applies to both administrative and legislative branches of government. The picture we have seen clearly suggests not only that our policy makers are poor judges of the public's wants, but that the system they are charged with operating is not responsive to the priorities as assigned by the public. To this point, then, the evidence would seem to suggest that, with respect to correctional system goals and their implementation, those whom we charge with public responsibility are failing to meet that charge.

We prefer a less cynical interpretation, and in fact feel that the data better fit a model of 'pluralistic ignorance' — a term commonly used to describe situations in which persons underestimate the extent to which others share their beliefs and sentiments (Merton, 1968; O'Gorman, 1975; O'Gorman and Garry, 1976). We also examined the relation between policy makers' perception of the public will and their perception of the functioning of our present correctional system. The relation was high and positive (rho = .78). It appears that correctional policy may indeed be made and implemented in accordance with the public will, as the policy makers perceive that will. This, of course, is the critical issue: the extent to which policy makers misperceive or misunderstand the views of the public may determine the extent to which public policy will be non-responsive to the public will. If existing mechanisms used by policy makers to assess public opinion are inadequate, it is important that policy makers recognize this limitation. As Riley and Rose (1980: p. 347) suggest:

> If the model of a representative democracy is indeed operative, then providing decision-makers with empirical data obtained by using scientific survey techniques [could and] should lead to greater responsiveness to public opinion.

Summary and conclusions

Conflict theory argues that the criminal justice system, in its definition of laws and policies, reflects the views or values of those in society who have power over others. Consensus theory, on the other hand, argues that society functions largely through a shared set of values and beliefs. The latter model suggests that there are few differences in values between those who rule and those ruled; the state is seen as value-neutral, and existing simply to carry out the values and wishes of society.

Support for either perspective historically has been mixed, and results of the investigations presented in this chapter contribute to this. Through examination of a novel method of assessing judged offence seriousness (which often has been studied in efforts to support the consensus perspective), we have shown that people's judgements of this critical concept may well differ. Clearly, the opinions of incarcerated felons — known rule violators — differ from those of a very heterogeneous sample of college students. It also is the case that those who enforce (e.g., police officers, prison guards, and parole/probation officers) and administer (e.g., judges and criminal attorneys) the law differ from each other, from felons, and from students. Interestingly, those having criminal justice system involvement view all types of offences as relatively less serious than do those not having such involvement. It is our opinion that these findings cast some doubt on the commonly held notion that groups do *not* differ with respect to their assessments of law-violating behaviour.

Our studies of correctional policy, however, do not seem to lend strong support to a conflict model. We did find a striking lack of correspondence between the public will and policy makers' perceptions of that will; but we also found that the public and the policy-maker sample actually were rather close in their assessments of correctional goals and strategies for change. Pluralistic ignorance is not conflict; and cannot, we think, stand as support for a conflict model. Rather, we would focus attention on the 'ignorance', which perhaps leads to a policy muddle.

It is only through the application of social science methods to these continuing debates of criminal justice policy that we may hope to better model the muddle, and perhaps to increase both the coherence of our criminal justice policies and their responsiveness to the public will.

Notes

1. The problem with a correlational approach, of course, is that the product-moment correlation coefficient *(r)* is independent of both unit of origin and

interval width. Hence, for example, two groups' judgements could be highly correlated even though the groups' judgements could differ with respect to (a) origin, (b) unit size, or (c) both. The use of regression coefficients (as was done by Rossi et al.) to assess differences among groups with respect to judged seriousness could ameliorate this problem since these coefficients represent differences in slope.

2. Note that even this apparently simple 'common metric' is problematic. For example, is it possible to equate time spent in county jails with time spent in state prisons? Or time spent in maximum security with time in minimum security? Should we consider a sentence of two years given to a 70-year-old man to be equivalent to two years given to a 20-year-old man, even if both are to the same institution?
3. The complete list of items is available from the first author. Example items appear in later tables.
4. The intercorrelations of scale values of the 162 offence descriptions based on the arithmetic mean, the median, the geometric mean, and on the results of the successive intervals scaling procedure all exceed .98. This suggests that end effects were relatively mild, and that substantive conclusions should not be affected simply by the measure of central tendency employed.
5. In our study, the offence description read 'A juvenile is repeatedly truant'. In the Sellin and Wolfgang study, the description was given as 'A juvenile plays hooky from school and thereby becomes an offender'.
6. Subjects were selected for inclusion in either sample using a probabilistically weighted random sample generator. As each subject is considered for inclusion independently of all others, sub-samples are not of precisely the same size.
7. The analyses which follow are, of course, conservative since the *n*/variables ratio is somewhat low. This could reduce the stability of any resulting structure.
8. Detailed tables describing all analyses are available from the first author.
9. It could be the case, of course, that these dimensions are small in terms of the proportion of the overall variance for which they account precisely because there were relatively few items available to define them.
10. Note that this procedure does not 'force' orthogonality of scales, as would be the case if factor scores were used to construct the scales.
11. Chi-squared on 30 degrees of freedom = 389.2; $p < .001$.
12. Chi-squared on 20 degrees of freedom = 164.7; $p < .001$.
13. Lambda = .88: Chi-squared on 12 degrees of freedom = 66.8: $p < .001$.
14. Because of budgetary restrictions, we did not of course interview all such persons. In this sense, then, this can be considered a sample of the larger policy-making group. We believe that our sample is biased toward the 'heavily involved' portion of this larger group.
15. However, a rural–urban–suburban locational analysis yielded little in the way of important differences.
16. The approach is described in detail in Gottfredson and Taylor, (1982).
17. With only four ranks, one must obtain a value of rho equal to 1.00 to achieve traditional levels of statistical significance. It should be pointed out, however, that the data discussed here represent mean ranks, and are based on very large numbers of cases. Accordingly, the ranks discussed may be considered to be quite stable. Where differences between mean ranks did not exceed at least one standard error in magnitude, ranks are represented as tied. Our use of rho is intended simply as an aid to interpretation.

References

Berk, R.A., and Rossi, P.H. (1977), *Prison Reform and State Elites,* Cambridge, MA: Ballinger.

Blair, G.W. (1956) *The Measurement of Mind and Matter*, New York: Philosophical Library.

Box, S., and Hale, C. (1982), 'Economic crisis and the rising prisoner population in England and Wales', *Crime and Social Justice*, (Summer), 20–35.

Chambliss, W., and Seidman, R. (1982), *Law, Order and Power*, Reading, Mass: Addison-Wesley.

Conklin, J.E. (1971), 'Criminal environment and support for the law', *Law and Society Review*, **6**(2), 247–259.

Cullen, F.T., Link, B.G., Travis, III, L., and Wozniak, J. (1985), 'Consensus in crime seriousness: empirical reality or methodological artifact?', *Criminology*, **23**(1), 99–118.

Dahrendorf, R. (1959), *Class and Class Conflict in Industrial Society*, Stanford: Stanford University Press.

Dershowitz, A. (1976), 'Background paper', in Report of the Twentieth Century Fund Task Force on Criminal Sentencing, *Fair and Certain Punishment*, New York: McGraw-Hill.

Devlin, P. (1965), *The Enforcement of Morals*, New York: Oxford University Press.

Diederich, G., Messick, S., and Tucker, L. (1957, 'A general least squares solution for successive intervals' *Psychometrika*, **22**, 159–173.

Figlio, R.M. (1979), 'The national survey of crime severity: some general findings', Philadelphia, PA: University of Pennsylvania (unpublished).

Gottfredson, S.D., and Taylor, R.B. (1982), *America's Correctional Crisis*, Final Report to the National Institute of Justice, Washington, DC: National Institute of Justice.

Gottfredson, S.D., and Taylor, R.B. (1983), *The Correctional Crisis*, Washington, DC: National Institute of Justice.

Gottfredson, S.D., and Taylor, R.B. (1984), 'Public policy and prison populations: measuring opinions about reform', *Judicature*, **68**(4–5), 190–201.

Gottfredson, S.D., and Taylor, R.B. (1987), 'Attitudes of correctional policymakers and the public', S.D. Gottfredson and S. McConville (eds) *America's Correctional Crisis*, Westport, CT: Greenwood Press.

Gottfredson, S.D., Young, K.L., and Laufer, W.S. (1980), 'Additivity and interactions in offence seriousness scales', *Journal of Research in Crime and Delinquency*, **17**, 26–41.

Harmon, H. (1967), *Modern Factor Analysis*, Chicago, Ill: University of Chicago Press.

Harris, L. (1968), 'Changing public attitudes toward crime and corrections', *Federal Probation*, **32**, 9–16.

Hedlund, R.D., and Friesma, H.P. (1972), 'Representative perceptions of constituency opinion', *Journal of Politics*, **34**, 730–752.

Kleinig, J. (1973) *Punishment and Desert*, The Hague: Martinus-Nijhoff.

Kornhauser, R.P. (1978), *Social Sources of Delinquency*, Chicago: University of Chicago Press.

Levi, M., and Jones, S. (1985), 'Public and police perceptions of crime seriousness in England and Wales', *British Journal of Criminology*, **25**(31), 234–250.

Liska, A.E., Lawrence, J.J., and Benson, M. (1981), 'Perspectives on the legal order: the capacity for social control', *American Journal of Sociology*, **87**(2), 413–426.

Liska, W.E., and Tausig, M. (1979), 'Theoretical interpretations of social class and racial differentials in legal decision-making for juveniles', *Sociological Quarterly*, (Spring), 197–207.

Luttbeg, N.R. (1968), 'Political linkage in a large society', *Public Opinion and Public Policy: Models of Political Linkages*, Homewood, Ill: Dorsey.

Macoby, E.E., Johnson, J.P., and Church, R.M. (1958), 'Community integration and the social control of juvenile delinquency', *Journal of Social Issues*, **14**, 38–51.

McCarthy, B., and Smith, B.L. (1986), 'The conceptualization of discrimination in the juvenile justice process: the impact of administrative factors and screening decisions on juvenile court dispositions', *Criminology*, **24**(1), 41–64.

Merton, R.K. (1961), 'Social problems and social theory', R.K. Merton and R. Nisbet (eds), *Contemporary Social Problems*, New York: Harcourt, Brace and World.
Merton, R.K. (1968), *Social Theory and Social Structure*, New York: Free Press.
Miethe, T.D. (1982), 'Public consensus on crime seriousness: normative structure or methodological artifact?', *Criminology*, **20**(3–4), 515–526.
Miller, W.E., and Stokes, D.E. (1963), 'Constituency influence in Congress', *American Political Science Review*, **57**, 46–56.
Morris, N. (1974), *The Future of Imprisonment*, Chicago: University of Chicago Press.
O'Gorman, H.J. (1975), 'Pluralistic ignorance and white estimates of white support for racial segregation', *Public Opinion Quarterly*, **39**, 313–330.
O'Gorman, H.J., and Garry, S.L. (1976), 'Pluralistic ignorance: a replication and extension', *Public Opinion Quarterly*, **40**, 449–458.
Quinney, R. (1970), *The Social Reality of Crime*, Boston: Little Brown.
Riley, P.J., and Rose, McN. (1980), 'Public opinion vs. elite opinion on correctional reform', *Journal of Criminal Justice*, **8**, 345–356.
Rossi, P.H., and Henry, J.P. (1980), 'Seriousness: a measure for all purposes?', M. W. Klein and K.S. Teilmann (eds), *Handbook of Criminal Justice Evaluation*, Beverly Hills, CA: Sage.
Rossi, P.H., Waite, E., Bose, C., and Berk, R. (1974), 'The seriousness of crime: normative structure and individual differences', *American Sociological Review*, **39**, 224–237.
Sellin, T., and Wolfgang, M. (1964), *The Measurement of Delinquency*, New York: Wiley.
Sparks, R., Genn, H., and Dodd, D. (1977), *Surveying Victims*, New York: Wiley.
Torgerson, W. (1958), *Theory and Methods of Scaling*, New York: Wiley.
Vold, G. B. (1958), *Theoretical Criminology*, Oxford: Oxford University Press.
von Hirsch, A. (1976), *Doing Justice: The Choice of Punishments*, New York: Hill-Wang.
Walker, M. (1978), 'Measuring the seriousness of crimes', *British Journal of Criminology*, **18**, 348–364.

3 Does the severity of sentences affect public disapproval? An experiment in England*

Nigel Walker and Catherine Marsh

The hypothesis

Scepticism about the efficacy of attempts to deter or correct offenders has driven theorists in two directions. One is 'just deserts'; the other is the denunciatory justification, sometimes called 'the expressive theory'. Although usually credited to Durkheim, this has been independently held by English lawyers — including one who wrote in the first half of the eighteenth century — and particularly by judges, of whom Fitzjames Stephen and Lord Denning are the most notable examples. They believe that an important function of the penalties of the criminal law is to denounce: that is, express condemnation (usually 'society's condemnation') of the offence. Lord Denning went so far as to tell the Royal Commission on Capital Punishment that this is the 'ultimate justification'.[1] However that may be, most 'denouncers' seem to believe that the point of expressing condemnation through the penalty is to increase (or at least maintain) public disapproval of the offence in question, In *R.* v. *Sargeant*[2] the Court of Appeal (Criminal Division) said: '... society, through the courts, must show its abhorrence of particular types of crime ... The courts do not have to reflect public opinion. On the other hand the courts must not disregard it. Perhaps the main duty of the courts is to *lead* public opinion' (our italics).

*This is a revised version of an article originally published in the *British Journal of Criminology* (1984), **24** (1), 27–48. We record our gratitude to the Social Science Research Council (as it then was called) for the grant which made the fieldwork possible; to NOP Market Research Limited for expert advice as well as professional service; to the Audio-Visual Unit of Cambridge University for videotaping our briefing sessions for the pilot interviewers; to Professor Leonard Berkowitz for helpful comments at the planning stage; to Professor Tony Bottoms, Dr David Farrington, Professor Hyman Gross and Mrs Monica Walker for comments on a draft of the report; and to Mr Brian Omotan of the Cambridge University Computing Service for help with some of the magnetic tapes.

Relevance for sentencing policy

Since the Court was considering Sargeant's sentence, the implication is that members of the public who believe a given type of offence to be severely penalized will, at least for a time, disapprove of it more than those who believe the penalty to be something markedly less severe. This implication is important for sentencing policy, especially when it forms part of the philosophy of the Court of Appeal, because it justifies a tough sentencing policy in a way that is independent of any belief in deterrence, correction or just deserts.

Fortunately, it also seems susceptible to empirical investigation. In the late 1970s Walker experimented with groups of undergraduate law students, asking them to indicate on paper how much they disapproved of various examples of criminal conduct, while systematically giving difficult sub-groups of his subjects different information about the nature of the sentence which the offender had received (Walker, 1981). Marsh followed these experiments with a small number of house-to-house interviews on similar lines, conducted by students. These experiments did not support the belief that differences in the severity of sentences influenced subjects' disapproval; but both of us felt that more rigorous testing was needed, using house-to-house interviews conducted by trained and thoroughly briefed interviewers.

The samples

A grant from the Social Science Research Council enabled us to contract with NOP Market Research Limited for a pilot study in the Cambridge area, followed by 1,000 interviews in three constituencies: St Helen's (in the north of England), Solihull (in the Midlands) and Basildon (on the outskirts of London).[3] The interviews were restricted to one parent of either sex in households where at least one child under the age of 20 was living at home, and where no member of the household was in work connected with law-enforcement. NOP were also kind enough to include one or two attitudinal questions in one of their periodic 'omnibus' surveys of adults aged 18 or older, irrespective of their parental status, with reassuringly similar results. The investigation was an experiment, not what Cook and Campbell (1979) have called 'a passive observation programme', so that the most important feature of its design was not the representativeness[4] of the sample, but the success of the random assignment of respondents to the different conditions used in the experiment.

The interviews

Interviews lasted, on average, for about 25 minutes: the pilot study suggested that longer interviews tended to bore respondents. The first question concerned respondents' agreement or disagreement with 10 standard propositions (e.g. 'divorce should be made easier to get'), in order to measure their 'liberality'. The next asked them to rank types of sentence in order of 'toughness'. Questions 3–10 were about the frequency with which respondents read newspapers or heard news on television or radio, and the extent of their recollection of news about specific trials and sentences. Next, respondents were shown the 'newspaper cuttings' in the appendix and asked questions about them. Questions were also asked, without newspaper cuttings, about non-use of seat-belts, which was due to become an offence early in 1983. Questions 27–35 were concerned with the effects of opinion polls on respondents' views about the availability of abortion.[5] The final questions dealt with matters such as respondents' age, education and occupation. Before the interview ended respondents were told that some of the details in the newspaper cuttings had been altered for the purpose of the survey.

Randomizing the independent variables

Interviews also recorded information about respondents' sexes, ages, occupational groups[6] and employment status, educational attainments and religious affiliations, chiefly in case these might be associated with different levels of disapproval of the incidents in our newspaper cuttings. At an early stage of the analysis we investigated the extent to which the method of sampling[7] had achieved a random distribution of such characteristics between the four versions of the interview, and in this analysis we included the independent attitudinal variables, such as our measures of 'liberality' and the ranking of standard penalties (discussed later). Significance tests confirmed that the distributions showed no sign of bias.[8] This meant that even if an independent variable was associated with our respondents' attitudes to our newspaper cuttings — and in particular their disapproval scores — it was unnecessary to make any adjustment to allow for this when we were comparing the scores in the four versions of the interview.

Attention to trial reports

If, as denouncers believe, sentences convey a message to the public, it is only by way of the news media that this message could reach a sufficient number to be worth consideration. Only a few people attend trials or hear by word of mouth of the sentences imposed on an offender. After we had asked how often respondents read local or national papers, and got news from television or the radio, we asked 'How often would you say you read or hear about court cases?' 'Most days' was the response of 43 per cent;[9] 'quite often' of 23 per cent; 'occasionally' of 32 per cent; and only 2.5 per cent said 'never'. When asked, however, 'Do you remember any details about any local or national court case?' 42 per cent could not, 31 per cent claimed to remember details of one case but no more, while 27 per cent claimed to recall details of a second case (they were not asked about more than two). The 58 per cent who said they could recall details were asked what the sentence was; but only 39 per cent, (i.e. about two-thirds of the 58 per cent) could do so, and only 13 per cent (i.e. about half of the 27 per cent) could do so in a second case.[10] It does not seem that the sentences which are reported by the news media are remembered by the majority of parents: a serious problem for denouncers.

When it was possible to identify the case, the respondent's recollection of the sentence was usually correct; but chiefly because most of the identifiable cases involved serious violence and a sentence of imprisonment for 'life'. Most frequently recalled, by 282 subjects, was *Sutcliffe* ('the Yorkshire Ripper'). The trial (and acquittal) of several prison officers as a result of Prosser's death in custody was recalled by 43, and a 'fantasy-murder' by an ex-patient from a mental hospital was recalled by 41. With these exceptions, however, the remembered cases were very miscellaneous: 592 respondents mentioned 291 different cases.

In no case was there an indication that a penalty was recalled because it seemed too severe; but in several cases a sentence was mentioned with a comment to the effect that it seemed lenient. We record this with hesitation, because our subjects were not asked why they recalled a sentence: a question which would have been of very doubtful value. We expected quite a number to mention the case in which a judge had been much criticized for merely fining a man who had raped a hitch-hiker; but only one respondent mentioned him, and he was unsure whether the sentence was a fine or suspended imprisonment.

Ranking penalties

People's disapproval is unlikely to be influenced by a sentence if they are not sure whether it is tough or lenient : so we investigated this. Seven penalties in common use were listed on seven cards, which were given to subjects in a randomly shuffled pack, with instructions to arrange it so that 'the toughest' was first, 'the mildest' was last and the rest in order between. The result is shown in Table 3.1.

The table has several features of interest. It shows, for example, how the usual presentation, mean rankings, and a less usual one,

Table 3.1 Ranking of the seven common sentences by 1,046 subjects

Sentence	Most frequent order (*N* = 98)	Most often assigned place (*N*s in brackets)	Mean rankings
Imprisonment: 12 months	1st	1st (959)	1.2
Imprisonment: 1 month	2nd	2nd (900)	2.2
Fine: £100	3rd	3rd (451)	4.0
Fine: £40	4th	4th (364)	5.3
Community service	5th	5th (261)	5.0
Probation	6th	6th (309)	5.0
Suspended sentence	7th	7th (401)	5.4

most frequent placings, can give a different order. In this case, mean rankings place the £40 fine sixth whereas its most frequent placing was fourth.

It is clear that for the great majority of our subjects a prison sentence was 'toughest', but that after that their unanimity decreased. There were no less than 23 different orderings of the seven penalties. Some were the result of mere carelessness: for example, the 2 per cent who ranked the shorter prison sentence as tougher than the longer one.[11]

It would be unsafe, however, to dismiss as merely careless the 3 per cent who gave first place to the £100 fine, or the 3 per cent who gave it to community service. For some of our respondents a heavy fine may indeed have been a 'tougher' prospect than imprisonment. Unanimity was somewhat increased — more precisely, the number of different orderings was reduced from 23 to 12 — by disregarding community service. The biggest reductions, however, were achieved by disregarding probation or suspended sentence, either of which reduced the number of different orderings to nine.

One of our concerns, however, was to identify the types of sentence which could be used in experiments such as ours to symbolize the opposite of 'toughness'. Clearly we had been right to assume that a prison sentence would symbolize toughness; but had we been right to assume that probation was the best symbol of leniency? The obvious competitor in Table 3.1 is the suspended sentence. Would it have been better to use it? At first sight there seemed to be little to choose between the two. The suspended sentence was placed fifth, sixth or seventh by more respondents than was probation (744 compared with 662); but it was also placed first, second or third by more (180 compared with 160). What was clearly in favour of probation, however, was the distribution of rankings. From the point of view of randomization (see the earlier section on this) probation rankings were much more evenly distributed ($p = 0.5$) between the respondents to the four different versions of the interview than were suspended sentence rankings ($p = 0.07$). Probation seems, after all, to have been the most fortunate possible choice. From the denouncer's point of view, however, it is worth noting that there is no measure in the court's repertoire[12] which stands for leniency in everyone's eyes.

The 'newspaper cuttings'

The most important part of the interview consisted of showing respondents five 'newspaper cuttings' (see appendix). These described examples of violence, vandalism and criminal dishonesty, and were based on incidents which had been reported in the press in recent years. They were specially composed for the survey so as to resemble newspaper cuttings in style and setting, while omitting any indication of the sentence or the sentencer's attitude to the offence, so that this could be given as supplementary information by the interviewer, in accordance with the experimental design (see Table 3.3). The exact wording of the questions can be seen in *The British Journal of Criminology*, vol. 1, 1984, pp. 43–47. The stories in the cuttings had to be:

- of sufficient interest to engage respondents' attention;
- of such a kind that either a prison sentence or probation was a credible disposal;
- not too long or complicated for respondents who were used to short, simple news items;
- not too numerous: the pilot survey had shown that about five cuttings were as many as respondents could read without loss of interest;
- concerned with offences which were not of the gravest nature: the pilot survey had confirmed, for example, that a violent mugging was so strongly disapproved of by nearly all respondents that no significant effect could be expected.

In short, we were trying to present respondents with stories which, though concerned with incidents that were not trivial, provided reasonable scope for the operation of the effect which the Court of Appeal in *Sargeant* called 'leading public opinion'. We even went to the length of constructing two of the stories — those involving the 'ex-boxer' and the 'booby-trapped greenhouse' — so that respondents would not find it easy to decide how far to disapprove of what the offender had done, since it seemed possible that the 'expressive effect' might be confined to such situations.

Expected penalties and 'cynicism'

After respondents had been shown each cutting the interviewer asked what penalty the offender should have received, and then what penalty the respondent thought that he 'actually did get'.[13] This was done partly in order to make sure that when respondents were *told* what he actually got they took note of it, partly in order to enable us to look for any interactions between expectations and information. The results, however, were interesting in themselves. The most straightforward example was the 'computer fraud'. Eight hundred subjects (78 per cent) thought he *should* have been sent to prison; but of those 800 only 67 per cent *expected* this sentence: the remaining third expected something more lenient. Even more striking were the expectations in the case of the owner of 'the booby-trapped greenhouse': 63 per cent thought he *should* have been discharged without penalty or given a suspended sentence; but of that 63 per cent only 28 per cent *expected* one of those disposals, and nearly three-quarters *expected* a more severe measure. In every case very substantial numbers did not expect the defendant to get what in their view he should have got. For want of a better term of art we call this 'cynicism'. 'Cynical' members of the public are unlikely to be as respectful of sentences as the denunciatory theory would require.

The disapproval scale

In order to measure respondents' disapproval of each incident we provided a 'disapproval scale' on the back of each cutting, so that at the appropriate stage they simply turned over the card and selected the phrase which came nearest to their feeling. Various types and wordings[14] of the scale had been tried at earlier stages, including purely numerical scales: Table 3.2 shows the version finally used, with the distribution of respondents after being shown the 'ex-boxer . . .' cutting.

The geography and demography of disapproval

Some of the differences in mean disapproval scores seem worth mentioning. We sub-divided respondents into eight sex–age–occupation groups: men or women under 34 or over 33, and in 'middle' or 'working-class' occupational groupings. Their mean

Table 3.2 *Respondents' disapproval of 'accepting a challenge to a fight like the ex-boxer did'*

	Choices
I do not disapprove at all	142
I disapprove very little	124
I disapprove a little	177
I disapprove quite a bit	145
I disapprove fairly strongly	127
I disapprove strongly	152
I disapprove very strongly	165
(Don't know)[15]	23
	1,055

scores did not differ significantly for 'the booby-trapped greenhouse' or 'computer fraud', perhaps because most respondents were very tolerant of what the greenhouse owner did and very censorious of what the bank employee did. For the other items, however — 'the hungry husband', the 'ex-boxer', the 'telephone vandal' and non-use of seat-belts — there were significant differences. Younger working-class men and women were least censorious of the ex-boxer's conduct. Older working-class women were the most tolerant of the hungry husband's assault on his neglectful wife, although all groups were fairly censorious. Young middle-class men and women were more tolerant than others about the vandalizing of the public telephone. Working-class respondents — with the exception of older women — were more tolerant of the decision not to use a seat-belt. The differences between mean scores in Solihull, St Helen's and Basildon were not striking, and in any case seemed to be due to small differences in the demographic make-up of subjects from the three constituencies.

Free comments

After indicating the strength of their disappoval, respondents were asked 'Is there anything else you would like to say about what the (vandal) did?'[16] They were not pressed to add anything, but roughly three in four commented on one or other of the offences. What they said could be sub-divided into about eight categories:

- the offence was serious;

- it was stupid or unjustifiable (especially said of the assault by the hungry husband);
- the offender was taking the law into his own hands (especially said of the greenhouse-owner);
- he had the right to do what he did (again especially said of the greenhouse-owner);
- the respondent sympathized with the offender;
- the victim was to blame (especially said of the challenger of the ex-boxer);
- society was to blame (in a few comments on the telephone vandal and one comment on the hungry husband);
- the police were to blame (in two comments on the booby-trapped greenhouse, meaning presumably that they should have detected the thief before the booby-trap was set).

Both the frequency and the nature of the comments confirmed that respondents were sufficiently interested in our 'newspaper cuttings', and also that they were differentiating between the culpability of the various defendants.

The experimental questions

The form of the experimental questions can be studied in the article in *The British Journal of Criminology*. The design of the four versions resulted in the showing of the newspaper cuttings in differing orders, so that each was followed by information of four differing kinds. For example, the 'telephone vandal' was followed by the statement that 'judges have recently agreed to take a less serious view of this sort of case' or '. . . a more serious view . . .', or by the information that the vandal 'was sent to prison for six months' or '. . . got a probation order'. Every cutting was followed, in one version or another, by information to the effect that the offender had been imprisoned or put on probation; and every cutting except 'computer fraud' was in some other version followed by information about judges' views or the disapproval of 'people like yourself'. The exception, 'computer fraud', was always shown last, either without any information about sentence, judges' views or peer disapproval, or with the statement that the bank employee had been imprisoned or put on probation. The design, and the resulting mean disapproval scores, can be studied in Table 3.3.[17]

We also confirmed that we had succeeded in our efforts to make the 'ex-boxer' and the 'booby-trapped greenhouse' more morally ambiguous than the other stories. The standard deviations of the disapproval scores were markedly the largest for these two stories. This is important, because of the possibility that, even if information

Table 3.3 Means scores of disapproval of various crimes under different experimental conditions

Disapproval was measured on a scale where 1 represented 'I do not disapprove at all' and 7 represented 'I disapprove very strongly'.

	EXPERIMENT						
	i) varying sentence			ii) varying judge's views		iii) varying peer's disapproval	
Cutting†	probation	prison	no info.	less serious	more serious	disapprove a little	disapprove strongly
Telephone vandal	6.4	6.5		6.1	6.2		
Ex-boxer	3.9	4.1				4.0*	4.3*
Hungry husband	5.7	5.9				5.2	5.1
Booby-trapped greenhouse	2.9	3.2		2.9	2.8		
Computer fraud	6.0	6.1	6.2				

Notes: Each mean is based on between 256 and 264 individuals. *T*-tests were performed on each of the experimental comparisons (analysis of variance in the case of computer fraud); only the asterisked comparison attained significance ($p = 0.04$); other p-values were 0.11 or greater.

†Cuttings are shown in the appendix.

about sentences has no influence on disapproval of straightforward offences, it might help people to make up their minds in ambiguous cases. We shall see later whether this was so.

Judges' views

After being shown the 'booby-trapped greenhouse' 263 subjects were told that the judge had taken a 'serious view' of this case, while 264 were told the opposite. In the case of the 'telephone vandal' the information was deliberately varied to 'judges have recently agreed to take a more serious view of this sort of case' (or the contrary), since it seemed possible that a statement about judicial policy might be effective even if the stated view of a single judge was not.

Disapproval of the telephone vandalism was high: 83 per cent chose 'strongly' or 'very strongly'. Yet, as Table 3.3 shows, the information that judges had agreed to take this less seriously did not result in a significantly lower mean score. Conversely, though disapproval of the greenhouse owner was low, the news that the judge had taken a serious view of this case did not raise the score. This is particularly interesting because the story was one of those which had been designed with an eye to moral ambiguity, so that respondents might have been expected to welcome a 'lead'. Yet whatever made up their minds it was not, apparently, what we told them about the judge's views. Perhaps if the judge had made some striking remark (such as 'that boy might have been killed') this would have influenced parents; but what we were testing was the effect of a routine expression of censure by the judge or the judiciary, which in these cases seemed to be nil. In other words, even a direct statement of the judicial view (as distinct from a symbolic statement by way of sentence) does not seem to have the effect for which denouncers hope.

Peers' disapproval

Both the early experiments with undergraduates in law faculties and the Berkowitz-Walker experiment (1967) had led us to expect some effect if respondents were told what their peers felt. So they were shown two cuttings, 'hungry husband' and 'ex-boxer', asking them first how much they thought 'other people like yourself disapprove', then telling them that in fact those other people disapproved 'a little' or 'strongly'. Finally respondents were asked how much they themselves disapproved.

It was interesting to compare their own scores with those which they attributed to people like themselves. Of those who attributed strong disapproval (i.e. scores 6 or 7) to others, 65 per cent themselves chose those scores, whether the subject was the hungry husband or the ex-boxer. Roughly the same was true of those who attributed low degrees of disapproval to others.[18] On the other hand, of those who attributed intermediate degrees of disapproval to others, much lower percentages chose similar scores for themselves (34 per cent in the case of 'hungry husband' and 44 per cent for 'ex-boxer'). In short, respondents who attributed extremes of disapproval to others were more likely to hold extreme views themselves. This could be the result either of the projection of subjects' views on to others, or conformity with what they believed to be the strongly held views of others, although the latter hypothesis does not explain what led them to that belief.

Information about peers' disapproval did affect respondents' own disapproval in the case of the 'ex-boxer' ($p = 0.04$). When we excluded parents who attributed extreme views to peers (and were therefore likely to hold such views themselves) the significance of the effect increased ($p = 0.017$). 'Ex-boxer' was the other story which had been designed with an eye to moral ambiguity, and it seems likely that respondents who attributed intermediate degrees of disapproval to others were themselves sufficiently unsure of the right answer to take a lead from the actual views of other people. This phenomenon, however, was not observable in the case of the hungry husband: peers' ratings seemed to make no difference, even when parents who attributed extreme views to peers were excluded. Perhaps the explanation is that the morality of the story was less ambiguous, as we intended: perhaps it simply came closer to home. However that may be, the differing scores for the 'ex-boxer' story did meet one possible criticism of our experimental manipulations: namely that they were too crude or insensitive to pick up the weak effects which were the most that could be expected in real life. These scores show that this is over-stated, and that disapproval in morally ambiguous situations can be affected, even in our sort of experiment, by at least one kind of manipulated information, namely about the disapproval of 'people like yourself'.

Seat-belts and 'criminalization'

The seat-belt questions were similarly reassuring. At the time of the survey Parliament had decided to make non-use of safety-belts in the front seats of vehicles an offence, but the law had not yet been brought into operation or publicized.[19] We were thus able to tell respondents that this would soon be an offence, and to ask them how much they disapproved of 'deciding not to wear a seat-belt at the moment' and 'when it becomes an offence'. In one version of the interview they were given no information about the penalty;

Table 3.4 Disapproval of 'deciding not to wear a seat-belt at the moment' and (in brackets) 'when it becomes an offence'

Maximum penalty	Number of respondents	Mean disapproval score	Standard deviation
Not stated	263	3.17 (4.51)	2.39 (2.27)
'up to a fine of £50'	527	2.90 (4.32)	2.26 (2.40)
'up to a month in prison'	264	3.01 (4.34)	2.29 (2.36)

in another version they were told that the penalty would be 'anything up to a month in prison', and in the remaining two versions they were told that it would be 'anything up to a fine of £50'. The results are in Table 3.4.

As can be seen, there were no significant differences between the scores of those who were given no information or different information about the maximum penalty. On the other hand, there were marked differences between their scores for 'at the moment' and 'when it becomes an offence'. These differences are consistent with the findings of the Berkowitz–Walker experiments (1967), in which subjects were given differing information about the illegality of lending money for betting and non-interference with suicide: being told that it was criminal was associated with stronger disapproval. An objection to our procedure is that the order in which respondents were asked how much they disapproved — first 'at the moment', then 'when it becomes an offence' — more or less invites them to express stronger disapproval in the latter case;[20] but the Berkowitz–Walker experiment was not open to this objection. The seat-belt scores are entirely consistent with the 'declaratory' theory that disapproval of at least some types of conduct is influenced by declaring it criminal; but that must be distinguished from the denunciatory theory about the effect of sentences, which in this case seemed absent. At the same time, this part of the experiment again demonstrated that it was sensitive enough to detect an effect.

Do sentences 'lead' public opinion?

It was, however, the possible effect of the sentence upon respondents' disapproval that was the main focus of our study, since this is presumably what judges have in mind when they believe that they are leading public opinion. So in one or other version of the interview

Table 3.5 Respondents who expected the greenhouse-owner to get no penalty

	Disapproval levels		
but were told he got	1 or 2	3, 4, 5 or 6	Number
Imprisonment	71%	29%	24
Probation	40%	60%	30

$\chi^2 = 3.94$: ($p < 0.05$)

respondents, having been shown the cutting, were asked first what sentence the offender should have got, then what sentence they expected, with the results already mentioned. Thus, whether or not they paid any attention to sentences reported by the news media, they could hardly help noting the sentence which they were then told this offender had received. To make sure of this, however, they were then asked what they thought of that sentence.[21] In real life it must be exceptional for readers to pay so much attention to the sentence; but our purpose was to give the expressive hypothesis every chance by making sure that in these cases our readers did.

Table 3.3 shows that the results did not provide support for the expressive hypothesis. Differences between mean disapproval scores in the 'prison' and 'probation' conditions were very small, and nowhere near an acceptable level of significance. The most that can be pointed out is that they were all in the predicted direction, so that it is *possible* that the scores of a small number of parents were influenced by the sentence. This cannot, however, be inferred from the figures, which merely fail to rule out this possibility. And there was at least one result which made it seem rather unlikely. The highest mean score for the 'computer fraud' was found amongst respondents who had been given no information about the penalty.

One finding, however, suggested that in certain circumstances a severe sentence might even *lower* disapproval: a 'back-lash effect'. Most disapproval scores in the case of 'the booby-trapped greenhouse' were low. No less that 54 respondents expected the booby-trapper to receive no penalty. Those who were told that he had been imprisoned were more likely to express little or no disapproval than those who were told that he had been put on probation (see Table 3.5).

There was a similar distribution in the other ambiguous case — 'ex-boxer' — but the numbers were smaller (43) and the difference less marked, so that the level of significance was lower. Taken together, however, the distributions suggest that in such cases a sentence which seems too severe may induce some people to express less disapproval than they would otherwise.

Summary

- it is only a substantial minority of parents who are interested in news media reports of criminal trials;
- not all of this minority can recall particular cases to the extent of remembering the sentence;
- for the great majority, a prison sentence stands for 'toughness';
- a somewhat smaller majority regarded probation as 'mild', but probation was the best choice as a symbol of leniency for the purpose of our experiment;
- comparison of the sentences which they thought should have been awarded for the offences described in the newspaper cuttings with those which they expected to be awarded suggested that many did not have much respect for the sentencing system;
- information about the judicial view of the seriousness of the offences did not influence their disapproval, even in a morally ambiguous case;
- but information about peers' disapproval did have the expected effect, though only in a morally ambiguous case;
- the information that non-use of seat-belts would soon be an offence seemed to increase their disapproval of it;
- the information that an offender had been imprisoned or put on probation did not affect the disapproval of enough parents to make anything like a significant difference to their mean disapproval scores;
- on the whole, parents seemed to be making up their own minds about the culpability of the actions described in our cuttings, and were not often influenced.

Discussion

The survey was not a plebiscite but an experiment. It went to considerable lengths to create conditions in which the severity or leniency of a sentence should be expected — by denouncers — to affect parents' disapproval, for example by drawing attention to the sentence to a greater extent than do newspaper reports, and by including morally ambiguous stories amongst the cuttings. It succeeded in eliciting evidence that peers' views and 'criminalization' could, in some circumstances, affect disapproval, but failed to do the same when the manipulated variable was information about the sentence or about judicial disapproval. It is conceivable, of course, that some subjects are affected in the way posited by denouncers, but that these subjects are so few in number that the effect is undetectable.

It is also conceivable that to achieve the effect it is necessary to draw subjects' attention to a succession of examples of similarly severe (or lenient) sentences for the same sort of offence: a possibility which might conceivably be tested experimentally. What has to be remembered, however, is that in real life news media reports of sentences do not seem to make much impression, even when they are strikingly lenient or severe, and that the news media cannot be expected to give repeated publicity to series of sentences which merely exemplify sentencing policy. The denunciatory theory has the attraction of appearing to justify a tough sentencing policy in a way which is independent of 'just deserts' or a belief in general deterrence, but the empirical facts make it most unlikely that the theory is realistic.

Notes

1. For a fuller account and discussion of variants of the expressive theory see Walker, 1981.
2. (1974) 60 Cr.App.R. 74.
3. In the event, the main survey, carried out in late June 1982, yielded 1,055 completed interview schedules. The number of interviews conducted in each ward of each constituency was proportional to its size. Controls were set on age, sex and employment status, using information from NOP's national random surveys. Wards being small ensured a degree of control over social class. Interviewers were instructed to interview only one parent of either sex in each household where there was at least one child under the age of 20 living at home (on the assumption that any influence of sentences is likely to be greatest amongst families in which adults are in a position to be concerned about the conduct of the young and to discuss such matters with them). Interviewers were also told to exclude households in which anyone worked for the police, the courts, prisons, the probation service or any part of the legal profession. There was about one refusal for every household in which an interview was achieved; but only in one up-market part of St Helen's did an interviewer encounter a markedly high refusal-rate. No other problems were reported by interviewers. In 43 interviews the interviewer was accompanied by a supervisor; and in addition 71 interviews were confirmed by a supervisor's personal visit, and 15 more by a telephone call.
4. Whatever 'representativeness' means: see Kruskal and Mosteller, (1979).
5. The subject of a separate article by Marsh.
6. Using the social gradings of the Institute of Practitioners in Advertising.
7. See note 3.
8. Out of 42 independent variables, only one (the ranking of the suspended sentence) was distributed in a way that was significant at even the 0.07 level, and this variable played no part in our experiment (see 'Ranking penalties').
9. Less often in the case of young men and elderly women from occupational groups D and E.
10. If they recalled that the trial was still continuing, or had resulted in a 'not guilty' verdict, this was counted as recalling the sentence: otherwise the percentages would have exaggerated the extent of failure to recall.
11. Only 35 of our subjects used orderings which could be called irrational, e.g. placing the shorter prison sentence higher than the longer one.
12. It would have been implausible to tell our subjects that each of the offenders

in our newspaper cuttings had been 'discharged'; and some people confuse a discharge with an acquittal.

13. The exceptions were Questions 11 and 13, which were used to test possible effects of telling respondents not what the sentence was but what the judge's view or the reaction of 'people like yourself' had been.
14. For example, we rejected 'how serious ...' because this seemed to give too much weight to the harm done. A purely numerical scale might have encouraged an assumption of equal interval width, but many respondents would not have found it easy to use. In any case, the relative robustness of *t*-tests provides some reassurance even when intervals are not of equal width (Lieberman, 1971).
15. Since we did not want to encourage this response, it was not printed on the card.
16. But not in the case of the computer fraud or non-use of seat-belts, by which stage there was a danger of boring respondents.
17. We also tested for significant interactions between our experimentally varied conditions and disapproval scores within each demographic group: but there were none.
18. But the percentage in the case of the hungry husband was only 50 per cent.
19. We ourselves had to make several enquiries in order to find out the proposed date of operation of the new law and the maximum penalty provided (a £50 fine). We were, by the way, extremely lucky: a few weeks after our survey the new provision did receive publicity.
20. Even if we had reversed the question in some versions, and asked first how much respondents would disapprove when non-use became an offence, and then how much they disapproved at present, it would still have been arguable that they would feel obliged to choose lower degrees of disapproval in answer to the second part of the question.
21. Except in the case of the computer fraud, since in one version they were not told what his sentence was.

References

Berkowitz, L. and Walker, N. (1967), 'Laws and Moral Judgments', *Sociometry*, **30**, 410–422.

Cook, T. D. and Campbell, D. T. (1979), *Quasi-Experimentation*, Chicago: Rand McNally.

Kruskal, W. and Mosteller, F. (1979), '... Representative Sampling, I, II and III', *International Statistical Review*, **47**, 13–24, 111–127, 245–265.

Lieberman, B. (1971), *Contemporary Problems in Statistics*, London: Oxford University Press.

Marsh, C. (1977), 'Does Sentencing Affect Moral Judgments?', Unpublished report available from the author.

Marsh, C. (1984), 'Back on the Bandwagon: the Effect of Opinion Polls on Public Opinion', *British Journal of Political Science*, **15**, 113–136.

Walker, N. (1981), 'The Ultimate Justification' in *Crime, Proof and Punishment: Essays in Memory of Sir Rupert Cross* (ed. C. F. H. Tapper), London: Butterworths.

Walker, N. and Argyle, M. (1964), 'Does the Law Affect Moral Judgments?', *British Journal of Criminology*, **4**, 570–581

Ex-Boxer breaks Challenger's Jaw

A broken jaw was the result of a challenge to a fight outside a Northtown public house. But the man who challenged Robert Brown (30), did not know he had been a welterweight boxer. Brown pleaded guilty to causing actual bodily harm outside the Rose and Crown. He told the court he thought the other man knew he was a boxer.

Computer Fraud Exposed

A bank employee who cheated thousands of customers by using his computer skills was brought to book in court yesterday. Sidney Smith (30) pleaded guilty to stealing more than £7,000 by instructing the computer to deduct any odd pence from cheques paid into customers' accounts and pay them into his own account.

TELEPHONE VANDAL CAUGHT

A man who smashed up telephone kiosks when he could not get his calls through was identified by a traffic warden who was waiting to make her own call from a box. Pleading guilty to criminal damage, Robert Jenkins (20) said he lost his temper when his girlfriend's office refused to put him through to her.

The Case of the Hungry Husband

Gossiping with her neighbours all day ended in violence for a Scottish housewife in Westville when her husband came home to find the house dirty and no meal ready for him.

'She had all day to get me a meal ready and clean the place up a bit' said Bertram Wilson (24), who pleaded guilty to assaulting his wife. 'It wasn't the first time, and I just lashed out'. Mrs Wilson sustained a cut lip, requiring a stitch.

The Booby-Trapped Greenhouse

Arthur Jackson suffered so many thefts of plants and tools from his greenhouse that he booby-trapped it, injuring a teenage thief.

Pleading guilty to causing actual bodily harm, Jackson (31) said that after putting up with repeated thefts from his greenhouse over a period of years he fixed up a piece of timber so that it would fall on anyone who opened the door without inserting a peg. Two nights later he heard a crash and found a boy lying in the greenhouse, with a cut in his head that required three stitches. The boy admitted several thefts from the greenhouse.

4 Pragmatism, ideology and crime control: three Dutch surveys

Jan J.M. van Dijk and Carl H.D. Steinmetz

It is widely believed that the demand from large sectors of the public in Western societies for tougher sentences stems from personal experience of crime. From this viewpoint, support for repressive criminal policies is a logical response to personal concerns about crime (Thomas and Foster, 1975; Figgie Report, 1980). Studies in the USA, Canada and Germany have raised doubts about the validity of this view (Taylor et al., 1979; Fattah, 1979; Stephan, 1977; Tyler and Weber, 1982; Brillon, 1983). Attitudes towards crime control seem to be largely determined by preconceived ideas about crime and justice which are little affected by personal experiences or concerns. In this chapter we shall analyse attitudes towards crime control amongst the Dutch public. Our first question concerns the hypothesis that crime causes punitiveness. We shall see whether the obvious increase in various types of crime in the Netherlands has affected public opinion on criminal policy. In particular, we shall explore the relationship between personal experience of crime and attitudes towards ways of controlling crime. We shall then examine whether personal experience of crime affects people's support for increased government expenditure on crime control.

Repression and prevention

In 1975 the Research and Documentation Centre of the Ministry of Justice in the Netherlands conducted a national survey on attitudes towards crime and crime control (Van Dijk, 1978). Essential parts of this study were replicated as an annex to the Dutch national victim survey of 1982 and as a separate survey in 1985.

In all the studies respondents were asked to evaluate three repressive methods of crime control (incarceration, heavier punishment and work camps) and three preventive methods (reform, social assistance and job programmes for ex-convicts). Support for repressive and preventive methods appeared to be negatively related. Those who support repressive methods tend to be sceptical about preventive ones and *vice versa*. Positive opinions about repressive and preventive

Table 4.1 *Degree of urbanization, victimization, risk perception, educational level and age, as independent variables and support for either a preventive or a repressive policy as a dependent variable*

	Chi²	dF	p	Cramer's V	Direction of association
Attitude towards crime control (a high score indicates a positive attitude towards repression)					
by degree of urbanization	51	8	<.01	.07	positive
by risk perception	4	4	n.s.	—	—
by victimization	65	4	<.01	.08	negative
by educational level	554	8	<.01	.17	negative
by age	557	12	<.01	.14	positive

Source: Dutch National Victim Survey 1982, CBS/RDC
N = 10,000

policies, however, are far from mutually exclusive; for instance, half of the respondents in favour of repressive measures are equally supportive of preventive measures.[1]

A scale was constructed to reflect people's support for repressive ways of tackling crime. Respondents with low scores were exclusively supportive of preventive measures, those with moderate scores tended to support both approaches and high scores indicated an exclusive preference for repressive policies (25 per cent of the sample). To test the assumption that such attitudes reflect personal concerns about crimes, the scale was cross-tabulated against three previously developed measures for exposure to crime — the extent of urbanization of respondents' neighbourhoods, their experience as victims of crime and their perceptions of the risks of crime, which were based upon two items (van Dijk and Steinmetz, 1983).[2] We know from previous analyses that these measures are strongly interrelated. If contact with crime generates a preference for repressive criminal policies, we would expect to find positive relationships between the two measures of contact with crime and the one for concern about crime with our prevention–repression scale. The results are presented in Table 4.1.

Table 4.1 indicates that support for repressive options is somewhat greater in the more densely populated areas in Holland — the three largest cities, which show particularly high crime rates. However, the scale is not related in any way to risk perception as an indicator of concern about crime. Surprisingly, those who have been victims of crime express a preference for preventive measures (and tend to reject tougher punishment). These data do not support the hypothesis that crime causes punitiveness.

Further analysis showed that repressive or preventive attitudes towards crime control are strongly related to educational level and age (see Table 4.1). The well-educated young tend to favour repression less than others. Scepticism about repressive criminal policies seems to grow with level of education. Also our 1975 and 1985 findings show that attitudes toward crime control are weakly related to political preferences. For example, those who vote for parties on the extreme left only support preventive measures.

Taken together, our data suggest that preferences for preventive or repressive methods of crime control depend more on basic political or ideological preferences than on personal experience of crime (see also Faugeron et al., 1980). In the Netherlands these attitudes are closely related to educational level. The hypothesis that experiences of crime have little impact on public attitudes towards crime control in the Netherlands is also supported by historical data. Since 1975 the national victimization rates as well as several indicators of 'fear of crime' have shown a clear upward trend. However, as Table 4.2 shows, support for repressive approaches to crime control did not increase at all over this period. Support for rehabilitative approaches declined, but a majority of the population still supports such measures.

Special questions in the 1985 survey

In the 1985 survey respondents were asked several additional questions about situational crime prevention measures (Berghuis and Essers, 1986). The majority of the sample supported measures such as increased surveillance in public transport, obligatory installation of security hardware in new buildings, the opening of more bicycle sheds, more staff in department stores etc. A third would still support such measures even if they led to higher costs for consumers. Support for such measures is clearly related to age: older people are more in favour of a 'monitored' society than the young. No relationship was found between personal exposure to crime and support for situational crime prevention. Here again, opinion about criminal policy seems to be surprisingly little affected by personal concerns or experiences.

In 1985 an attempt was made to gauge the public's attitudes

Table 4.2 Victimization rates, crime rates, fear of crime and attitude toward crime control in the Netherlands, 1975 and early 1980s

	1975	1982	1985
Victimized[1] last year			
— burglary in a dwelling	1.1%	2.2%	2.4%
— pickpocketing	1.7%	2.4%	2.8%
Crime rates per 100,000[2]	4,000	8,000	9,000
Perception of higher victimization risks[3]	43%	56%	56%
Incarceration (suitable method of tackling crime)[3]	72%	68%	71%
Support reintroduction of capital punishment[4]	47%	38%	40%
Reform by education (suitable method of tackling crime)[3]	55%	67%	57%
Percentage supporting social work counselling as suitable method of tackling crime[3]	71%	79%	62%

1 RDC victimization survey 1975; NCS, CBS/RDC 1982 and 1985
2 Police Statistics Central Bureau of Statistics 1975, 1983 and 1985
3 RDC/Victim survey of 1975 and NCS 1982, 1985 CBS/RDC, RDC special survey
4 National social indicator surveys of the Bureau for Social and Cultural Planning, 1975 and 1981, The Hague

towards sentencing using a special set of questions. Respondents were invited to suggest a sentence for seven typical cases which were described briefly. We have compared the suggestions with the actual sentences which were passed in 1983 for crimes of the same category (see Table 4.3).

Attitudes to increased expenditure on crime control

In our 1982 victim survey we included a series of questions on central government expenditure on crime control. The first question was: 'Do you think that the government spends too much, too little or just the right amount on combating crime and dealing with the consequences?' Fifty-four per cent of the sample said that they would welcome an increase in expenditure. In 1985 this figure had increased to 77 per cent. Thirty-two cent would even be prepared to pay more taxes for this purpose.

Table 4.3 Comparison of sentencing suggestions in the 1985 survey and actual sentences in 1983 in the Netherlands

	Survey suggestions		Court practice	
	% proposing unconditional prison sentence	Suggested length of prison sentence*	% sentenced to unconditional prison sentence	Length of prison sentence**
Crime				
Bicycle theft	14	up to 1 yr	23	up to 4 mths
Damage to property	20	up to 1 yr	7	up to 2 mths
Burglary	55	3 mths–5 yrs	42	up to 6 mths
Aggravated assault	60	3 mths–5 yrs	54	up to 1 yr
Rape	65	3 mths–5 yrs	71	1 mth–1.5 yr
Attempted homicide	78	1 yr–5 yrs	85	up to 4.5 yrs
Heroin dealing	86	≥5 yrs	70	up to 2.5 yrs

N = 1,700
*At least 67 per cent of those who suggested an unconditional prison sentence stayed within this range.
**At least 67 per cent of actual prison sentences lie within this range.

All respondents in the 1982 survey were subsequently asked to assess the way the budget was allocated between the police, the prison service, probation, the courts and crime victims (see Table 4.4).

A cross-tabulation between attitudes to expenditure and our scale of preferences for preventive or repressive policies showed a negative association (Chi^2 = 191; dF = 8; V = 0.10; $p<0.01$). In other words, those in favour of repressive policies are less inclined than others to support more expenditure on crime control. Further analysis showed that respondents supporting repressive or preventive policies were equally in favour of increased expenditure on services for the victims of crime. Those who supported repressive policies favoured reducing the budget of the probation service and extending that of the police and, to a lesser degree, the prison system. Those in favour of preventive policies want only to extend the probation service budget. Allocating more money to the courts appeals to neither group.

In the 1985 survey respondents were asked to allocate a hypo-

Table 4.4 *Preferences for spending on crime control overall, and on different parts of the criminal justice system*

	More spending (%)	Same amount (%)	Less spending (%)	
Total crime control budget	54	32	14	100
Branches:				
Help for victims	88	11	1	100
Police	72	25	3	100
Prisons	51	39	10	100
Help for offenders	37	35	28	100
Courts	28	61	11	100

Source: Dutch National Crime Survey 1982 CBS/RDC

Table 4.5 *Allocation of an additional budget of 100 million Guilders between types of expenditure by a national sample of the Dutch population in 1985*

	Guilders (millions)
Expanding the prison service	19.9
More neighbourhood police units	18.2
More services for victims	17.9
Situational crime prevention	16.4
More detectives, prosecutors or judges	14.4
More social aid to offenders	8.7
Other	4.5
	100 million

N = 1,700
Source: Berghuis and Essers (1986)

thetical extra budget of 100 million Guilders.[3] The collective allocation decisions of the sample are presented in Table 4.5. The results in Table 4.5 are in agreement with the general finding that a large

Table 4.6 Degree of urbanization, victimization and risk perception as independent variables and support for higher spending on crime control as the dependent variable

	Chi^2	dF	p	Cramer's V	Direction of association
Support for higher expenditures					
by degree of urbanization	27	4	<.01	.60	positive
by risk perception	83	2	<.01	.10	positive
by victimization	32	2	<.01	.06	positive

Source: Dutch National Victim Survey 1982, CBS/RDC
N = 10,000

majority of the Dutch public supports a criminal policy which is a mixture of preventive and repressive elements.

Public support for extra expenditure on crime control

The public's preferences about the *quality* or tone of their government's criminal policies seem to be little affected by personal experience of crime. But it is conceivable that direct experience of crime may change attitudes about the *quantity* of government effort directed against crime. We were therefore interested in a possible relationship between our measures of exposure to crime and attitudes towards extra expenditure on crime control. The results of these cross-tabulations are presented in Table 4.6.

Support for more spending on crime control is related positively to all three measures (extent of urbanization, risk perception and victimization). These findings show that citizens who are personally exposed to crime favour increasing the budget for crime control more than others. It should be noted, however, that the relationship is rather weak. Opinions about the allocation of government budgets and/or about taxes are obviously determined by a variety of other factors such as financial situation and political beliefs (Berghuis and Essers, 1986).

The conclusion that personal contact with crime may induce some citizens to advocate greater expenditure on crime control is further supported by the finding that such support increased drastically in the Netherlands between 1982 and 1985 — a period when, as we have seen, crime was on the increase.

The relationships between exposure to crime and support for extra expenditure differ markedly from those between exposure and preference for prevention or repression presented in Table 4.1. Perception of risk is positively related to support for extra spending on crime control, but not to preference for prevention or repression; personal experience as a victim is positively related to support for extra spending, and negatively to preference for repression.

Further analysis showed that the positive relationship between exposure to crime and support for higher budgets exists both amongst those favouring repression and those favouring prevention. The latter are generally more willing to support extra expenditure, and when they are personally concerned about crime this tendency is reinforced. Those who prefer a repressive approach to crime are less willing to support higher expenditure. When they are personally victimized or are otherwise exposed to crime they change their minds and support increased spending on crime control (see Figure 4.1).

Finally, we looked at attitudes towards budget allocation amongst those who had been victimized or otherwise concerned about crime, according to their views about repression and prevention. Those favouring prevention supported higher spending on probation in particular. Recent victims in favour of repression were especially in favour of additional spending on the police and prisons. We found no evidence of convergence of opinions about methods of tackling crime amongst those who are personally exposed to crime. Both repressive and preventive groups remain faithful to their convictions. Both, however, are ready to spend more on putting their convictions into practice.

Conclusions

To sum up, the Dutch surveys produce results which question the common-sense theory that repressive attitudes are a pragmatic response to concern about crime arising from personal experiences — the hypothesis that crime causes punitiveness. Our results suggest that support for preventive or repressive crime control policies is little affected by personal contact with crime. Such opinions seem to be based on ideas which are part of one's view of the world; people stick to their ideologies when personally threatened by crime. In the case of the Dutch public, this means that there is continued support for a criminal policy which emphasizes both preventive and repressive measures (see also Downes, 1986). It does not follow from this that the public does not respond politically at all to a heightened concern about crime. Those who feel threatened by crime favour extra government spending on crime control, regardless of their criminological position. However, the way the money should

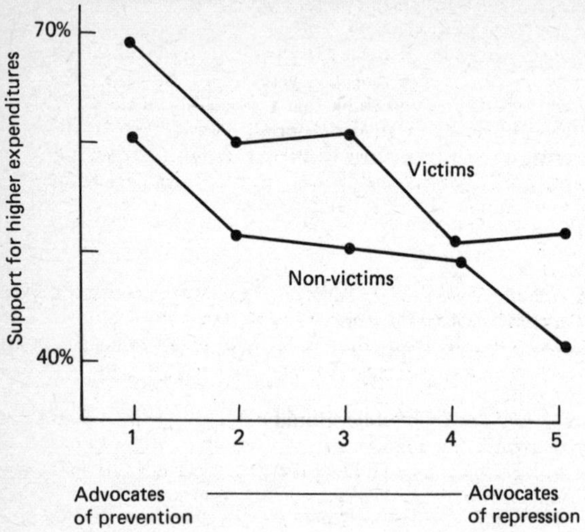

Source: survey CBS/RDC, 1982.
Figure 4.1 *Attitudes of victims and non-victims to extra spending on crime control, by victimization and preference for repressive or preventive policies*

be spent — on the police, the prison system or the probation service — still reflects their basic ideologies about crime control.

The dynamics of public opinion about crime control put those responsible for such policies in a quandary. In a period when concern about crime is high, people support higher expenditure on crime control. But opinions as to the precise allocation of this additional budget are as divergent as ever. Ministers of Justice who want to respond to the public's personal concern about crime walk on a tightrope. The best strategy seems to lie in presenting a policy which is a mixture of soft and tough opinions. Such a policy will appeal to both ideological camps and most easily gain majority support.

Notes

1. Questions on support for preventive and repressive ways of tackling crime: 'Crime

can be tackled in many ways. I will mention some of them. Please indicate each time your opinion of: (1) re-education of offenders; (2) incarceration of offenders; (3) heavier punishments; (4) social aid; (5) labour camps; (6) more employment opportunities for ex-convicts; and (7) obligation to settle damage by offenders.' [Very suitable, suitable, not suitable, unsuitable, not unsuitable, very unsuitable] (Translation).

2. Questions on perception of risks: 'Do you have the feeling that today you have a greater or smaller chance than two years ago of becoming the victim of some criminal offence? Or do you think that the chances did not change?' [A greater chance, the same chance, a smaller chance] (Translation).

   'How often do you ever consider the possibility of becoming a victim of any criminal offence?' [Never, hardly ever, sometimes, regularly, often] (Translation).

3. About £30 million in May 1987 (editors' note).

References

Berghuis, A. C. and Essers, J. J. A. (1986) 'Criminaliteitsbestrijding en Publieke Opinie', *Tijdschrift voor Criminologie,* July, **28,** 159–179.

Brillon, Y. (1983), 'La peur du crime et les tendences repressive du public envers les criminels', *Revue internationale de criminologie et de police technique,* **36,** October/December, 12–59.

Dijk, J. J. M. van (1978), 'Public attitudes towards crime in the Netherlands', *Victimology,* **3,** (3/4), 265–273.

Dijk, J. J. M. and Steinmetz, C. H. D. (1983), 'Victimisation surveys: beyond measuring the volume of crime', *Victimology,* **8,** (1/2), 291–309.

Downes, D. M. (1986), *Contrasts in Tolerance: postwar penal policy in the Netherlands and England and Wales,* London: London School of Economics.

Fattah, E. A. (1979), 'Perceptions of violence, concern about crime, fear of crime and attitudes to the death penalty', *Canadian Journal of Criminology,* **21** (1), January, 22–38.

Figgie Report (1980), *The Figgie Report on Fear of Crime: America Afraid, Part I,* New York: Research and Forecasts Inc.

Faugeron, C., Moreau-Capdeveille, G., Turmaine, M. (1980), *Réponses à la déviance et groupes sociaux,* Paris: Service d'Etudes Penale et Criminologique, Ministère de la Justice.

Shaw, S. (1982), *The People's Justice: a major poll of attitudes on crime and punishment,* London: Prison Reform Trust.

Stephan, E. (1979), 'Einstellung zur Todesstrafe: die Bedeutung von schichtspezifischer Sozialisation und von Personlichkeitsmerkmalen, *Zeitschrift für die gesammte Strafrechtswissenschaft,* **27,** (4), 1046–1067.

Taylor, D.G., Schepple, K. L. and Stinchcombe, A. L. (1979), 'Salience of crime and support for harsher criminal sanctions', *Social Problems,* **26,** (4), April, 413–424.

Thomas, C. W. and Foster, S. C. (1975), 'A sociological perspective on public support for capital punishment', *American Journal of Orthopsychiatry,* **46,** (4), July, 641–657.

Tyler, T. R. and Weber, R. (1982), 'Support for the death penalty: instrumental response to crime or symbolic attitude?', *Law and Society Review,* **17,** (1), 21–45.

5 Punitiveness, status and ideology in three Canadian provinces

Yves Brillon

The present analysis* is based on data obtained during a comprehensive study on *Attitudes of the Canadian Public Toward Crime Policies* (Brillon, Louis-Guérin and Lamarche, 1984). So far, there has been little research done in Canada that has gone beyond determining public opinion in general to discover the attitudes of different social groups that explain their reactions to crime and to the administration of justice. It is a knowledge of these basic attitudes, however, and of their sociological distribution, that will provide legislators, administrators and researchers with an explanation of people's resistance to change and innovation and inform them of the goals and objectives the public assigns the agencies of the criminal justice system and their expectations concerning the many aspects of its administration.

It is to acquire this knowledge that we undertook our investigations. We have studied social concepts concerning crime and sought to identify the ideology behind individual and collective action. We therefore focused on a study of the relationship between the individual and crime in general. We examined people's punitive attitudes in both their socio-cultural and ideological context, taking into consideration the connection that may exist between their view of the world, their image of the criminal and how he should be dealt with.

Punitive orientation of the population or attitudes of the citizens toward the severity of sentences

Very roughly, we can assume that the attitudes of the public towards

*This is a revised version, translated by D. Crelinsten, of an article published in the *Canadian Journal of Criminology* (1984), **26,** (3). For more details, see the final report of the pilot enquiry: Y. Brillon, C. Louis-Guérin and M.-C. Lamarche (1984), *Attitudes of the Canadian Public Toward Crime Policies* Cahier No. 1A; Les Cahiers de Recherches Criminologiques (310 pages). CICC Université de Montréal. It was done at the request of the Department of the Solicitor General of Canada, which financed it. The 'theoretical' sample was made up of a highly urbanized population from Montreal, Toronto and Winnipeg (N = 614) and a rural population from the provinces of Quebec, Ontario and Manitoba (N = 203). The total sample comprised 817 subjects. The ideas expressed here are solely those of the author.

crime policies depend on two major perceptions:

(a) its perception of (or experience with) criminality as a real or potential menace; this perception could be of a nature that would create a reaction on the part of the population (fear of crime, dread of victimization, suspicion, the desire for revenge against criminals, expectations of protection, security, the suppression of crime, prevention and the rehabilitation of delinquents, etc., by the penal agencies);

(b) its perception of the criminal justice system as a more or less adequate response, first, to the pursuit of the objectives assigned to it (protection of the social order, the punishment or rehabilitation of criminals, the compensation of victims) and next, to its methods of functioning (satisfaction with the methods used, the tasks accomplished, the effectiveness of the efforts made, their deontology, etc.).

In this schema, the 'punitive/non-punitive' attitude becomes a dual reality in the sense that it can be modulated both by the view we have of crime or the criminal (images which can be more or less exact depending on whether they are based or not on experiential knowledge) and by the image we have (it, too, being marked or not by experience with criminal agencies) of the system of criminal justice, whether as a whole or in its individual components: the police, the courts, probation, correctional institutions, parole.

It seems that the idea of punishment cannot be dissociated from that of criminal justice, or even justice itself. When an individual or a community has one of its rights attacked, the court charged with settling the dispute must have a coercive power that can, as a last resort, force the author of the infraction to give satisfaction to the injured party. This coercive power implies the possibility of resorting to punitive measures if the offender refuses to comply with the decision of the legitimate authority.

Attitudes to the severity of the sentences pronounced by the courts

In the field of criminal justice, the 'punishment' or 'penalty' is not only used as a measure of constraint intended to force the delinquent to make reparation for the harm done. It is only one element of the sentence pronounced by the court. In fact, as the origin of the word indicates, the 'penal' law is basically a 'punitive' law.

And on this point there seems to be a very large consensus among the population. However, where there is a great difference of opinion is on the question of the function of punishment. Asked about the most important objective of sentences, people answered as shown in Table 5.1.

Table 5.1 The importance accorded by the population to the various objectives sought by the criminal justice system in giving sentences

Choices of the sample by percentage	Objective considered most important
31.4	To discourage people from committing crimes
25.0	To protect citizens against crime
19.1	To punish those who commit crimes
14.7	To enable criminals to return to a normal life
7.0	To compensate for the harm done to victims
2.0	To enable society to take revenge on those who commit crimes
0.7	Do not know
100.0	

Question: 'In handing down sentences, the criminal justice system has different objectives. Among the following objectives (card shown) which, in your opinion, is the most important?'

Looking at Table 5.1, we see that citizens expect that the decisions taken by judges will have a deterrent effect on future delinquents (31.4 per cent) and will give them real protection (25 per cent). In short, punishment is seen much more as intended to protect the public than as a measure of expiation imposed on the criminal (19.1 per cent). And it is a relatively small proportion of the sample who consider the most important objective of the sentence to be social reintegration (14.7 per cent), reparation for the harm done to the victim (7 per cent) and public vengeance (2.1 per cent).

In general, the public seems to define both the object of the sentence and the type of punishment in terms of what will best ensure its own safety. This seems to correspond, in great part at least, to imprisonment that is long enough and hard enough to instil fear, and widely enough used to isolate and neutralize the greatest number of criminals. It is by this gauge of the effectiveness of imprisonment that the criminal justice system is evaluated.

The Figgie Report (1980) shows that although in the USA the attitudes toward the police are very positive, this is not true of the people's feelings about the system of criminal justice. Our research shows the same result. The lukewarm attitude of Americans toward the courts is evidenced by the following: eight out of ten citizens think that the prison sentences now given do not succeed in discouraging crime; a large majority of persons believe that it is impossible to help those who commit crimes or control criminality with the existing judicial system; on the other hand, 66 per cent of Americans are of the opinion that the death penalty could effectively discourage the commission of murder.

In general, among the people questioned in the USA, there is a large consensus on the need to resort to much more severe and more punitive sentences to control crime, and even to achieve a certain rehabilitation of delinquents. Thus there are only 3 per cent (against 95 per cent) of the persons questioned who consider the courts too severe. This coincides with the results obtained in September 1980 in Canada by the Centre de Recherche sur l'Opinion Publique (CROP) and by our own research; these two studies show that 2 per cent and 4.2 per cent of their samples, respectively, share the opinion that, in Canada, the courts are too severe. The same holds true in France, where a survey done by the SOFRES, in February 1977, showed that for 84 per cent of the French, the justice system was too lenient; an opinion which, according to Peyrefitte (1981), has not been disproved by any more recent survey.

In the USA, opinion surveys show that the proportion of persons who think that the punishment inflicted is not severe enough has been increasing continually over the past 15 years, and at a fairly rapid rate. According to the data of Stinchcombe et al. (1980), who present the results of 12 surveys which from 1965 to 1978 dealt with this question of the severity of the courts, we find that in 1965, 49 per cent of Americans were of the opinion that the sentences were not harsh enough, a percentage that rises to 63 per cent in 1968, to 78 per cent in 1974, and reaches 85 per cent in 1978. During this same period, the rate of violent crimes (murders, rapes, thefts with violence and grave assaults) that amounted to 189 per 100,000 inhabitants in 1964, jumped to 482 in 1975. This comes to an increase, in ten years, of 255 per cent. The same phenomenon can be observed in Canada, where between 1964 and 1974, the rate of violent crimes more than doubled, going from 40 to 98 per 100,000 inhabitants.

On a parallel with these figures are those relating to the fear of crime (fear that is measured here by the fear of going out alone at night in one's own neighbourhood). An analysis of the principal surveys that were made in the USA between 1965 and 1977 show that, for men, the feeling of fear tended to spread to a larger and larger population, but at a relatively slow rate: 18.4 per cent in 1965 and 23.4 per cent in 1977. During the same period, the surveys carried out by Stinchcombe (1980) show that, among women, the percentage who were fearful was much higher: it was around 50 per cent between 1965 and 1968, and around 63 per cent from 1973 to 1977.

Without wishing to draw a direct line of cause and effect between these three phenomena — the increase in crimes of violence, the heightened fear among the population and the rise in punitive attitudes — the fact remains that Peyrefitte's remark, for France, seems highly pertinent:

> To begin with, major criminality soared between 1970 and 1980: hold-ups, swindlings, murders and assassinations, rapes and armed robberies. Assuredly, it represents only 1.5% of all crimes and infractions; but it is this that, making the headlines in the newspapers, is the fuse that has set off the increasing feeling of insecurity (1980, p. 334). (Free translation)

Even though violent crimes constitute only a small portion of the total volume of criminality (10 per cent in Canada and a little more in the USA), the fact remains that it is frightening and that its rapid increase makes it more visible to the general public. Thus it is not the most frequent crimes that create anxiety but those that are more serious, because the nature of the consequences they entail can arouse anxiety and distress. This greater visibility of violent crimes, then, following their marked increase, by making a vast number of people feel insecure, seems to have some influence in creating punitive or stringent attitudes in people.

This does not mean to say that the most punitively oriented persons are those who are the most frightened; it means that with the increased fear of crime, more and more people picture criminals as violent individuals who require more radical correctional measures. In other words, when citizens are asked if, in general, they think the courts are too severe, severe enough or not severe enough, most of their replies are in terms of dangerous criminals, contrary to Stinchcombe's hypothesis: 'Presumably . . ., the question of harsher courts encourages people to fill in their picture of the average court, the average crime, the average criminal, and perhaps the average victim and to make an overall judgment' (Stinchcombe et al., 1980, p. 143).

This, in any case, is the finding of the CROP survey (Omnibus-1980-5-3) and of our enquiry (GRAC, April 1981) where, with regard to the severity of punishment, we obtained very similar results; these are shown in Table 5.2 and their analysis confirms the hypothesis just advanced.

In both cases, people were asked to specify what type of criminal they were thinking of when giving their opinion on the severity of the sentences. For the CROP sample, 41 per cent of the people

Table 5.2 *Comparative distribution of the opinions of a sample of the Canadian population (CROP, 1980; N 979) and a sample from the provinces of Quebec, Ontario and Manitoba (GRAC, 1981; N 817) regarding the severity of sentences*

Opinions	Percentages	
The sentences pronounced by the court are:	CROP	GRAC
too severe	2	4.2
just severe enough	18	17.5
not severe enough	70	72
don't know	0	6.4
Total	100	100

Question: 'In general, would you say that the sentences handed down by the courts are *too severe, just severe enough, not severe enough*?'

had murderers in mind, 5 per cent rapists and 14 per cent violent criminals (authors of kidnapping, physical assault, armed robbery, recidivists, etc.). We get 60 per cent of respondents, then, who think of a crime of violence and 70 per cent who believe that the courts are not severe enough. The same conclusion is arrived at from our own data: 32.3 per cent of those surveyed thought of various forms of assassination and murder, 9.7 per cent of rape and 22.1 per cent of serious criminality, that is, of crimes committed by 'real criminals' (premeditated acts, sadistic acts, thefts with violence, repeated criminality, recidivism, etc.). Thus 64.1 per cent of the persons interviewed referred to 'big' crimes, whereas 72 per cent of them considered the courts of justice too lenient.

It seems evident, then, that among the population, it is the violent criminal, the recidivist, the incurable offender who serves as the standard for judging the severity of the courts and judges. And it is no doubt because of this that the punitive attitude of the public is expressed almost exclusively in terms of imprisonment, the only punishment that seems able to make life in society safe because it eliminates the evil, or the threat of evil, in its midst – the criminal.

If we analyse the opinions of respondents with regard to long sentences of imprisonment, we see confirmation of their tendency to consider prison the ideal method of ensuring public order by playing the double role of deterring offenders and protecting the citizens. Thus, among our sample, we find 38 per cent who strongly (16.8 per cent) or somewhat (21.1 per cent) agree with the fact that it would be 'inhuman to keep people in prison for twenty-five years'. On the other hand, 58 per cent of the people somewhat (30.3 per cent) or strongly (27.6 per cent) disagree with this point of view.

Similarly, only a minority of 18.8 per cent of persons either strongly (5.7 per cent) or somewhat (13.1 per cent) agree that 'life in prison should be easier'. On the contrary, more than two-thirds (72.1 per cent) of the population are somewhat (35.5 per cent) or strongly (36.6 per cent) against improvement of the living conditions of prisoners. This is due, of course, to the fact that half of the individuals questioned (50.6 per cent) have a singularly luxurious image of the correctional institutions, for they think that 'today, the prisons are veritable hotels'. But this also shows a desire on the part of the public to be assured that prison sentences are disagreeable and difficult enough to discourage crime and to deter criminals.

It follows that punitiveness is directly connected with the functions that the population assigns to the system of criminal justice. And among these functions, as we have already seen, those that emerge the most often are 'deterrence' and 'protection'. Punitiveness, as a general way of thinking, seems to be focused more on victimization, that is, on the consequences of the act (perceived as a serious attack against the public safety) than on the criminals. This means that, for the people questioned, punishment should serve more to eliminate a threat to the social order than to apprehend deviant individuals in order to punish them, to get them to reform or become rehabilitated. These objectives of punishment seem to be subsidiary to 'putting away' the delinquent, 'keeping him out of harm's way'.

A study conducted in California in August 1981 by the National Council on Crime and Delinquency shows that, for 78 per cent of 1,018 persons interviewed, one of the main reasons for sending offenders to prison lies in the fact that 'it is the way justice keeps its promise that those who commit crimes will get the punishment they deserve'. This view of prison on the part of the Californian population confirms what our own data seem to show, namely that the public, in its majority, identifies 'criminal justice' with 'prison'. And implicitly, this popular view corroborates the idea that the concept of 'criminal justice' would also evoke, for most people, a grave criminality for which imprisonment would be the proper punishment. In spite of the disadvantages it can sometimes entail, prison, as Foucault says, is seen as the 'deplorable solution which we could not do without' (1975, p. 234).

Threshold of tolerance toward crime and criminals

At the present time, in various societies, there seems to be a sort of shifting of expectations with regard to the institutions of detention. The prison image seems to evoke in people not so much the idea of imprisonment (deprivation of liberty and the correction of criminals) as of 'confinement' (putting them in a place which they cannot leave). In effect, coming back to the California survey, we note that the persons questioned agreed, almost unanimously (93 per cent), that recourse to penalties of imprisonment 'removes the criminal from the community and protects citizens from further crimes that might be committed by that person'. Although a relatively large number of citizens (67 per cent) thought that incarceration 'deters other people from committing crimes because they are shown an example that crime does not pay', the proportion of those who believed the prison 'places the criminal in an environment where he can be reformed through job training, work experience, education and similar programs' went down to 58 per cent; the proportion of Californians who saw imprisonment as 'society's way of getting even with the criminal for what has been done to the victim' fell to 50 per cent and those who perceived the prison as 'a harsh experience that will discourage that person from committing another crime', shifted to 42 per cent. And for the whole of the USA, the Figgie Report shows that only 48 per cent of the people think that prison sentences discourage crime.

It is this that brings us to understand that the punitive attitude starts with a perception of dangerousness and gives rise to a demand for ostracism. For the general population, it is as if delinquents were divided into two categories: the dangerous and the not dangerous, the 'real' criminals and the others. All this leads us to believe that for the public, it is the criterion of dangerousness that determines the threshold of tolerance toward the delinquent. As soon as the danger perceived is seen as a sufficient threat, the reaction toward the deviant is one of rejection. Hence a marked preference on the part of the population for penalties of imprisonment as soon as the criminal act is considered sufficiently menacing. What our Canadian sample confirms as the indication of dangerousness is the act itself rather than the personality of its author.

For example, for an occasional petty theft, 5.4 per cent of people would like to see a prison sentence, 52.9 per cent probation and 40.6 per cent a fine. If there is recidivism and someone has committed a number of petty thefts without violence, many more people favour prison (19.5 per cent), almost half the sample (47.1 per cent) probation and a third (32.2 per cent) a fine. For an armed robbery, even if it is the delinquent's first offence, a large majority of citizens

(74.6 per cent) would want the judges to resort to imprisonment whereas 16.4 per cent would accept probation and only 6.4 per cent a fine.

After the type of crime, there are elements which, in the eyes of the persons questioned, constitute the dangerousness of an act, the first being premeditation (the element chosen by 27.1 per cent as the most important factor, and one which the judge should take into account when handing down his sentence). Next in order of importance are the way in which the crime was perpetrated (the most important factor for 23.6 per cent of the respondents), the motivation (20.4 per cent), recidivism (16 per cent), the personality and social milieu of the accused (8.8 per cent), and the age and sex of the victim (2.6 per cent).

All this leads us to the conclusion that the popular penal philosophy — at least as it appears — could be reduced to two basic statements: there are some delinquents who represent a danger to life in society and others who do not: and there are some delinquents who should be removed from society and some who can be tolerated. It is this point of view, it seems, which influences the opinions of a large portion of individuals on the subject of the death penalty.

Attitudes toward the death penalty

Capital punishment, for many persons, is a form of ostracism which, in the most serious cases, becomes a supplement to imprisonment. For some, it is the surest way of ensuring public safety and for others, the most humane way of ridding society of a dangerous criminal. Table 5.3 shows the distribution, among the population, of opinions on the death penalty.

Among the population, there are 15.8 per cent of persons who are totally against the very principle of capital punishment, and who oppose it ideologically, and 83.5 per cent who, to various degrees, accept it as an exceptional or necessary recourse. Among the latter, 29.9 per cent are opposed to it save when it proves necessary, 31.4 per cent are in favour of it except in a few cases where it is not necessary, and finally, 22.2 per cent form a hard core of people who say they are strongly in favour of it.

In the case of murder, the gravity of the act — if we are to go by the proportion of persons who would be in favour of applying the death penalty — is judged more or less great according to the following criteria:

- the age of the criminal: 34.1 per cent of the people are in favour of resorting to the death penalty if the murderer is a youth, and 53.7 per cent if the accused is an adult;

Table 5.3 Distribution, in the sample, of the different opinions on the death penalty

%	Opinions
15.8	I am opposed to the death penalty under any circumstances
29.9	I am opposed to the death penalty except in a few cases where it may be appropriate
31.4	I am generally in favour of the death penalty except in a few cases where it may not be appropriate
22.2	I am strongly in favour of the death penalty as an appropriate measure
0.7	I don't know

Question: 'Which of the following alternatives (card shown) describes your attitude toward the death penalty . . .?

- whether the act is impulsive or premeditated: 34.4 per cent of the population are in favour of the death penalty when a person has killed his/her spouse in a fit of anger, 76 per cent when a person commits premeditated murder and 79.8 per cent when a person has killed more than once (in this last case — which has the largest consensus — the idea of recidivism implicitly includes that of premeditation);
- The personality of the criminal and the type of victim: for murder in general, committed by an adult, 57.7 per cent of the respondents advocate the elimination of the criminal. If the victim is a policeman or prison guard, 70.9 per cent of the sample would want the guilty party condemned to death. In this last case, the difference in the answers was always attributed exclusively to the status of the victim. And it is mainly on the basis of this aspect that the death penalty was re-established in Canada as a measure believed necessary to protect (by deterrence) the lives of policemen and prison guards.

The response of the population is ambiguous, however, and it is impossible to know if it relates to the type of victim or the type of criminal. In effect, the question of the death sentence being applied to the murderer of a policeman or guard is attributed to the image of a 'more dangerous' criminal than is the case when it is a matter of an 'ordinary' murder. To kill a police officer or a guard, a person must either have committed another crime and be pursued by the police, or must already be a prisoner in a correctional institution. This murder shows a criminal who is not new to the game.

Surveys on capital punishment in the USA have shown a decided increase in the population favouring this measure: in 1936, 62 per cent of Americans declared themselves in favour of the death sentence and in 1977, the proportion reached 67 per cent. Stinchcombe (1980) compares — as mentioned before — the increase in violent crimes, the spreading fear among the population and, what appears to be a result of these phenomena, the increase in punitive attitudes: demands for harsher sentences and the death sentence. He notes that, among the persons who find that the sentences are not severe enough, there are 24.3 per cent more who support the death penalty than among those who think the penalties are adequate. The latter, in turn, are 10.1 per cent more numerous in advocating the death penalty than the persons who think that the courts are too severe in their judgements.

In spite of the parallel between the rise in the number of persons who are afraid of crime and that of the indices of severity of the sentences, Stinchcombe is unable to establish any connection whatsoever between fear and punitiveness. The recent data in the Figgie Report (1980) incidentally confirms this absence of correlation:

> With regard to *both* types of fear (concrete and formless), almost equal members of the fearful and non-fearful favor the death penalty and long prison sentences. The fearless are no more likely than the fearful to believe that long prison sentences discourage crime (p. 127).

Further on we shall try to clarify this ambiguity and to answer the following question: how is it that, in the last 15 years, there are more and more people who are afraid of crime, that there are more and more people who demand the death penalty and longer prison sentences and yet there is no connection between the persons who are afraid and those who ask for the imposition of more severe sanctions by the courts?

Where the death penalty is concerned, the data in the Figgie Report show clearly enough that feelings of fear are not factors that determine or explain the degree of people's punishment orientation. On the contrary, certain groups, that of men and that of whites, who are much less afraid, are much more in favour of recourse to capital punishment: among Americans, there are 76 per cent of men against 68 per cent of women who are for the death penalty (gamma .20) and 73 per cent of whites against 64 per cent of blacks (gamma .22). The same study indicates, furthermore, that the elderly are more for the death penalty than the young (76 per cent of those 60 and over compared with 67 per cent of young people from 18 to 29). The same relationship exists between married persons (or who have been married) and single persons: 73 per cent of the former are in favour of the death penalty against 63 per cent of the latter.

Our study confirms the absence of any connection between fear and the desire to punish. Thus if we consider the persons who would accept the application of the death penalty, even in exceptional cases, we get the following results: 83 per cent of women and 84 per cent of men; 74 per cent of young people from 18 to 31 years of age compared with 87 per cent of persons 62 and over; 81 per cent of city residents against 91 per cent of rural dwellers. These last figures reveal the independence of fear and severity, for many more people in the villages feel safer than in the cities (96 per cent against 88 per cent), do not fear being robbed (76 per cent rural against 57 per cent urban residents) and have no fear of being attacked where they live (83 per cent against 76 per cent). And yet they are more inclined (10 per cent more among the rural dwellers) to favour recourse to the death penalty.

The authors of the Figgie Report, in view of their results, conclude that 'support for the death penalty is a dominant sentiment which seems to uniformly reflect the ethos of what was once popularly called the "establishment", and which is defined demographically as older, white, male and married'. To interpret our data according to this same logic, we would have to add 'rural' to the definition of the 'establishment', which does not make much sense. However, and it is from this perspective that we will study punitiveness, it is probable that attitudes toward sanctions have nothing to do with demographic characteristics, sentiments or emotional traits, but that they come from particular public images. From this point of view, the connection between the 'establishment' and 'rural' variables could well be found in a more 'authoritarian' and more 'conservative' view of the world.

Scale of punitive/non-punitive attitudes

To analyse the punitive/non-punitive attitudes of the population questioned, we used the components we have just described, namely:

- views of the sentences pronounced by the court: are they too severe (1) just severe enough (2) or not severe enough (3)?
- opinions regarding very long sentences: 'It's inhuman to keep criminals in prison for twenty-five years' (strongly agree 1; somewhat agree 2; somewhat disagree 3; strongly disagree 4);
- opinions *vis-à-vis* measures to improve the conditions of detention: 'prison life should be made easier' (strongly agree 1; somewhat agree 2; somewhat disagree 3; strongly disagree 4);

- opinions concerning the death penalty: strongly against (1); somewhat against (2); somewhat in favour (3); strongly in favour (4).

Based on these four components, a scale of punitiveness was designed. For each subject, the score for each of the questions was added together. Next, the subjects, according to the score obtained, were regrouped into five categories, distributed in increasing order according to their degree of punitiveness. The distribution is shown in Table 5.4.

The questions on which this punitiveness scale is based, besides being closely inter-associated (the alpha coefficient is 0.66), offer the advantage of integrating people's severity concerning both the sentences pronounced by the courts and the conditions of detention, and of also taking into account the 'punitive' nature attributed by members of the public to long sentences of imprisonment and the death penalty. Because the scale is not limited to only one aspect of severity, this gives a better picture of the numerous and complex factors that underlie the punitive attitude.

Structured in this way, the measuring instrument offers more flexibility and makes it possible to better explain the population's reaction to criminals. It too often happens that we presume there is extreme severity among the public since more than 70 per cent of the people find that judges are too lenient, and just as many, if not more, are in favour of the death penalty. What we forget to take into consideration is the fact that this severity is most often directed only toward the most dangerous criminals; and these constitute but a very small minority of individuals responsible for particularly repugnant acts. It seems wrong, then, to think that the population — at least a portion of it — demands more severe sentences for all crimes (even the less serious ones). We must not forget that in the eyes of a large part of the population, the desired severity of the sentences shows a need to be 'protected' much more than to 'chastise' or 'punish'. This is a most important point and should be at the very basis of every crime policy. The pseudo-punitive attitude of the public may only be a reflection of the criminal justice system's inability to prevent crime and rehabilitate delinquents.

Factors connected with punitive attitudes

By cross-tabulating the scale of punitiveness with most of the variables in our questionnaire as well as with the scales that were constructed, we can identify certain characteristics of the groups in our sample that are the most severe and the most punitive *vis-à-vis* criminals.

Table 5.4 *Distribution of the sample population according to its increasing degrees of punitiveness*

Degree of punitiveness		Number	Percentages
Low	1	85	10.4
	2	113	13.8
	3	234	28.6
	4	234	28.6
High	5	151	18.6
Total		817	100.0

Questions: (a) 'In general, would you say that the sentences handed down by the courts are too severe? . . . just severe enough? . . . not severe enough?'

(b) 'Here are a number of opinions about prisons and penitentiaries. Do you strongly agree, somewhat agree, somewhat disagree or strongly disagree with each of these? (cards shown):

(i) It is inhuman to keep criminals in prison for twenty-five years

(ii) Prison life should be made easier.

(c) 'Which of the following alternatives describes your attitude toward the death penalty? (card shown)

I am opposed to the death penalty under any circumstances

I am opposed to the death penalty except in a few cases where it may be appropriate

I am generally in favour of the death penalty except in a few cases in which it may not be appropriate

I am strongly in favour of the death penalty as an appropriate measure.

The first thing to note is the total absence of any connection that can be established between punitiveness, on the one hand, and sex (gamma .01), victimization (gamma .09), a feeling of security (gamma .02), fear of going out alone at night because of crime (gamma .03), fear of being robbed (gamma .09) or of being attacked at home (gamma .05), on the other. Thus we are able to confirm certain of the conclusions arrived at by Stinchcombe et al. (1980), namely:

- first, that women, who are less often the victims of violent crimes, are more fearful but not more punitive than the rest of the population;

- second, that persons who had been victimized do not have a greater tendency to favour more punitive measures than those who had not.

We have already mentioned that the Figgie Report (1980) also established the absence of a relationship between the fear of crime and attitudes toward the death sentence (gamma .06 and gamma .04 according to whether the fear is concrete or formless); and toward long prison sentences. Despite the fact that since 1965, in the USA and elsewhere, there has been an ever-increasing rise in both the percentage of persons who say they have a fear of crime and that of people who would like to see harsher sanctions against criminals, there is no direct relationship between the two phenomena.

People have become more punitive in later years than they were before because, it seems, the increase in violent criminality has made their image of the delinquent become analogous with the dangerous criminal. Whether they have any fear or not, people have the same image of the offender, and it is in terms of this image and not of fear that their punitiveness is manifested. In other words, a large majority of the persons questioned (64 per cent of our sample) are thinking of murderers, rapists and violent criminals when they consider the sentences not harsh enough. Consequently, the punitive attitudes of the population are a reflection of the gravity of the crimes which it uses as a gauge to evaluate the severity of the sanctions and not the fact that these serious crimes elicit, for some more than others, a fear of crime or a dread of victimization (both of which, for example, are greater among women, elderly persons and city people). If, then, the fear is emotional, punitive or non-punitive attitudes are due much more to a way of seeing things. At least this is what we will try to show by pointing out the factors that characterize the most punitive groups of individuals.

Socio-demographic indicators show that, among the most punitive people, proportionately, there are:[2]

- more people with very high incomes (57 per cent of persons earning $35,000 and more) than persons with low incomes (41 per cent under $20,000);
- a much higher percentage of owner-occupiers (56 per cent) than tenants (37 per cent);
- 57 per cent and 55 per cent of the members of the sample who live in Ontario and Manitoba, respectively, compared with 32 per cent of those who live in Quebec;
- more English Canadians or those from other ethnic groups (55

per cent of them in both categories) than French Canadians (31 per cent);
- more elderly persons (54 per cent of people 62 years of age and over) than young people (35 per cent of those under 30);
- more rural residents (52 per cent) than city residents (45 per cent);
- more people with little education (50 per cent) than persons who are well educated (31 per cent).

These variables are fairly closely connected. First of all, it is interesting to note that the socio-demographic characteristic that shows the strongest correlation with punitiveness is the status owner/tenant (gamma = .36). Then, in decreasing order of association, comes the province (gamma = .32), ethnicity (gamma = .29), income (gamma = .22), age (gamma = .17), scholarity (gamma = .17) and place of residence (rural/urban gamma = .15).

The most punitive persons, then, are people who, in the highest proportions, are owners, live in Ontario or Manitoba, are English-speaking, have a high income, are elderly, live in rural areas and are less well-educated. These different factors obviously overlap. For example, in our sample, only 38 per cent are proprietors in Quebec, whereas 55 per cent are in Ontario and 74 per cent in Manitoba. Also, it is in Quebec, of course, that we find almost all the French (83 per cent against 4 per cent in Ontario and 5 per cent in Manitoba). Furthermore, where income is concerned, we find that there are more than three times fewer persons in Quebec who receive salaries of $35,000 and more (5 per cent compared to 25 per cent in Ontario, and 26 per cent in Manitoba). In the case of low incomes the proportions take a reversed curve: 69 per cent of Quebecois, 41 per cent of Ontarians and 37 per cent of Manitobans earn less than $20,000. Finally, we note that of young people from 18 to 31, 33 per cent are home owners whereas among those 62 and over, the rate is 53 per cent; also there are many more villagers who own their own homes (80 per cent) than city residents (45 per cent).

To sum up, the social groups that are the most wealthy are at the same time those seen to be the most punitive. And these groups have several dominant traits in common: they have high incomes, are proprietors, English-speaking and elderly. Schooling and place of residence (rural/urban) figure here as well, but to a lesser degree.

With regard to more general attitudes, we find that the groups or individuals who display the most punitive attitudes are those who prove to be the least liberal. In fact, in our sample, the persons who want criminal justice to be more severe with delinquents are largely those who have a more rigid, more conservative and less tolerant view of the world. For example, the more severe people are:

1. the more they are in favour (68 per cent of them against 48 per cent of the less punitive) of a more authoritarian government to better ensure public order (gamma = .31);
2. the more they think (64 per cent against 49 per cent) that women who have children should stay at home to look after them (gamma = .22);
3. the more they are of the opinion (58 per cent compared with 50 per cent for the others) that people today have no respect for anything (gamma = .14);
4. the more they believe (85 per cent against 72 per cent of those who have a low degree of punitiveness) that if things are bad today, it is because the family no longer plays the same role that it used to (gamma = .28);
5. the more numerous they are (47 per cent against 26 per cent) in rejecting the idea that in our society homosexuals should be accepted like everyone else (gamma = .36).

However, these five questions, which serve to distribute our population according to 'conservative/liberal' attitudes, afford a high enough degree of cohesion to serve as an index (the coefficient alpha is .66). By separating our sample according to the degree of punitiveness and liberalism, we can establish a direct equation between the two scales, as Table 5.5 shows.

According to Table 5.5, among the most punitive people there is a higher percentage of 'conservatives' (56 per cent), for among the same group of individuals, only 34 per cent are 'liberals'. The opposite distribution occurs for the persons who have a low degree of punitiveness: 44 per cent tend toward conservatism whereas 66 per cent express more liberal opinions. In view of these data, it is clear that the persons who are in favour of harsher sentences (persons who are very much 'pro-police', incidentally) are at the same time less tolerant. They are more for an authoritarian government (capable of guaranteeing law and order), for maintaining traditional values (such as respect, the continuity of the family where the woman remains the central pivot), and are much less open to accepting certain deviances (such as homosexuality).

It seems logical, then, to find among punitive and conservative people those who are culturally the most deeply rooted in the past, in ancestral values and institutions, and who are most in favour of maintaining the established order and acquired rights, namely,

Table 5.5 Relationship between punitiveness and liberalism

Degree of punitiveness	Degree of liberalism and openness to change	
	More conservative (%)	More liberal (%)
Low	44	66
High	56	34
(Number of respondents)	(492)	(329)
% of the sample	60	40
Gamma .34		

Scale components (5 questions): 'Here are various opinions about the society we live in. Do you strongly agree, somewhat agree, somewhat disagree or strongly disagree with each of them?' (card):

(a) 'We need a stronger government to maintain law and order'. (Strongly agree, somewhat agree, somewhat disagree, strongly disagree, don't know.)
(b) 'Women who have children should stay at home to look after them'. (Strongly agree, somewhat agree, somewhat disagree, strongly disagree, don't know.)
(c) 'There is no respect for anything these days'. (Strongly agree, somewhat agree, somewhat disagree, strongly disagree, don't know.)
(d) 'If things aren't going well today, it's because the family does not play the same role that it used to'. (Strongly agree, somewhat agree, somewhat disagree, strongly disagree, don't know.)
(e) 'Homosexuals should be accepted in our society like everybody else'. (Strongly agree, somewhat agree, somewhat disagree, strongly disagree, don't know.)

the 'haves' (that is, those who own property and who have high incomes), the elderly and rural residents.

Attitudes of the population toward the rehabilitation and social reinstatement of delinquents and criminals

The first part of this chapter focused on the attitudes of citizens regarding severity of sentences. Since most people have dangerous criminals in mind when they evaluate the adequacy of the punishments imposed by the courts, it is evident that a majority of respondents think they are not harsh enough. Studied from this angle, the data gathered during the present survey overestimate the punitiveness of the population. Since the images of crime and the criminal which the persons questioned have in mind are those of the most violent delinquents, namely those who have committed murder, rape, grave assault or theft with violence, their attitudes toward rehabilitation are not very clear.

Because the persons who find the sentences too lenient are also those who are most numerous in thinking of criminals as incorrigible and hardened recidivists, it is not surprising to find that it is also these most punitive people who believe least in the rehabilitation of delinquents.

Relationship between punitive attitudes and attitudes toward the rehabilitation of criminals

In our sample, it is among the persons who have shown themselves to be the most punitive that we find the greatest pessimism regarding the proportion of criminals who can be rehabilitated, that is, can be influenced to return to a normal life in society. Among the people with a high degree of punitiveness, there are 81 per cent who think that not one (4 per cent) or only a few (77 per cent) prisoners, can be rehabilitated, 17 per cent who think that most criminals can be, and 2 per cent who believe that all delinquents have the potential for reintegration in society. In comparison, among the less punitive persons, there are none who think that no delinquent can be salvaged, there are 35 per cent (twice as many as for the other group) who are of the opinion that most of the authors of crimes and infractions are capable of changing their way of life and 3 per cent who are sufficiently optimistic to hope that all offenders can somehow find the straight and narrow path. Thus the correlation between attitudes toward the severity of sentences and those regarding the ability of delinquents to reform is very strong: gamma = .45.

The data just analysed show us the proportion of delinquents who, according to whether people are more or less punitive, are considered to have some chance of being reformed by society. Another more specific question concerned the possibilities of rehabilitating a true criminal ('even a hardened criminal is not beyond redemption'). The object of the question was both to assess people's determinism regarding criminogenesis and their pessimism concerning the 'redemption' capacity of individuals as well as of the penal institutions. As we logically expected, 53 per cent of the most punitive individuals rejected any possibility that the hardened criminal could be rehabilitated. Here, too, the relationship between punitiveness and pessimism regarding rehabilitation is fairly high: gamma = .33.

Image of the prison and punitiveness

What has just been said depends as much on the image people have of crime and criminals as on the repressive or therapeutic measures adopted by the penal system. We have seen, for example, that generally speaking the persons who consider the sentences too lenient are a majority of those who are most preoccupied by crime (to the point of resorting more to various ways of protecting themselves) and who see the criminal as a violent person, a recidivist and incurable. For the less punitive individuals the picture is quite the opposite (it is of young delinquents, criminals committing their first offence who are not dangerous and who can be rehabilitated).

To be able to analyse thoroughly the 'punitive/non-punitive' attitudes of the population, then, it would be completely wrong, and unfair, to limit the study (as many surveys do) to only the public's evaluation of the severity of the sentences pronounced by the courts. If the population considers punishment either too severe or not severe enough, it is essential to know in terms of what type of criminal (this is what we discussed at the beginning of the chapter) and what manner of sentence. It seems self-evident that people's punitive attitudes can only be assessed in relation to their idea of punishment. Furthermore, since in the minds of most people there is a strong association between 'penal sentences' and 'imprisonment', it is impossible to focus on the punitiveness of the public without knowing the public's perception of prison.

The public's image of prison institutions is polarized around two stereotypes: the paradise-like prison–hotel — and the nightmarish concentration camp. It would seem logical that people's conception of prison would have an influence on the degree of their punitiveness. For example, among the population that we surveyed, there are a little more than half (58 per cent) who believe that 'today the prisons are veritable hotels'. The others (42 per cent) have a more sombre, a more unpleasant picture of custodial institutions.

The answers to the questions evaluating the severity of the respondents show, without any doubt, that the persons who see the prisons as 'hotels' are those who, in largest proportion, feel that the sentences are not harsh enough (gamma = .47). Among them, there are 85 per cent (compared to 58 per cent for the others) who say that the sentences pronounced by judges are not severe enough. Thus there is a direct relationship between the degree of punitiveness and the fact of thinking that life in prison is more

Table 5.6 Relation between the degree of punitiveness and whether or not people consider prisons 'veritable hotels'

Degree of punitiveness	'The prisons are veritable hotels'	
	Agree (%)	Do not agree (%)
Low	40	71
High	60	29
(Number of respondents)	(473)	(344)
% of the total sample	58	42
Gamma .47		

Question: 'The prisons today are like hotels' (Strongly agree, somewhat agree, somewhat disagree, strongly disagree.)

or less painful. Table 5.6 illustrates this close connection between punitiveness and people's image of the prison.

The results presented in Table 5.6 show that seven persons out of ten (71 per cent) among the less punitive individuals do not think that the prisons are like hotels. Consequently, it is those who have the most negative view of imprisonment who are the least severe. The contrary is obviously true for the people who have a high degree of punitiveness: 60 per cent tend to minimize the negative and deprivational aspects of imprisonment. Thus a correlation emerges between the image of the criminal, punitiveness and impression of the prison. The most punitive people are those who, when judging the severity of sentences, have the most dangerous criminals in mind, and who refer to the prisons as 'veritable hotels'.

This correlation could mean that it is the image of the prison that actually conditions both the individual's punitive attitude as well as the desire to see the courts act with much more severity. It seems more logical, however, to believe that the conditioning takes the opposite direction. It would be the 'punitiveness' rather, as a basic attitude, that would lead people to see life in prison as more or less easy-going, more or less 'pleasant'.

It is among the punitive people, those who see the prisons as too lenient, too 'comfortable' that we also find those who have least confidence in the rehabilitation of delinquents. And, based on what was said at the beginning of this chapter, this is consistent with the fear they have of crime (they are more worried about crime

Table 5.7 Relationship between liberalism and the prison image

Degree of liberalism and openness to change	'The prisons are veritable hotels'	
	Agree (%)	Do not agree (%)
More conservative	71	45
More liberal	29	55
(Number of respondents)	(473)	(344)
% of the total sample	58	42
Gamma .43		

than the others) and of the criminals themselves. They see the latter as 'dangerous', 'hardened' criminals, 'incurable' and 'violent' (gamma = .32 between the prison image and confidence in rehabilitation). According to them, only incarceration can succeed, provided it is long enough. These persons are also (and perhaps their image of prison life and punitive tendencies are due to this) much more conservative (71 per cent compared with 45 per cent for those who do not call the prisons 'veritable hotels'). The gamma here is very high between the prison image and liberalism; it is −.43, and Table 5.7 explains the distribution of these two variables.

The image of the prison, then, as the word itself implies, is largely 'imaginary'. It is based on each person's perception of the world and of his fellow human beings. The fact that it is so closely associated with 'conservatism/liberalism' indicates that people 'see' prison in terms of their punitiveness, with the result that there is a correlation between their demand for severe sentences and the way they evaluate the deterrent aspect of these 'sentences'. As the data already show, this means that the most punitive persons are also those who have the least punitive image of life in prison. And it is precisely because they want more severe sentences that they tend to view prison life as easy and not very likely to discourage criminals. All the more so since when they think of 'criminals', they refer to cruel, impenitent and incurable individuals.

It is not surprising, then, to find among the people who see the prisons as hotels those who are most opposed to alternative measures to imprisonment. The largest proportion of them are against both parole and halfway houses. In Table 5.8, we show the distribution of our population's opinions concerning these two measures, a distri-

Table 5.8 View of the prison and attitudes toward alternatives to imprisonment

Opinions concerning parole and halfway houses	'The prisons are veritable hotels'	
	Agree (%)	Do not agree (%)
1 *Parole*		
For, in every case	4	13
For, in certain cases	80	84
Against, in every case	16	3
Gamma = .52; r = .28		
2 *Halfway houses*		
For, in every case	15	27
For, in certain cases	79	70
Against, in every case	6	3
Gamma = .34; r = .21		
(Number of respondents)	(473)	(344)
% of the total sample	58	42

Questions:

(a) 'The parole system allows a prisoner to be released under supervision before his sentence has been fully served. In general, would you say you are for or against release on parole? (... for it for every case; ... for it for certain cases; ... against it for any case; ... don't know).'

(b) 'Some prisoners can be released before the end of their sentence and be sent to halfway houses. They live there under supervision while being allowed to participate in various activities outside the house which make it possible for them to readapt later to a normal life. In general, are you for or against halfway houses? (... for them for every case; ... for them for certain cases; ... against them for any case; ... don't know).

bution that varies according to the way the respondents view the prisons.

Clearly, in both the case of parole and that of halfway houses, the majority of the sample advocates recourse to these measures 'in certain cases'. We note, however, that among the people who have a more negative view of prison institutions, the percentage of those who would be in favour of these measures for 'all' delinquents is higher than the others (13 per cent and 27 per cent respectively are in favour of parole and halfway houses for all prisoners against 4 per cent and 15 per cent in the rest of the sample). It is at the extremities of the scales that the opinions are intensified. The persons who conceive the prisons as hotels are five times more numerous (16 per cent against 3 per cent) in being against parole 'in every case' and twice as numerous (6 per cent against 3 per cent) concerning halfway houses. And here again we see confirmation of the fact that the most conservative people tend to see criminality in terms of 'violent criminals' and hence to demand more repressive measures and a stricter filtering of the use of alternatives to incarceration.

Conceptions of prison life and the degree of punitiveness

We saw previously that most citizens seemed to expect the courts to provide sanctions that would afford them 'security' rather than exact penalties aimed to 'punish' or 'chastise' criminals. From this point of view, we can confirm that punitiveness seems to come somewhere between the view of the dangerousness of the criminals and the need to isolate the most menacing among them. Since, on the other hand, people have few illusions about the therapeutic potential of correctional institutions, it seems valid to claim that — for the population as a whole — the key concept that underlies the penal philosophy is 'deterrence'.

This can be deduced from the fact that nearly six persons out of ten among those interviewed (56 per cent) think that the primary objectives of criminal justice are to discourage people from committing crimes and to protect the citizens against any attempt on their person or property. It must be noted, however, that for 21 per cent of respondents, the goal of sentences is primarily either to 'punish those who commit crimes' (19.1 per cent) or 'to permit society to take revenge' (two per cent) on offenders. These are among the most punitive of the respondents and therefore among those who would like to see prison life as harsh as possible in order to bring 'hardened' and 'incorrigible' criminals to their knees and to reform.

Thus there is a very strong correlation between the degree of punitiveness and the conditions that people advocate for prison life. The more punitive people are:

- the more they are opposed to prisoners with light sentences being allowed to work in companies outside the prison (30 per cent of the more punitive against 13 per cent of the less punitive: gamma = .44 and r = .38);

- the more they are against prisoners being paid the same salary as workers outside the prison and also paying toward a pension (44 per cent of the punitive in comparison with 26 per cent of the non-punitive: gamma = .29 and r = .28);
- the more they demand that prisoners be obliged to work, without a salary, in the prison shops (52 per cent against 28 per cent of the less punitive: gamma = .42 and r = .38);
- the more they object to prisoners being allowed to have sexual relations with their husbands or wives in prison (55 per cent of the punitive persons against 23 per cent of the others: gamma = .52 and r = .47);
- the more they are against granting prisoners the right to vote (64 per cent against 35 per cent: gamma = .51 and r = .48);
- the more they are opposed to prisoners having frequent leaves to see their families (77 per cent against 37 per cent of the less punitive persons: gamma = .64 and r = .58);
- the more they are inclined to demand more guards in the prisons (75 per cent against 57 per cent: gamma = .23 and r = .22).

There can be no doubt about the relationship between punitiveness and detention. The persons in our sample who show a high degree of punitiveness are, first of all, those who want judges to hand down more sentences of imprisonment, and secondly, would like these sentences to be more severe, that is, longer and harsher. Thus they have a more repressive conception of life 'inside'. What is wanted by the persons who demand more severity on the part of the courts (and who are also those who 'imagine' that the prisons are like hotels: 74 per cent of these punitive persons have this image) is that custodial institutions 'deter' criminals and prevent recidivism.

To achieve this end, they do not wish the prisoners to have what they consider privileges (salaries, the right to vote, sexual relations with their husbands or wives, family leaves) but, on the contrary, would have prisoners confined to a more disciplined, more ascetic and more arduous way of life. The answers to the questions concerning prisoners' living conditions show that punitive persons feel a certain nostalgia for the 'houses of correction' of the past. They seem to want all prison activities to be centred on 'work', the latter being perceived (and this clearly emerged from the in-depth interviews held during the qualitative stage of research) as 'redeeming', 'character moulding' and 'therapeutic'.

Conclusion

An analysis of public attitudes toward penal and correctional measures enabled us to establish some basic data which can be summed up as follows:

- the degree of punitiveness shown by an individual has nothing to do with sex, fear of crime or victimization, or even actual victimization;
- the degree of punitiveness seems, rather, to be connected with socio-economic status (income, province, property ownership) where these factors are directly associated with an ideology or world view: thus we were able to establish a link between the position of respondents on scales of 'conservatism/liberalism' and punitiveness:
- the degree of punitiveness conditions the image people have of prison institutions as well as their image of the criminal: the more punitive they are, the more they tend to use 'the violent criminal' as their point of reference to justify the laxness of the prisons and to demand more repressive sentences.

Finally, it would seem that punitiveness is a basic attitude (derived perhaps from authoritarianism, from anomie and a certain intolerance . . . in short, from a way of seeing people and situations) which is inherent in people's personality. As such, it cannot be explained by how people perceive the phenomenon of crime or by the image people have of the system of criminal justice. On the contrary, it would seem to function as an important modulating element which itself plays a basic and active role in how people see crime, the criminal and criminality, and on the other hand, in their perceptions of the penal system and the way it reacts *vis-à-vis* crime and the criminal.

Notes

1. Group Research on Attitudes toward Criminality. The survey took place in April 1981. For the analysis of the data, see Brillon et al. (1984).
2. The people defined as the most punitive are those situated at the levels of 4 and 5 on the scale of punitiveness. They represent 47.2 per cent of the sample.

References

Brillon, Y., Louis-Guérin, C. and La Marche, M.-C. (1984), *Attitudes of the Canadian Public Toward Crime Policies*, Cahier No 1A, Les Cahiers de Recherches Criminologiques, C.I.C. Université de Montréal.

Centre de Recherche sur l'Opinion Publique, Inc. (1972), *Les normes sociales*, Rapport final, Montréal, June; (1980), *Sondage omnibus*, Omnibus 1980-5-3 Montréal.

Figgie Report (The) (1980), *America Afraid*, The Figgie Report on Fear of Crime, Part I: The General Public A-T-O Inc., Ohio.

Foucault, M. (1975), *Surveiller et punir, Naissance de la prison*, Gallimaud, Paris.

National Council on Crime and Delinquency (1981), *Attitudes of Californians Toward*

Prisons and Jails, Punishment and Some Other Aspects of the Criminal Justice System, Summary Tables, NCCD., Research Center, California.
Peyrefitte, A. (1981), *Les chevaux du Lac Ladoga*, Plon, Paris.
Stinchcombe, L. A. et al. (1980), *Crime and Punishment: Changing Attitudes in America*, Jossey-Boss Publishers, San Francisco–Washington–London.

6 Public punitiveness and public knowledge of the facts: some Canadian surveys

Anthony N. Doob and Julian Roberts

In Canada, as in many countries, the general public does not appear to be completely content with the way in which sentencing takes place. According to the recently released report of the Canadian Sentencing Commission (1987), many ordinary Canadians share the same views as those who have relatively close ties with the criminal justice system — as judges, lawyers, prosecutors, or defendants — that there are problems with sentencing. However, these others do not always identify the problems as being the same as those identified by the public at large.

Our starting point in this exploration of the Canadian public's view of sentencing will be two quite disparate findings which, at first glance, appear to be contradictory. (All the estimates of Canadians' views of crime and sentencing reported in this paper, unless otherwise specified, come from nationwide polls of at least 1,000 respondents, carried out by the Gallup organization largely in 1982, 1983, 1985, and 1986.) The first finding is that a substantial portion of Canadians believe that sentences are not severe enough (see Table 6.1).

Interestingly enough, in one of the more recent polls (1985), respondents were asked to indicate their view of sentences for particular groups. As noted in Table 6.1, only 2 per cent of respondents thought that sentences were generally too severe. Yet 19 per cent of these same respondents thought that sentences for native Canadians were too harsh and 43 per cent thought that sentences for poor people were too harsh.

Respondents were also asked whether offenders convicted of particular offences were treated more harshly or more leniently than they deserve (see Table 6.2).

Clearly a substantial portion of the public thinks that all sentences for all categories of offences are too lenient. This is most true, however, for violent and sex crimes, and for drinking driving offences.

Table 6.1 Opinions of sentences, 1966–1987

Year	Too severe (%)	About right (%)	Not severe enough (%)	Don't know (%)
1966	7	29	43	21
1969	2	22	58	18
1975	4	13	73	10
1980	4	19	63	14
1983	1	17	80	2
1985	2	25	65	8
1986	2	27	61	10
1987	3	12	78	7

Question: 'In general, would you say that the sentences handed down by the courts are too severe, about right, or not severe enough?' (Pre-1983 and 1987 data were obtained from the Gallup organization in Canada.)

Table 6.2 Opinions of sentences for particular offences (1985)

	Too harsh (%)	Appropriate (%)	Too lenient (%)	Don't know (%)
Violent offences	2	25	69	4
Property offences	5	46	43	6
Drinking and driving	4	23	71	3
Sex offences	2	11	83	4
Drug related offences	9	28	56	6

Question: 'Now I would like you to indicate if offenders convicted of the following types of offences are treated more harshly or more leniently than they deserve.'

The overall finding is that since the late 1960s a majority of Canadians feel that sentences are not severe enough.

The second finding, which should be contrasted with the public's view that sentences are too lenient, is quite simple. Respondents were asked the following question: 'Canada's prisons are becoming over-crowded. Two solutions that have been proposed are the following: (a) build more prisons, and (b) sentence more offenders to alternatives to imprisonment such as probation, restitution, community service orders and fines. In which direction would you favour the government spending its money?' The consensus was clear: most Canadians (70 per cent of the respondents) appear to favour spending money on developing sanctions other than imprisonment (Canadian Sentencing Commission, 1987, p. 53). It appears when one looks at this question alone that Canadians are not quite as harsh in their views as the questions about sentence harshness would suggest.

Obviously, there is a large number of explanations for the apparently conflicting results of these two questions. One obvious one is that the desire for harsher sentences is not a strongly held desire: people want harsher sentences only if there is no cost. Another more interesting hypothesis is that people are, in fact, thinking about quite different things when they answer the two questions. This chapter will suggest that this latter explanation is correct. More generally, the chapter will explore the views of Canadians concerning sentencing, coming to the conclusion that Canadian views, as they presently stand, are not as harsh as they might be seen to be.

In the latter part of the chapter, we will present evidence suggesting that mass media coverage of sentencing gives people in Canada a distorted view of this part of their criminal justice system. Finally, we will suggest that reforms of sentencing should be sensitive to the underlying views of the public and should not slavishly follow the surface view which people are often compelled to express, given the simplistic nature of some opinion polls.

It should be pointed out that excessive leniency is not the only problem with sentencing that members of the Canadians public perceive. Canadians were asked if they perceived unwarranted disparity to be a problem in sentencing. The results are in Table 6.3. Clearly unwarranted disparity is seen to be a problem by most Canadians.

How do Canadians view crime in Canada?

In order to understand how Canadians view sentencing, it is first necessary, we feel, to have some understanding of what people in Canada think about crime. We now have quite a bit of information about this. Put simply, the views of most Canadians bear only a slight resemblance to what (official) crime really looks like. As is well established in most western countries, most crime consists of offences against property. This is not, however, the view that Canadians have. In 1982 and 1983, Canadians were asked how much

Table 6.3 Perceptions of unwarranted sentencing disparity (1985)

	(%)
Yes, it is a problem:	73
No, it is not a problem:	15
Don't know, not stated	12
Total	100

Question: 'One topic that has been discussed recently concerns sentencing disparity. This refers to the possibility that similar offenders, convicted of similar offences, sometimes receive dissimilar sentences. From what you know about sentencing in Canada, do you think this is a problem or not?'

Table 6.4 Estimate of proportion of crime involving violence

	1983	1982
	(%)	(%)
Accurate (0–9%)	3	4
Small overestimate (10–29%)	15	15
Large overestimate (30–100%)	74	74
Don't know, not stated	8	7
Total:	100	100

Question: 'In your opinion, of every 100 crimes committed in Canada, what percentage involve violence — for example, where the victim was beaten up, raped, robbed at gun-point, and so on?'

crime involved violence. As can be seen in Table 6.4, most respondents substantially overestimated the amount of crime involving violence. In Canada it appears reasonable to estimate that under 10 per cent of crime involves violence. Almost three-quarters of Canadians severely overestimated this proportion.

In Canada, capital punishment was abolished in 1976. (At the time of writing this chapter, a resolution was being debated in Parliament to begin the process of considering the return of the death penalty.) Since 1976, the number and rate of murders and all homicides has fluctuated from year to year, but has, overall,

Table 6.5 *Estimate of first offender recidivism: violent offenders (1983)*

	(%)
Underestimate (0–9%)	2
Correct (10–29%)	12
Small overestimate (30–59%)	35
Large overestimate (60–100%)	45
Don't know/No response	6
Total:	100

Question: 'Of 100 first time offenders convicted of crimes involving violence, what percentage do you think will be convicted again for any criminal offence within the next five years?'

Table 6.6 *Estimate of first offender recidivism: property offenders (1983)*

	(%)
Underestimate (0–19%)	9
Correct (20–39%)	21
Small overestimate (40–59%)	29
Large overestimate (60–100%)	34
Don't know/No response	7
Total:	100

Question: 'Of 100 first time offenders convicted of property offences, what percentage do you think will be convicted again for any criminal offence within the next five years?'

either decreased or stayed the same. Yet in 1982, 67 per cent of Canadians thought that murder had increased since the abolition of capital punishment.

Another contrast between public knowledge and reality becomes apparent when considering views about criminals. We asked Canadians to estimate what they saw as the likelihood that first offenders would recidivate. The results, in Tables 6.5 and 6.6, clearly demonstrate that most Canadians overestimate the likelihood of recidivism.

Canadians' views of their criminal justice system are equally uninformed. Without going into detail, on any of seven fairly common offences (e.g. robbery, break and enter, theft) fewer than 15 per cent of Canadians were at all accurate in their knowledge of statutory maximum penalties. This is not surprising, given that our maximum penalties are much higher than normal sentences are. In addition, even though there had been a fair amount of publicity about one minimum penalty which had recently changed, Canadians knew almost nothing about which offences had minimum penalties and what they were. Finally, not surprisingly, Canadians had little knowledge about actual levels of penalties imposed by the court. This last finding is hardly surprising since, among other things, there is no easy way for anyone — criminologist, policy maker, journalist, or lay member of the public — to find out what sentencing looks like in Canada, since comprehensive published data have not been available for 15 years. (In order to get any data at all, the Canadian Sentencing Commission had to go to extraordinary efforts to put together incomplete data from a large variety of sources.)

What is the public thinking about when they say that sentences are too lenient?

Clearly the majority of Canadians overestimate, and a substantial number of Canadians seriously overestimate, the proportion of first offenders who will be re-convicted. Canadians overestimate the amount of crime that involves violence. They think that homicide is increasing when it is not. Other examples can be cited. For example, they perceive the parole boards to be releasing more inmates than in fact is the case.

These data demonstrate that the view that Canadians have of crime is distorted. Their apparent harshness then, in 'wanting' more severe penalties can, even on the basis of these findings alone, be questioned. If the public's view of crime is that there is an ever-increasing amount of violent crime; that violent crime is a substantial portion of crime, that offenders — particularly violent offenders — are very likely to recidivate, then it is not surprising that they say they want harsher sentences.

We asked respondents what kind of offender they were thinking of when they indicated whether they thought that sentences were too lenient, too harsh, or about right. Their responses, broken down by their view of sentences, are shown in Table 6.7. Those who think sentences are too lenient are more likely to be thinking of violent or repeat offenders.

When asked what should be considered in sentencing someone, we see that offence seriousness, harm to the victim, premeditation,

Table 6.7 Type of offender in mind when evaluating sentences (1983)

	Violent (%)	Repeat (%)	Various (%)	All (%)	Total (%)
View of sentences					
OK/Too harsh	21	10	29	39	100
Too lenient	45	18	6	31	100

Question: 'What type of criminal were you thinking of when you answered this last question?' Percentages exclude the 5 per cent who did not respond. Chi square = 103, $p < .01$. 'Various' includes juvenile delinquents, first offenders, and property offenders.

and the record of the offender, seemed most relevant (see Table 6.8). The responses to this question give one the feeling that the public is thinking about serious crimes involving harm to persons.

Respondents who indicated that they thought that sentences were too lenient were asked in one survey to rate the importance of five reasons for making sentences harsher. The results are shown in Table 6.9.

The primary reason, it seems, for feeling that sentences should be longer is that the punishments are not perceived to fit the crime. The utilitarian concerns are obviously seen as being important by most respondents. However, proportionality appears to be dominant. It may be, then, that the public views sentences for different crimes as being too similar and does not perceive (or believe) there to be enough variation in the way in which different people convicted of different offences are sentenced.

Do Canadians really want harsh sentences?

On the face of it, most of the data we have thus far presented suggest that people simply want harsher sentences. There is a hint, though, that Canadians' views are not completely undifferentiated. As noted above, in Table 6.2, a bare majority of Canadians apparently feel that sentences for property offences (by far the largest category of offences in Canada) are being dealt with either appropriately or too harshly.

Similarly, if one looks to the broad, utilitarian goal of 'protection of the public' (a purpose of sentencing rejected by the Canadian

Table 6.8 What should a judge consider in sentencing? (1983)

	% listing factor	
	first	second
Whether crime is premeditated or planned	22	16
Criminal record	16	18
Harm to victim	16	13
Whether offence is violent	15	17
Likelihood of recidivism	11	9
Age of offender	4	5
Frequency of this crime in community	3	3
Whether offender shows remorse	3	5
Whether offender has provided restitution to victim	3	4
Whether crime is racially motivated	1	2
Whether offender is working	<1	<1
Don't know, not stated	5	7
Total	100	100

Question: 'Which of the following do you think should be the single most important factor [second most important factor] to be considered by a judge in sentencing someone convicted of a criminal offence?' (The choices were presented to the respondents in one of two different random orders.)

Sentencing Commission), it is clear that respondents see this purpose as being fulfilled in different ways, depending on the nature of the offence (see Table 6.10).

Imprisonment, then, is not seen as necessarily the best way of dealing with all offenders. In particular, these questions suggest that imprisonment is not seen as the appropriate penalty in order to achieve the utilitarian goal of 'protecting the public' from those who commit minor offences.

The question of what the most appropriate sentence should be for non-violent offences, however, needs to be looked at more directly. In 1983, we questioned Canadians about what is probably seen as one of the most serious non-violent property crimes – breaking and entering a dwelling (see Table 6.11).

Clearly, most Canadians do not feel that imprisonment is appropriate for first offenders who have committed one of the most serious

Table 6.9 Reasons of those believing that sentences are not severe enough for making sentences harsher (1986)

	% rating it as very important (8–10 on 10-point scale)
Offenders deserve more punishment	76
To express society's disapproval of the criminal behaviour	68
Deter potential offenders	63
Deter the offender	62
Incapacitation	57

Question: 'Here are some reasons why sentences should be made more severe. As I read each one to you please rate the reason from 1 to 10 on its importance to your belief that sentences should be more severe. To do this you should rate a reason as "1" if it is not at all important to you or you should rate it as "10" if it is very important to you, or you may use any number in between.' (Reasons were described to respondents in more detail than noted.)

property crimes. Interestingly enough, however, when asked whether they would want the offender to be given a community service order instead of the sentence they had just suggested, most felt that they would want it to be considered (see Table 6.12).

Although respondents' willingness to consider a reparative sanction did not vary according to their overall view of leniency of sentencing, it did relate rather strongly to their initial choice of sentence (see Table 6.13).

What we find most notable about these findings is not that willingness to consider a reparative sanction varied with the originally chosen sanction, but rather that over three-quarters of those who initially favoured prison felt that at least in some cases consideration should be given to a reparative sanction.

These results would seem to imply that people do not favour imprisonment for property offences. However, one must be cautious in this interpretation. When asked to indicate their feelings about imprisonment *per se*, the majority felt that imprisonment was appropriate for this very same offence.

The difference between the results of the question in Table 6.14 and the question (asked three years earlier) which asked only about

Table 6.10 *Most appropriate sentence to protect the public for minor or major offences (1986)*

	Minor offences (%)	Major offences (%)
A fine	13	2
Probation	22	8
Community service order	53	10
Imprison more people	5	33
Imprison people for longer	4	43
Not stated	3	5
Total:	100	100

Question: 'For most offences in the Criminal Code a judge has a choice as to the kind of sentence to impose. Consider the case of relatively minor crimes such as theft under $200 and consider more serious crimes such as assault. Assuming for the moment that the aim of sentencing is protection of the public, please choose the *most* appropriate sentence to achieve that aim.'

(*Note:* Sentence types were defined in more detail for respondents.)

Table 6.11 *Most appropriate sentence for first offender, breaking and entering a dwelling (1983)*

	(%)
Probation	39
Fine	26
Fine and probation	3
Prison	29
Don't know/can't say	3
Total:	100

Question: 'Which of the following sentences would you most prefer to be given to a first offender convicted of breaking and entering into a private home and stealing things worth $250?'

Table 6.12 Preference for reparative sanction for first time breaking and entering (1983)

	% giving this response	Cumulative %
Yes, in all cases	30	30
Yes, in most cases	31	61
Yes, in some cases	27	88
Only in very rare cases	6	94
Never	4	98
Don't know, not stated	2	100
Total:	100	

Question: 'Now, instead of [answer chosen in preceding question] would you be in favour of having the offender be ordered by the court to do a certain number of hours of work beneficial to the community or the victim or in some other way pay back the victim for the harm done?'

Table 6.13 Willingness to consider reparative sanction as a function of respondent's initial choice of sanction (1983)

	Initial choice of sanction (%)			
	Fine	Probation	Fine & Probation	Prison
Yes, in all cases	42	36	31	17
Yes, in most cases	30	38	41	24
Yes, in some cases	24	23	25	36
Only in very rare cases	3	3	3	14
Never	2	<1	0	10
Total:	100	100	100	100

Note: Chi square = 143.4, $p < .01$ (Questions were those noted in Tables 6.11 and 6.12.)

Table 6.14 Opinion regarding imprisonment for various offences (1986)

	Sentence to a prison term (%)		
	Yes	No	Don't know
Assault	74	21	5
Theft over $200	64	30	6
B&E private dwelling	63	32	5
Impaired driving	60	35	5
Robbery	59	34	7
B&E business premises	56	39	5
Theft under $200	17	79	4

Question: 'There are a number of different sentences an offender can be given other than a term of imprisonment. These include a fine, a period of probation and/or community service. In the case of an adult offender with no previous convictions, please tell me, for each offence I read to you, whether in your opinion, and generally speaking, the offender should or should not be sentenced to a term of imprisonment.'

the appropriate sentence for a minor break and enter of a dwelling (Table 6.11) is notable. In the earlier version of what on its face appears to be a similar question, only 29 per cent favoured prison, yet when asked the question in a slightly different way, 63 per cent favoured prison for the same offence. Since the proportion of the population thinking that sentences were too lenient had decreased during the same period (See Table 6.1), it seems unlikely that the difference is due to a real change in attitude.

Much more likely is that the results in the latter survey (Table 6.14) reflect the fact that the question centred on prison. Had the question centred on any other sanction, it is possible that a sizeable proportion would have favoured that, as well. Favouring prison in the abstract is easy. In the earlier attempt to measure attitudes (Table 6.11) we did not suggest any particular sanction; hence opinion was more divided. And, as shown in Tables 6.12 and 6.13, when people were challenged about whether they really held the view strongly that a particular sanction was appropriate, it became clear very quickly that their initial view was not strongly held.

The lesson, we feel, is clear even though the results may not

Table 6.15 Opinion regarding most effective way to control crime (1986)

	Sentences are		
	Too lenient (%)	About right (%)	Overall (%)
Make sentences harsher	35	17	27
Reduce unemployment	42	44	41
Increase social programmes	7	15	10
Increase non-imprisonment options	12	21	13
Increase number of police	4	3	4
Other/don't know/not stated	—	—	5
Total:	100	100	100

Question: 'Which of the ways listed on this card would in your view be the single most effective way to control crime?'

Note: Choices noted in the table are slightly abbreviated forms of what were shown to the respondents. Breakdown by view of sentences excluded the non-respondents, etc. Chi-square of view of sentence severity by best solution to crime = 41, $p < .01$.

be: views of appropriate penalties for at least some crimes are not strongly held. In particular, views that the harshest penalty — imprisonment — should be imposed may simply reflect the salience of imprisonment as a sanction in our society or the fact that imprisonment was salient in the way in which the question was asked.

Do Canadians view harsh sentencing as a solution to crime?
We started this chapter with what appeared to be a set of contradictory findings. Most Canadians see sentences as being too lenient, but most do not think that additional money should be spent building prisons to house additional prisoners.

We have already pointed out (See Table 6.9) that Canadians endorse all of the standard justifications for making sentences harsher. However, this should not be interpreted as meaning that Canadians look to the courts as the institution that can control crime effectively. In 1986, the public was asked its view of the most effective way to control crime. The overall results, and a breakdown by the overall view of sentencing is shown in Table 6.15.

Clearly most Canadians do not look exclusively to the sentencing process to solve the problems of crime. Only slightly more than a quarter of respondents thought that making sentences harsher was the best solution for crime. Those who view sentences generally as being too lenient were more likely to see harsher sentences as the most effective way of controlling crime. However, even within this group, harsher sentences were not seen as the best way to control crime: reducing unemployment was seen as being more effective.

Instead of looking to punishment as a way of controlling crime, most Canadians look to programmes to reduce unemployment as well as to other social programmes. Most criminologists would probably agree that harsher penalties would be unlikely to help control crime. Interestingly enough, almost nobody saw the solution of hiring more police as an effective way of controlling crime.

To sum up then, it appears that although a majority of Canadians think that sentences are too lenient, this proportion has varied somewhat in recent years. Although Canadians say that they want the courts to be harsher, this view does not carry over to other areas. Thus, they say that they want substantial numbers of people imprisoned for various offences — including property offences — but when imprisonment is offered as one of several choices of sanction, they choose imprisonment to a much lesser extent and for the most part are willing to consider alternatives to imprisonment. Finally, even among those who view sentences as being too lenient, harsher sentences are not seen as the most effective way of controlling crime. In this context, the finding that Canadians would rather spend money on sentences which do not remove the offender from the community than they would on building new prisons makes a good deal of sense.

How do Canadians acquire their view of sentencing?

Not surprisingly, when Canadians are asked to indicate the source of their information about the sentencing of offenders, they indicate that they are most likely to receive it from the mass media. Television, in particular, is named as the primary source for most people (see Table 6.16).

There is a good bit of research (e.g., Tversky and Kahneman, 1973; Hamill, Wilson, and Nisbett, 1980) that supports the view that single case information is much more vivid, memorable, and thus influential in the inferences we draw than is 'statistical' base-rate information. Given that most people (95 per cent) indicate that they receive their information about sentencing from the mass media, it is interesting to see if people can recall an instance of a sentence that is too lenient. As can be seen in Table 6.17, most people can

Table 6.16 Primary source of information about sentencing (1986)

Television news	53
Newspapers	31
Radio news	11
Friends/acquaintances	2
Gov't pub./attend court	1
Other/don't know, etc.	2
Total:	100

Question: 'Although you may hear about sentences from a variety of sources, from which one of these sources do you get most of your information about the sentencing of offenders in Canada?'

Table 6.17 Type of lenient sentence recalled (1986)

	All respondents (%)	Excluding those who didn't recall one (%)
Homicide	28	42
Sexual assault	16	23
Impaired driving	7	11
Assault	6	9
Theft/robbery	3	4
Drugs	2	4
Child abuse	2	3
Other	3	4
Have not seen/heard and don't know	39	—
Total:	106	

Question: 'If you have recently seen/heard in the news of a sentence that was too lenient, what was the crime that was committed?' Percentages add to more than 100 due to multiple responses from a few respondents.

recall a sentence which was too lenient and, surprisingly, the largest number of those who did recall one recalled a case of homicide.

It is remarkable, in one sense, and predictable in another, that sentences for homicide are the most likely to be recalled as lenient. The mandatory sentence for first and second degree murder in

Canada is life imprisonment. It is unlikely that this sentence is seen as too lenient even though people in Canada appear (on simple questions asked in simple ways) to favour bringing back capital punishment. It is possible that people are referring to manslaughter. For this offence the sentencing judge can impose any sentence up to and including life imprisonment.

What makes it understandable that violent offences — and in particular homicides — are remembered is that not only are they more dramatic and memorable, but they also are most likely to be reported in the news. The Canadian Sentencing Commission reported that in a study it carried out of over 800 sentencing stories in the newspapers of nine Canadian cities, over half of the stories dealt with offences involving violence and over half of these dealt with some form of homicide. In other words, the lenient sentences that people are most likely to remember deal with offences that constitute a tiny proportion of offences brought to court (Canadian Sentencing Commission, 1987, pp. 95–96).

Unfortunately, we know of no systematic research in Canada on the reporting of sentences by the electronic media. The reason for this is simple: it is much more difficult to sample and to research sentencing stories from radio and television than it is to analyse stories in the newspapers.

When one looks at newspaper stories about sentencing, probably the most salient thing about them is that they are, in almost all cases, short and provide little information. For example, in the study just referred to carried out by the Canadian Sentencing Commission (1987, p. 96), in 70 per cent of the over 800 stories examined, although the sentence was reported, no reasons for the particular sentence were reported. In two-thirds of the remaining stories only one reason for the sentence was reported in the news story. Given that the newspapers were disproportionately reporting serious offences with sentences of imprisonment, it seems likely that judges were saying a lot more about why they imposed the sentence they did. The public, from the newspapers at least, does not seem to be given the opportunity to evaluate the judges' logic in imposing the sentence.

When reactions to actual newspaper stories are examined, it is understandable that members of the public would view sentences as too lenient. In 1983, we gave a sample of Canadians (who, though not representative of the overall Canadian public on demographic characteristics, were representative of the public on views related to sentencing) a sample of newspaper stories of sentencing in Canada from Toronto newspapers (Doob and Roberts, 1983). The results of these ratings of 16 stories by 99 people (with each person seeing four stories) are shown in Table 6.18.

Table 6.18 Evaluation of newspaper stories

	(%)
Much too harsh	3
Too harsh	5
Slightly harsher than it should have been	8
About right	33
Slightly more lenient than it should have been	17
Too lenient	20
Much too lenient	14
Total:	100

Thirteen of the 16 stories were rated, on balance, as describing sentences that were too lenient. Equally relevant are the findings that almost everyone for each story that he/she read was at least somewhat confident about his/her rating. Indeed, 58 per cent of the ratings of the stories were made by people describing themselves as being 'very confident' about their rating. In 35 per cent of the ratings, the respondent indicated that he/she was somewhat confident; in only 7 per cent of the ratings was the respondent 'not at all confident.' This confidence existed notwithstanding the fact that the stories were very short.

Given that most people feel that sentences generally are too lenient (about 80 per cent of a comparable sample expressed this view), it is not surprising to find that when the generally held view was apparently supported by the article being rated (i.e., the sentence in the article was seen as too lenient), people were more confident about their views. The rank order correlation (across the 16 stories) between the percentage rating the sentence as too lenient and the percentage indicating that they were very confident about their evaluation of the sentence was significant (Spearman correlation = $+.50$, $p < .05$).

Are people getting adequate information about sentencing from the mass media?

Casual observation as well as systematic research (Canadian Sentencing Commission, 1987) reveals that newspapers are not reporting much information about a case; hence it seems likely that stories about sentences in newspapers will not be a good reflection of what went on in court. In order to contrast what people's views of sentencing would be if they had more complete information, we gave different groups of people (on a random basis) different accounts of the same sentencing hearings. Four separate studies (involving a total of 568 people) were run (Doob and Roberts, 1983).

The general structure of these studies was always the same. People were randomly assigned to read one of a number of accounts of a sentencing. After reading the account, they would indicate whether they thought that the sentence was appropriate. In some of the studies we were able to compare the reactions of different groups of people to different newspaper accounts of the same sentence and in some studies we were able to compare reactions to one or more newspaper accounts with the reaction to 'court-based' documents. These documents included transcripts and other documents (e.g., details of the offender's criminal record) that would have been discussed in court and which presumably formed the basis of the judge's sentence.

In all of the studies that compared different newspaper accounts of the same sentencing hearing, the reaction to the sentence depended on the account that was read. In other words, an identical sentence for the 'same' set of 'facts' was rated differently (in terms of its appropriateness) depending on which newspaper account was read. In addition, in all cases, the reactions to at least one of the newspaper accounts differed from the reactions to the court-based documents.

The last of the four studies in this series generated the most impressive results, in part because the case that it involved was one where the newspaper had not only given the case a good deal of prominence but also criticized the judge in an editorial (the following day) for giving the sentence he did. As shown in Table 6.19, there is no doubt whatsoever that readers of the newspaper would feel that the sentence was too lenient. What is important, however, is that people evaluating exactly the same sentence for the same man for the same offence when given the kind of information that the court had available to it saw this same sentence as too harsh. As shown in Table 6.20, the respondents were not happy with the manner in which the judge arrived at his decision if they read the news account. If, however, they had the court-based information available to them, they were considerably more content with the judge's decision.

Other results from this study help explain why the judge and the sentence were seen in such different lights by people who had read different accounts. As shown in Tables 6.21 and 6.22, both the offender and the offence were seen as worse by those whose source of information was the newspaper.

The accused in this case appealed his sentence notwithstanding the fact that his home-town newspaper had said it was already too light. It seems safe to assume that the newspaper was not happy

Table 6.19 *Evaluation of the sentence*

	Too harsh (%)	About right (%)	Too lenient (%)	Total (%)
Court-based documents	52	29	19	100
Newspaper	13	24	63	100

Question: 'What do you think of the sentence (21 months in prison) given to [offender's name] for the offence of assault causing bodily harm?' (Alternatives were: much too harsh, too harsh, slightly harsher than it should have been, about right, slightly more lenient than it should have been, too lenient, much too lenient.)

Note: Chi square = 28.1, $p < .01$.

Table 6.20 *Evaluation of whether the judge considered all appropriate factors*

	Yes (%)	Can't say (%)	No (%)	Total (%)
Court-based documents	59	17	24	100
Newspaper	29	25	46	100

Question: 'Do you think that the judge considered and gave proper weight to all of the appropriate factors in deciding his sentence?' (Alternatives were: definitely yes, probably yes, impossible to say, probably not, definitely not.)

Note: Chi square = 11.3, $p < .01$.

to report that the Court of Appeal had 'nearly halved' his sentence. The irony, of course, is that the readers of the news account probably agreed with the editorial stand taken by the newspaper and were probably quite upset to hear that the Ontario Court of Appeal had reduced the sentence. The Court of Appeal, on the other hand, would seem to have been quite well in step with public opinion

Figure 6.21 Evaluation of the offender

	Worse than average (%)	About average (%)	Better than average (%)	Total (%)
Court-based documents	36	42	22	100
Newspaper	76	17	7	100

Question: 'Compared to other people sentenced for criminal offences, how bad a criminal do you think [offender's name] was at the time of his sentencing?' (Alternatives were: one of the worst, worse than average, about average, not as bad as the average, much less bad than the average.)

Note: Chi square = 19.2 $p < .01$.

Table 6.22 Evaluation of the offence

	More serious than average (%)	About average (%)	Less serious than average (%)	Total (%)
Court-based documents	24	46	30	100
Newspaper	48	32	20	100

Question: 'Compared to other cases where people are found guilty of the same offence (assault causing bodily harm), how serious do you feel that [offender's name] actual offence was?' (Alternatives were: much more serious than average, more serious than average, about average, less serious than average, much less serious than average.)

Note: Chi square = 7.35 $p < .05$.

based on court documents in that they, like the public who had access to court-based information, thought that the original sentence was too harsh. The Court of Appeal, however, would appear to have been out of step with public opinion about the case as reported in the newspaper account.

We are left then with a serious and unresolved problem. Members of the public, it would appear, are getting information about the sentences of the court which leads them to feel that sentences are too lenient. These same members of the public, when given access to more complete or less selected accounts of the sentences, are more content with the decisions made by the trial judges. Public opinion about sentencing is likely to be shaped more by the news media than directly by events as they take place in courts. In short, people appear to be reacting not only to the actual sentence (which, in these studies, was constant across accounts) but also to the context in which the sentence is placed.

The public is aware of the deficiencies of information conveyed by the news media. The majority of Canadians who voiced an opinion to a question put to them in a 1986 poll, answered 'No' to the question 'Are the news media, in your view, providing the public with adequate information about sentencing?' Eight per cent voiced no opinion.

Conclusion

Sentencing in Canada is a complex process requiring the simultaneous consideration of a number of often competing principles. Nevertheless, most Canadians are willing to express views about sentencing. These views suggest that Canadians are not happy with the sentencing that occurs in their criminal courts. Many of these views relate to the level of severity of sentences. Although there is a good deal of variation in the Canadian public's assessment of the severity of sentences over the past 20 years, since 1969 a majority has always thought that sentences were too lenient.

This simple view, however, does not do justice to the public's actual views. As noted in this chapter, not only are these views based on inadequate information, but the public is, in fact, much more tolerant of leniency in sentencing (especially of non-violent offenders) than this simple view would suggest. One-dimensional questions give one-dimensional answers. The Canadian public's views of sentencing are in fact more complex. When asked simple questions about sentencing, especially the sentencing of violent offenders, Canadians seem to react with severity. When asked in a more appropriate way and when provided with more adequate information, it appears that Canadians respond in quite a sensitive manner.

Those policy makers, politicians, and others who justify advocating harsher penalties for criminal offenders on the basis that the public wants them are obviously relying on a superficial interpretation of

Table 6.23 Opinion on proportion of robbers who should be imprisoned as a function of respondents' opinion about sentence leniency

	Proportion of robbers who should be imprisoned			
	0–59%	60–79%	80–100%	Total
View of sentences:				
OK/too harsh	45	10	45	100
Too lenient	34	17	49	100

Note: Chi square = 9.57 $p < .01$

public opinion. Superficially they are correct, and to the extent that they wish to base policy recommendations on superficial views of public opinion, they obviously can find support in these findings.

However, the absurdity of using superficial findings about a process as complex as sentencing can be illustrated easily by one last set of findings. In Canada about 80–90 per cent of those convicted of robbery are sent to prison. In a 1983 poll, 86 per cent of respondents underestimated this figure, including 76 per cent who gave large underestimates (59 per cent or fewer robbers going to prison). In that same poll, respondents were asked 'Of every 100 persons convicted of any type of robbery, what percent do you think should be sent to prison?' Over half of those who expressed an opinion thought that fewer should go to prison than, in fact, do.

Indeed, as shown in Table 6.23, even among those who view sentences as being too lenient, about half recommend that a smaller portion go to prison than occurs at present.

The thoughtless policy maker, blindly following superficially expressed public opinion, would, therefore, not know whether to recommend harsher sentences (based on the opinion of sentences, generally, reported in Table 6.1) or more lenient sentences (based, for example, on findings such as those in Table 6.23). Both expressions of public opinion are obviously superficial. Both need to be understood in terms of what the public knows and understands.

Those policy makers, politicians, and others who wish to listen carefully to what members of the Canadian public really know and think about the sentencing of criminal offenders will find that the public's view of sentencing is not simple and shallow. To advocate generally harsher sentences on the basis of 'public opinion' is shallow, however. Such a view is not being sufficiently sensitive to what Canadians say when they are asked to express their views, based on reasonable information, in a more sensitive and thoughtful fashion.

Notes

Parts of this paper were taken from Doob and Roberts (1983). As noted in the text, the national surveys were carried out by the Gallup organization in the various years indicated in the text or tables. Those survey data collected in 1982 and 1983 were collected for the two Doob and Roberts papers. The 1985 and 1986 surveys were carried out for the Canadian Sentencing Commission. More information about the surveys and results can be found in the original publications.

The writing of this paper was facilitated by the Department of the Solicitor General, Canada, through its contribution to the operation of the Centre of Criminology, University of Toronto. In addition, we wish to thank the Department of Justice, Canada, for its direct and indirect support of the research described in this report. The views expressed in this paper are our own and do not necessarily reflect the views held by the Canadian Sentencing Commission or any department or ministry of the Government of Canada.

References

Canadian Sentencing Commission, *Sentencing Reform: A Canadian Approach*, Ottawa: Minister of Supply and Services Canada, 1987.

Doob, A. N. and Roberts, J. V. (1982), 'Crime: Some views of the Canadian public', Ottawa: Department of Justice, Canada.

Doob, A. N. and Roberts, J. V. (1983), 'An analysis of the public's view of sentencing', Ottawa: Department of Justice, Canada.

Hamill, R., Wilson, T. D., and Nisbett, R. E. (1980), 'Insensitivity to sample bias: generalizing from atypical cases', *Journal of Personality and Social Psychology*, **39**, 578–589.

Tversky, A. and Kahneman, D. (1973), 'Availability: a heuristic for judging frequency and probability,' *Cognitive Psychology*, **5**, 207–232.

7 Dealing with offenders: popular opinion and the views of victims in England and Wales*

Mike Hough and David Moxon

This chapter presents findings from the 1984 sweep of the *British Crime Survey (BCS)* on the views of the general public and of crime victims about punishment. A brief introductory review is also provided of the evidence from earlier polls and surveys in Britain. The chapter's scope is limited; it is concerned only with attitudes towards punishment and sentencing, paying attention to fear and concern about crime only so far as these affect attitudes to punishment. And it sets out simply to chart public opinion. It does not consider the formation of public attitudes – how opinion affects and is affected by politicians, pressure groups, mass media and the operation of the criminal justice system itself (see, e.g. Rock, 1979). Finally, it largely skirts philosophical issues about the nature of public opinion and technical ones about the measurement of opinion through sample surveys.

It has long been recognized that the legal system should command popular support, and some legal theorists, such as Dicey (1962), have placed particular emphasis on the dependence of law on public opinion. This is not to say that the criminal law has always marched in step with public opinion. The mandatory death sentences of the Black Act and other Draconian legislation of the eighteenth century certainly strained public tolerance (Thompson, 1975), whilst a modern-day referendum might well put capital punishment back on the statute book. People justify the mismatch, of course, with the argument (inherited from Burke) that it is the job of the elected representative to exercise his own intelligence on behalf of his constituents. But recently there has been more emphasis on the need to maintain confidence in the criminal justice system: greater importance is being attached to popular opinion about the criminal justice system in general and to sentencing policy in particular (see,

* This is a revised version of an article in the *Howard Journal* (1985) **24** (3), 160–175.

e.g. Home Office, 1984) — the assumption being that the sentences handed out by courts should be seen to be just deserts.

Whatever weight sentencers may accord to popular opinion, it is clear that the views of victims themselves have quite a different status. Obviously the courts could never accommodate the preferences of the most punitive victims, as the criminal law serves in part to protect offenders from vengeance, but legislators and sentencers are giving more consideration to the wants and needs of victims. This is reflected in growing support for disposals which are intended not simply to punish the offence against the law, but also to put right the wrong done to the victims. For example, the 1982 Criminal Justice Act enabled a compensation order to be made as a free-standing sentence; and there are experiments in progress on reparation and mediation. Further, it is increasingly often argued that victims should have more of a voice in the sentencing process.

This shift of focus from offender to victim reflects in part a scepticism amongst criminal justice practitioners about the criminal justice system's potential for deterring or rehabilitating those who pass through it. If deterrence or rehabilitation by themselves provide a shaky foundation for sentencing policy, little surprise that more priority is now given to maintaining the support of victims and the general public. Some might see a move in this direction as populism, others as a welcome whiff of democracy. Whatever the case, it is widely supposed that those involved in the administration of justice are less punitive than the public. Findings from the *British Crime Survey* call this belief into question; first, however, an overview of previous polls and surveys will suggest how such misconceptions about popular attitudes to punishment might have gained currency.

Previous surveys and polls

The British public has been polled a great deal on topics of law and order, but the most commonly asked questions are about crime as a social problem, the reasons for rising crime and about the police. Few polls or surveys have looked explicitly at public attitudes to sentencing, and fewer still have focused on victims.

Views of the general public

Polls on law and order paint a picture of a public which favours heavy sentencing. Thus, for example, in 1981 64 per cent of people thought that court sentences were too short, a figure which rose in 1982 to 67 per cent. In the same survey, around 60 per cent of people want the 'cat' brought back, with only 35 per cent feeling that we should 'continue to do without the cat'. And in 1983, 56 per cent of people felt that tougher sentences would 'greatly reduce the rate of crime generally' (Gallup, 1981, 1982; Marplan, 1983).

Polls of this sort are probably an accurate reflection of a widespread belief in deterrent principles — that heavier sentences will reduce crime. But the effectiveness and the equity of a sentencing policy are distinct, and these polls cannot tell us whether popular opinion sees current practice as inequitably lenient. Questions designed to find out whether offenders are generally thought to get their just deserts can only be sensibly asked if people hold accurate beliefs about current practice. There is good reason to think that they do not. Readily informative statistics are not available (let alone read widely); and the national media naturally dwell on the most sensational cases. Walker and Marsh (see Chapter 3) found that only 39 per cent of their sample could recall the sentence handed out in any single court case they had read or heard about via the media; as few as 13 per cent could recall the sentences in two such cases.

In interpreting these polls, one must also bear in mind some of the wording of the questions. For example 'continuing to do without the cat' is suggestive of making do. Questions asking generally about crime may put people in mind of serious crime, the comparatively rare offences committed by professional criminals, by the deranged and psychopaths, such as bank robberies, major burglaries, murder, rape and other very violent crimes, rather than the much more common crimes which impinge on everyday life — domestic burglaries involving comparatively small amounts, thefts of and from cars and vandalism (see also Chapter 6). Both common sense and research (Chapter 5) suggest that people regard serious crime in quite a different way from day-to-day offences.

Surveys focusing on specific offences point in this direction. Thus Gallup polls have found that around three-quarters of the adult population are in favour of capital punishment for the murder of policemen and soldiers and for the murder of a woman following sexual attack; around 40 per cent favour capital punishment for rape (Gallup, 1982). A broader spread of views emerges when less serious offences are included in the list. In a survey conducted by the Prison Reform Trust and *The Observer*, for example, the percentage of respondents favouring imprisonment as 'in general most appropriate' ranged from 88 per cent for rape and 70 per cent for mugging to 47 per cent for burglary, 35 per cent for vandalism and 8 per cent for shoplifting (Shaw, 1982).

Findings such as these, however, are insufficiently precise to answer the question whether sentencing is in line with public opinion — that is, whether people would see court sentences as fair. One way of answering this question is to ask people what they think of sentences handed out in a selection of case histories. The other — taken by the *BCS* — is to ask people to 'pass sentence' on a selection of hypothetical cases, and then compare the findings. Apart from Walker and Marsh's experiment described in Chapter 3, no survey of either sort had been carried out on a general population sample in this country before the 1984 *BCS*.

What victims want

Only two British studies before the *BCS* have examined victims' attitudes to punishment. Shapland et al. (1981) interviewed in depth a sample of some 280 victims of violent crime. Victims did not seem to the researchers to be very punitive. In response to general questions about sentencing levels, for example, a quarter of the sample felt that fewer people should be imprisoned; a marginally *smaller* number felt that more should be imprisoned. Questioned about their own cases, victims were on balance more punitive than the courts; comparing 135 court sentences to victims' preferences as stated to the researchers before the case reached court, 43 per cent were less severe than victims had hoped for, 33 per cent were as severe, and 23 per cent more severe.

A study by Maguire (1982) interviewed a sample of over 300 burglary victims. The researchers were surprised by the lack of vindictiveness among victims; fewer than 30 per cent thought that 'their' burglar should be sent to prison. They favoured restitution and community service, and also rehabilitative disposals. There were however some supporters of the birch, the stocks and violent personal revenge. Of course, the judgements in the survey were made, in the main, in ignorance of information about offenders. However, the study also asked victims about punishment in a number of hypothetical cases which provided details about offenders. People were lenient on first offenders, with only one in seven proposing prison either for 18-year-old offenders or for 30-year-olds. But if the 18-year-old had previous convictions, more than half favoured prison; for the 30-year-old, three-quarters were in favour. (Paradoxically, a far smaller proportion of those who believed themselves to be victims of professional burglars favoured prison for their own offender — only 31 per cent.) Similar findings have been found abroad (see especially Waller and Okihiro, 1978).

Findings from the *British Crime Survey*

The *British Crime Survey (BCS)* is a large sample survey designed primarily to estimate the extent of various types of crime; its count of crime differs from that in *Criminal Statistics* in that it includes incidents unreported to the police and unrecorded by the police.

So far, sweeps of the survey have been carried out in 1982 and 1984 (Hough and Mayhew, 1983; Hough and Mayhew, 1985) and the third sweep is planned for 1988.[1]

Besides counting crime, the survey asked respondents about their attitudes towards crime and about factors which affect their chances of becoming crime victims. The 1982 *BCS* contained only two questions on punishment, which asked crime victims how they would like to see 'their' offender dealt with. Though by no means definitive, the findings suggested more lenience and a greater public awareness of sentencing options than had been expected; and the 1984 survey set out to explore attitudes to punishment in more depth. As in 1982, all respondents identified as victims of crime in the previous year were asked how they would like their offender dealt with. Further questions about punishment were asked as part of a 'follow-up questionnaire', administered to a sub-sample of both victims and non-victims.

The findings presented below are drawn largely from the 1984 *BCS*. First, analysis of items in the follow-up is presented to shed light on the question whether current court practice and public opinion are in line. The chapter then moves on to examine victims' attitudes to the punishment of 'their' offenders and, finally, some of the factors which make for punitive and lenient attitudes are examined.[2]

Is sentencing practice in line with popular opinion?

Perhaps the first question addressed to this issue should be about the accuracy of popular beliefs: do people know what sorts of sentence are typically passed by the courts? The *BCS* asked only about burglary, and for this crime at least, they clearly do not. Respondents were asked whether a third, a half or two-thirds of convicted burglars aged 21 and over get sent to prison. Twelve per cent of the total sample felt unable to express an opinion; of those who answered the question, only 19 per cent selected the right answer, a half; 74 per cent answered a third, and 7 per cent two-thirds. In other words, most people overestimate the leniency of the courts towards burglars. The *BCS* asked only about burglary, but it is very possible that the same is true for other crimes as well.

Would *actual* court practice strike people as too lenient? The *BCS* tackled this question by getting people to 'pass sentence' in a number of hypothetical cases, and comparing the responses with sentences of the court. Respondents were asked about six offences committed by males, where the age of the offender was varied: half were asked about a 17-year-old offender with previous convictions and the other half about a 25-year-old, also with previous convictions. A question was also asked about a prostitute soliciting. Respondents were shown a menu of the main sentencing options available to the adult courts, though with some simplifications. For example, the term 'court warning' was used rather than absolute or conditional discharge; and in the case of 17-year-olds 'prison' was used as a proxy for youth custody (which replaced prison and borstal for young adults from May 1983) and detention centres. Answers were then compared to actual court practice for offenders of the relevant age group and offence category (see Tables 7.1 and 7.2).

Does this constitute a fair comparison? It should be remembered that the two sets of figures do *not* share the same base. In the first place, the decisions of the sample of 'lay sentencers' is made on a handful of cases, which provide basic information about the offender but no detail beyond offence category about the crimes themselves. The court statistics, on the other hand, represent sentencers' decisions in several thousand very varying cases; some of the variation between cases will stem from differences between sentencers, but most will arise from variations in the seriousness of offences. Where Table 7.1, for example, shows that 62 per cent of respondents would like to see burglars imprisoned this is not equivalent to a popular wish to see 62 per cent of burglars imprisoned; rather, it means that this proportion of the sample would like to see imprisonment as the modal sentence for burglary.

Comparison is made still more difficult by limits to the detail in which statistics could be provided on court practice. Respondents were asked about offenders *with previous convictions*: people think criminal history should be an important factor in sentencing (see Shaw, 1982) and this is probably reflected in the *BCS* 'sentences'. However the Home Office Statistical Department were unable to give a breakdown of disposals which included criminal history; the court figures in Tables 7.1 and 7.2 thus include first offenders. The majority of sentenced 17- and 25-year-olds probably do have previous convictions. The 1978 *Criminal Statistics* included tables comparing sentences for first offenders with sentences given to those having previous convictions, for different age groups. It can be inferred from these tables that around 60 per cent of 17-year-olds and 70 per cent of 25-year-olds have previous convictions. In summary, the comparison is far from perfect, but it can still offer a guide to whether opinion and practice are in step.

Table 7.1 shows respondents' preferences and court practice in respect of 25-year-old offenders. Bearing in mind that the comparisons must be suggestive more than conclusive, the table shows a fair degree of congruence between the courts and the public at least

Table 7.1 Sentences for 25-year-old offenders: preferences of BCS respondents compared to court practice for selected offences

	Robbery (%)	Burglary (%)	Shop-lifting (%)	Car theft (%)	Drugs (%)
BCS respondents' preferences (offender aged 25 with previous convictions)					
Prison	85	62	12	23	15
Discharge/caution	1	1	16	10	23
Community service	5	10	18	17	7
Other disposal	10	27	54	50	55
Total	100	100	100	100	100
Court practice for offenders aged 25 (including first offenders)					
Prison	92	61	10	31	11
Discharge/caution	1	2	11	6	11
Community service	1	8	5	11	2
Other disposal	6	29	74	52	76
Total	100	100	100	100	100

Question: 'On this card are the actions the police can take or the various sentences that a court can give to people. I am going to read out a number of different crimes and for each one I would like you to tell me what you think should have happened to the person committing the crime. You should assume in each case that this person is male, aged 25 and has previously been in trouble for similar crimes.'

Note: Weighted data; unweighted *n* = 3270
Court figures, relating to both Magistrates' and Crown Courts in 1983, provided by Home Office Statistical Department.
Source: British Crime Survey, 1984

in terms of the use of imprisonment. The vast majority of people would like to imprison 25-year-old robbers with previous convictions; and the vast majority of such offenders *are* sent to prison. The majority would not like to see offenders of this age imprisoned for shoplifting, car theft or use of cannabis, and indeed, in most of these cases, the offender stays out of prison.

Two offences have been excluded from Table 7.1 — rape and soliciting. In 1983 25-year-olds were found guilty in only nine rape cases, and it would be meaningless to compare the sentences of

Table 7.2 *Sentences for 17-year-old offenders: preferences of BCS respondents compared with court practice for selected offences*

	Robbery (%)	Burglary (%)	Shop-lifting (%)	Car theft (%)	Drugs (%)
BCS respondents' preferences (offender aged 17 with previous convictions)					
Custody	74	51	9	20	14
Discharge/caution	2	2	17	12	25
Community service	11	18	20	19	7
Other disposal	13	29	54	49	54
Total	100	100	100	100	100
Court practice for offenders aged 17 (including first offenders)					
Custody	81	45	5	22	2
Discharge/caution	3	7	23	10	25
Community service	8	16	6	15	1
Other disposal	8	32	66	53	72
Total	100	100	100	100	100

Question: 'On this card are the actions the police can take or the various sentences that a court can give to people. I am going to read out a number of different crimes and for each one I would like you to tell me what you think should have happened to the person committing the crime. You should assume in each case that this person is male, aged 17 and has previously been in trouble for similar crimes.'

Note: Weighted data; unweighted $n = 3300$
Court figures, relating to both Magistrates' and Crown Courts in 1983, provided by Home Office Statistical Department.
Source: British Crime Survey, 1984

these nine with the preferences expressed by *BCS* respondents; but a comparison can be made instead with court practice *vis-à-vis* all rapists aged 21 or over. The courts sent some 96 per cent of these offenders to prison in 1983, whilst the *BCS* shows 94 per cent of the public favouring imprisonment for rape. For soliciting, 18 per cent of the public chose a prison sentence, but this is no longer an option for the courts.

There was some, albeit minority, support for diversion, particularly for the less serious offences. It is surprising to find one in

12 respondents recommending formal or informal police warnings for shoplifters aged 25 with previous convictions. It is perhaps less unexpected to find one in seven in favour of cautioning cannabis users. (In each case the criminal justice system filtered out less than 2 per cent of males aged 25 through a formal caution in 1983.) And for those taken to court there was considerable support for discharges for these offences. A larger minority of respondents favoured some sort of reparation by offenders. A quarter would like to see burglars and car thieves pay compensation to victims, perform community service or both; the figure for shoplifters approached a third. Where compensation was suggested it was nearly always as an addition to another penalty — in under 2 per cent of cases was compensation recommended on its own.

Table 7.2 compares respondents' sentencing preferences with court practice in respect of 17-year-olds. Again, there is a good degree of congruence between the courts and the public in terms of the role of imprisonment. It is clear that both respondents and the courts respond to age as a mitigating factor in the sentencing process, and in a similar way. As compared with the 25-year-olds, both the courts and the public are less likely to favour imprisonment and more likely to opt for community service, or for a discharge or caution. Comparisons in relation to sentence length are not possible in relation to 1983 data due to the fact that borstal sentences were indeterminate between six months and two years.

In sum, and despite the shortcomings of the comparisons, the agreement revealed by the tables as to the kinds of cases which call for a prison sentence does suggest that sentencing practice is broadly in step with public opinion, at least in this very important respect.

The views of BCS victims

The *BCS* uncovers a very broad spread of crimes, from the very serious to the trivial; to talk of victims' views in aggregate would be misleading. Even within categories of offence this is true. Incidents of vandalism, for example, range from arson to defacing walls. Because of this, discussion here is restricted to two fairly homogeneous offence types — residential burglary involving loss, and theft of cars. These are, besides, well-reported crimes — the police were notified in 88 per cent of the burglaries and 99 per cent of the car thefts — and the picture is not altered in substance when the small proportion of unreported crimes is included in the analysis. It should be remembered that whilst victims are well aware of the circumstances of the offence, they are unlikely to have any information about offenders.

Table 7.3 Penalties specified by victims of burglary and car theft

	Burglaries (%)	Car thefts (%)
Year + in prison	19	8
Up to 1 year in prison	14	9
Fine	13	20
Community service	15	25
Probation, susp. sentence	17	14
Just compensation	7	4
Discharge or caution	10	12
Other/DK/depends	5	9
Total	100	100
Weighted data		
Unweighted *n:*	260	170

Percentages do not total 100% due to rounding
Question: 'On this card are the actions the police can take or the various sentences that a court can give to people. Which of these do you think should have happened to the person/people who did it?'

Source: British Crime Survey, 1984

The *BCS* tapped victims' attitudes to punishment in 1982 by asking an 'open-ended' question about penalties for their offenders; they were not asked to select a disposal from a list of options, but could choose anything they could think of. Respondents showed some awareness of the less obvious disposals — community service, probation, compensation — but 38 per cent of burglary victims and 31 per cent of victims of car theft opted for a prison sentence; fines were also popular. In 1984 respondents were offered a list of options on a card. When reminded in this way of alternatives to the obvious options, victims were less likely to select imprisonment and fines (see Table 7.3).

Given that no information is available for the majority of these offenders, it is impossible to say how closely victims' preferences are in line with practice; but it is clear that there is no substantial mismatch in terms of severity of sentence. The exception, as in the previous section, is in victims' preparedness to see offenders warned, either by the courts or the police, and in their enthusiasm for reparation. The 'compensation' category in Table 7.3 refers to victims who wanted reparation from the offender and nothing else; a further third of victims of both burglary and car theft wanted compensation *and* some other punishment. There seems to be a clear desire amongst victims that offenders should make some redress for the harm they have caused.

What determines attitudes to sentencing?

Some of the variation in attitudes to sentencing can be explained simply by generation and class differences. When the follow-up sample (of the general public) were asked about suitable punishments, people over 60 favoured long prison sentences more than those between 31 and 60, who in turn were more tough-minded than people under 30. This was true for all seven crimes which were asked about, and for both 17- and 25-year-old offenders. The proportion favouring *any length* of custodial sentence rose markedly with age for the less serious crimes: thus 18 per cent of the over 60s considered imprisonment appropriate for 25-year-old shoplifters as compared with 8 per cent of those aged 30 or under.

Turning to class, attitudes of manual workers and their families were tougher than those of non-manual workers — as measured by their preference for custodial sentences of a year or more — and this is especially marked for the so-called 'victimless crimes' — cannabis use and soliciting for prostitution. Non-manual workers were more likely to select discharge, community service, probation and suspended sentence. Table 7.4 shows how age and class affect preferences for long prison sentences in the case of burglary. Differences between the sexes were marginal except in the items about rape and soliciting. More men than women favoured custodial sentences of a year or more for rapists; and more women than men favoured imprisonment of any duration for the offence of soliciting.

Do fear and anxiety about crime lead to punitive attitudes? Answers to this question must take into account the fact that older people tend to favour heavier sentences than younger. Table 7.5 shows the percentage of *BCS* respondents favouring long prison sentences for 25-year-old burglars; it is clear that within each age-band, those who say they are 'very worried' about burglary are tougher on burglars than those who are less anxious. Similar patterns of findings emerge for the other offences covered by the follow-up questionnaire.

If Table 7.5 is an example of social research proving the obvious, findings about the relationship between *experience* as a victim and punitiveness are not. The *BCS* found no evidence to suggest that being a victim of crime makes for support for tough sentences. This was true when victims of all offences were considered together; and

Table 7.4 Attitudes to punishment of burglars: percentage of BCS respondents favouring custodial sentence of a year or more, by age and class

	Percentage of respondents favouring one or more years in prison for	
	17-year-old burglar (%)	25-year-old burglar (%)
Respondents aged 16–30	23	31
Respondents 31–60	27	37
Respondents aged 61 +	35	44
Non-manual	23	34
Manual	32	40
Weighted data		
Unweighted *n:*	3,274	3,253
Question: see Tables 7.1 and 7.2.		

Source: British Crime Survey, 1984

differences still failed to emerge when burglary victims were compared to others on their attitudes towards the punishment of burglars, and those who had had vehicles stolen were compared to others on attitudes towards car thieves. Thus 61 per cent of burglary victims thought that the hypothetical 25-year-old burglar should be imprisoned, as against 62 per cent of non-victims; 23 per cent of victims of car theft would imprison the 25-year-old car thief, in contrast to 22 per cent of non-victims. For the 17-year-old burglar, 54 per cent of victims opted for prison sentences and 51 per cent of non-victims; the respective figures for the 17-year-old car thief were both 20 per cent.

Victims were no more tough-minded than others in their responses to the hypothetical cases posed in the follow-up questionnaire, but obviously there was considerable variation amongst victims in attitudes towards the disposal of offenders in their own cases. Examining what makes some victims more lenient than others, analysis is restricted, as before, to burglary (involving loss) and vehicle theft; findings are thus based on small samples — 260 burglary victims and 170 victims of car theft. This said, for burglary victims no clear difference emerged between the sexes or between

Table 7.5 Attitudes to punishment of burglars: percentage of BCS respondents favouring custodial sentence of a year or more, by age and fear of burglary (25-year-old burglar)

	Very worried	Not very worried
	% favouring year or more in prison	% favouring year or more in prison
Respondents aged 16–30	36	30
Respondents aged 31–60	47	34
Respondents aged 61 +	57	40
Weighted data Unweighted *n:*	817	2,433

Question about punishment: see Table 7.1
Question about fear of burglary: 'Using one of the phrases on this card, can you tell me how worried you are about having your home broken into and something stolen?'

Source: British Crime Survey, 1984

different age-groups and classes; and for victims of car theft, the only such difference was that many more men than women favoured imprisonment of car thieves — 32 per cent as against 6 per cent. Not surprisingly, what differentiated victims' attitudes towards punishment of 'their' offenders most clearly was the severity of the crime. Those whose losses were high or whose property had been damaged proposed more severe sentences than others.

Summary and conclusions

The *BCS* offers findings which provide a corrective to widely held misconceptions about popular attitudes to punishment. To summarize the main findings:

- people seem to think the courts more lenient towards burglars than they actually are;
- public attitudes about appropriate sentences seem to be broadly in line with practice;

- there is some public support for diversion of minor offenders from the court process;
- the principle of reparation by offenders, either to individual victims or to the wider community, has some public support and the support of victims in particular;
- the older people are, the more tough-minded they are about punishment; and manual workers and their families generally favour tough sentences more than non-manual workers;
- those who are most fearful of crime tend to advocate heavier sentences than others;
- victims of crime are no more punitive than others.

These findings suggest that policy makers and courts can treat with a degree of scepticism the claims often made by the media that public opinion demands a tougher line with offenders. The *BCS* offers no evidence to suggest widespread dissatisfaction with sentencing practice amongst the public. If, as the results of the *BCS* suggest, opinion and practice are broadly in line, there is probably leeway to introduce more lenient or heavier sentences without losing public support.

Support for more lenient sentences, however, would probably be forthcoming only if the public were better informed about current practice. If people believe the courts to be more lenient than they actually are, they may well feel that heavier sentences are called for, and may find proposals for lighter sentences unacceptable. Confidence in the criminal justice system might perhaps be improved if people have a more accurate idea of sentencing levels.

According to the *BCS*, there is some support — especially among victims — for the principle of offender reparation, whether amends are made to the community or to the victim. Thus recent emphasis on reparation, exemplified by the introduction of the compensation order as a disposal in its own right, and by the extension of community service to 16-year-olds, fits well with the prevailing public mood.

The finding that those who are anxious about crime favour heavy sentences bears on policies to reduce fear of crime. The *BCS* cannot say whether anxiety about crime leads to support for tough sentencing or whether, more simply, certain sorts of people are both anxious and tough on offenders. It nevertheless raises the possibility that effective policies of fear reduction might lessen pressure for heavier sentences.

Notes

1. The first *BCS* had a sample of 11,000 people over the age of 15 in England and Wales and 6,000 in Scotland. The 1984 *BCS* was conducted only in England

and Wales, with a sample size of 11,000. The response rates were 80 per cent and 77 per cent respectively.

2. Most of the *BCS* findings in this chapter are drawn from the 'follow-up' sample of the 1984 *BCS*. This had a sample size of 6,600; it over-represents victims of crime, and data have been weighted to restore representativeness of the general public in England and Wales over the age of 15.

   Given the size of the follow-up sample, sampling error will be small. For example, a statistic of 20 per cent in Table 7.1, which is based on a sample of 3,270, would be unlikely to vary by more than 2 per cent if repeated samples of this size had been interviewed. (Design effects make the sampling error larger than for a simple random sample; a /deff of 1.4 has been assumed.)

   Where findings are presented on *victims'* attitudes towards the punishment of their own offenders, findings refer only to the victims of burglary involving loss (*BCS* offence code 52) and car theft (*BCS* offence code 60). The sample size here is small (430 in total), and findings may be subject to considerable sampling error.

   See NOP (1985) for full technical details about the survey design.

References

Dicey, A. V. (1962), *Lectures on the Relation between Law and Public Opinion in England during the 19th Century*, London: Macmillan.

Gallup (1981), *Gallup Political Index, No. 252, August 1981*, London: Social Surveys (Gallup Poll) Ltd.

Gallup (1982) *Gallup Political Index, No. 260, April 1982*, London: Social Surveys (Gallup Poll) Ltd.

Home Office (1984), *Criminal Justice: A Working Paper*, London: Home Office.

Hough, M. and Mayhew, P. (1983), *The British Crime Survey*, Home Office Research Study no. 76, London: HMSO.

Hough, M. and Mayhew, P. (1985), *The British Crime Survey*, Home Office Research Study no. 86, London: HMSO.

Maguire, M. (1982), *Burglary in a Dwelling*, London: Heinemann.

Marplan (1983), Survey carried out for BBC Broadcasting Research Department, 22–24 August, 1983.

NOP (1985), *British Crime Survey Technical Report*, London: NOP.

Rock, P. (1979), 'Public opinion and criminal legislation', *Public Opinion in Relation to Crime and Criminal Justice: Proceedings of the 13th Criminological Research Conference*, Strasbourg: Council of Europe.

Shapland, J. with Willmore, J. and Duff, P. (1981), *The Victim in the Criminal Justice System*, Oxford: Centre for Criminological Research.

Shaw, S. (1982), *The People's Justice: a major poll of public attitudes to crime and punishment*, London: Prison Reform Trust.

Thompson, E. P. (1975), *Whigs and Hunters*, London: Allen Lane.

Walker, N. and Marsh, C. (1984) 'Do sentences affect public disapproval?' *British Journal of Criminology*, **24** (1), 27–48.

Waller, I. and Okihiro, N. (1978), *Burglary: the victim and the public*, Toronto: University of Toronto Press.

8 How the public sees sentencing: an Australian survey

John Walker, Mark Collins and Paul Wilson

In Australia the systematic collection of comments and attitudes on crime and punishment is a rare event (see Wilson et al., 1986). Media polls often trivialize and sensationalize public opinion on criminal justice matters and this is very clearly seen directly after a horrendous crime, when views on the death penalty are sought (Potas and Walker, 1986). So, in order to obtain a more balanced overview of public opinion on crime and punishment, the Australian Institute of Criminology commissioned a survey in which a randomly selected cross-section of 2,551 members of the public was asked the appropriate sentence for each of 13 'offences' described to them.

The sentencing question was as follows: 'What do you think would be the appropriate sentence to be served by a person convicted of each of the following offences?':

1. A person breaks into a home and steals $1,000 worth of household goods.
2. A doctor cheats on claims he makes to a Commonwealth health insurance plan for patient services for an amount of $5,000.
3. A parent beats his child with his fists. The child is hurt and spends a few days in hospital.
4. A person smuggles heroin into the country for resale.
5. Two adult males willingly engage in a homosexual act in private.
6. A factory knowingly gets rid of its poisonous waste in a way that pollutes the city water supply. As a result one person dies.
7. A person cheats on their Commonwealth income tax return and avoids paying $5,000 in taxes.
8. A person steals $5 worth of goods from a shop.
9. A man beats his wife with his fists. As a result she spends a few days in hospital.
10. A person stabs a victim to death.
11. A person illegally receives social security cheques worth $1,000.
12. A person armed with a gun robs a bank of $5,000 during business hours. No one is physically hurt.

13. A worker had his leg caught in an unguarded piece of machinery because the employer knowingly failed to provide safety measures. As a result the worker lost his leg.

Respondents were shown a card listing the available forms of punishment, uncluding the option of 'No penalty' and that of capital punishment (even though capital punishment has not been available to courts in any Australian jurisdiction since 1984). They were first asked to specify the *form* of punishment appropriate to the offence under consideration, then to specify the *severity* (amount of fine, term of imprisonment etc.). No limits were placed on the severity of punishment.

As the results presented here clearly show, there is no single public view of sentencing, but many different views. These differences can result from variations in attitudes to the seriousness of crimes, the culpability of offenders or the punitiveness of sentences (i.e. some individuals rate a crime more seriously than others do while some will differ in their assessment of the culpability of an offender); and, even where individuals agree on seriousness of offence and culpability of offender, some may be more punitive in sentencing than others.

In combination, these three factors lead to wide differences of opinion between different community groups, and we set out below both the ranges of attitudes in the community as a whole, and the differences in attitudes between the various components of the Australian public.

The results

The average response shows broad agreement with typical court decisions, including a tendency to punish violent offenders by way of prison sentences and to punish property offenders with non-custodial penalties, particularly fines (see Tables 8.1 and 8.2). But there were significant areas in which public opinion appears to be at odds with court practice, sometimes being more punitive, sometimes less.

'Life' for murder and heroin trafficking

Life imprisonment is seen by the majority of the sample as appropriate for persons convicted of stabbing to death or of heroin trafficking. Significantly, only one in four respondents called for the death penalty for the stabbing and one in six for the drug offender. Table 8.2 shows that the courts also favour life imprisonment for murder, and it is not unknown for such a sentence to be imposed on major drug traffickers. In general, however, 'head' sentences of 10 years

Table 8.1 Most commonly selected sentence options for selected offences

	Offence	Preferred sentence options (percentages)								
		No penalty	Warning	Fine	Probation	CSO	Prison	Life	Death	Total
1	Stabbing to death	—	—	—	—	—	17	53	29	100
2	Heroin trafficking	—	—	—	1	2	42	36	18	100
3	Industrial pollution kills	—	2	57	2	3	28	6	—	100
4	Industrial negligence injury	1	4	66	3	2	22	2	—	100
5	Armed robbery	—	1	5	3	3	85	3	—	100
6	Child bashing	1	8	4	24	13	49	2	—	100
7	Wife bashing	1	12	7	23	17	40	1	—	100
8	Social security fraud	1	6	41	10	24	17	—	—	100
9	Medicare fraud	—	3	60	6	6	24	—	—	100
10	Income tax evasion	3	9	61	7	8	13	—	—	100
11	Break and enter	—	1	17	11	11	60	—	—	100
12	Male homosexuality	72	10	3	4	3	6	—	—	100
13	Shoplifting ($5)	3	51	11	15	11	8	—	—	100

Table 8.2 Actual sentencing patterns for selected offences

	Offence and statistical category		Level of court	Penalty types (percentages)						
				Warning	Fine	Probation	CSO	Prison	Life	Total
1	Stabbing to death	Murder	Higher courts	—	—	—	—	24	76	100
2	Heroin trafficking	Drugs import/export	Higher courts	—	5	15	—	80	—	100
3	Industrial pollution	Pollution of waters	Industrial courts	—	100	—	—	—	—	100
4	Industrial negligence	Industrial negligence	Industrial courts	—	100	—	—	—	—	100
5	Armed robbery	Armed robbery	Higher courts	—	—	15	5	80	—	100
6	Child bashing	Assault child	Lower courts	24	27	42	—	6	—	100
7	Wife bashing	Assault ABH	Lower courts	11	11	60	6	12	—	100
8	Social security fraud									
9	Medicare fraud	Fraud and misappropriation	Higher courts	4	1	59	8	29	—	100
10	Income tax fraud									
11	Break and enter	Break, enter and steal	Lower courts	2	10	46	10	32	—	100
12	Male homosexuality	No offence		—	—	—	—	—	—	—
13	Shoplifting	Shoplifting	Lower courts	15	68	12	1	3	—	100

Note: National court statistics are not yet available for comparative purposes. With the exception of the two industrial offences, these data are the percentages of persons sentenced in the various statistical categories in New South Wales in 1983 (New South Wales, 1983). The New South Wales sentencing patterns may not exactly represent those in other jurisdictions, but since they constitute almost 40 per cent of court cases in Australia they can be taken as an approximate guide. The corporate offence data were estimated from Braithwaite and Grabosky, which suggests that although 99 per cent of factory pollution or negligence cases result in a warning only, the most serious cases (such as those described here) would almost certainly result in a fine.

and above are commonly preferred over the indefinite life sentences for the drug offences, and the effective time to be served may be not very much less than if the original sentence were 'life' (Walker and Biles, 1983–1987).

Severe punishments for pollution and negligent employers

Respondents were distinctly more punitive than our current judges in sentencing persons convicted of the two corporate offences, namely, factory pollution and employer negligence causing severe injury to a worker. The most common sentence suggested was a fine of at least $50,000, but one in three demanded prison sentences where a person died from pollution, and one in five would also sentence the defendant to prison for causing the loss of an employee's leg. We also found that one in 12 respondents specified life imprisonment for the fatal pollution offence which, from other studies conducted by the Institute, is far in excess of any penalty ever handed down by an Australian court for any pollution offence. An industrial negligence case described in exactly the same terms as in our survey resulted in a fine of $250 in the Industrial Court of South Australia in 1982, while fines of up to $10,000 have been imposed for potentially fatal pollution offences (Braithwaite and Grabosky, 1985; Grabosky and Braithwaite, 1986).

Prison for armed robbery, domestic violence and burglary

Imprisonment was the almost unanimous choice of respondents for armed robbery, and was also the most common sentence type for domestic violence and burglary. Two to five years' gaol were suggested most frequently for armed robbers (25 per cent of respondents), while up to two-year terms were specified for domestic violence and burglary. The less punitive interviewees clearly regarded both prison and financial penalties as inappropriate for domestic violence — since they would often penalize the victim as well as the offender — and about one in three preferred terms of probation or community service orders. The courts appear to agree with this line of reasoning except in the most serious cases.

In regard to burglary of $1,000 of property, the community generally perceived this as a very minor offence in terms of seriousness. However, the level of punishment preferred by the respondents was quite high — commensurate, in fact, with offences rated three times as serious. Institute studies show that actual sentences of two years in prison for burglary are generally meted out by the courts only for persistent offenders (Potas, 1985), and Table 8.2 shows that community-based sentences are preferred in two-thirds of burglary cases in the lower courts.

Heavy fines for white-collar crime

Although the $1,000 social security offence is regarded as more serious than the $5,000 medical or tax frauds, the offender appears to be more leniently treated by the public. Almost two-fifths of the sample would give a person who commits a social security fraud a non-custodial sentence, while about the same proportion would hand down a fine, generally within the range $1,000–$2,000. Over one-fifth of the sample would allocate a community service order to the offender. In contrast, over half the sample would fine the other fraud offenders, with the most likely ranges being $5,000–$10,000 in the case of tax fraud and $5,000–$50,000 for the doctor.

Warning preferred for petty shoplifters

In the case of a $5 shoplifting offence, the respondents were mostly in favour of a police warning, with a wide range of other options supported by a small but not insignificant number of respondents. In view of the amount stolen ($5) the courts would probably agree with the majority of our respondents in this case.

Differing opinions about homosexuality

The consenting adult male homosexuals, whose activities are not illegal in most states of Australia, would be given no penalty by almost 60 per cent of the sample. By contrast, one in 20 would send them to prison.

Socio-demographic correlates of sentencing preferences

Further analysis was conducted to determine which socio-demographic variables (age, sex, education, voting preference, etc) were relevant to the determination of an individual's choice of sentence. The major findings were as follows.

The less-educated are more punitive

The variable eliciting the most systematic differences was the respondent's educational level. For 10 of the 13 offences, significant trends were evident across educational groups with regard to sentencing preferences. The only offences where education did not appear to influence opinions were shoplifting, breaking and entering, and armed robbery. For all other offences, the trend was for individuals with higher education to advocate much more lenient sentences than those with less formal education.

The first point to note in Figure 8.1 is the relative disinclination of the better educated to use the death penalty for stabbing and heroin trafficking. Of particular interest is the fact that for the offences involving cheating in social security, Medicare or taxation,

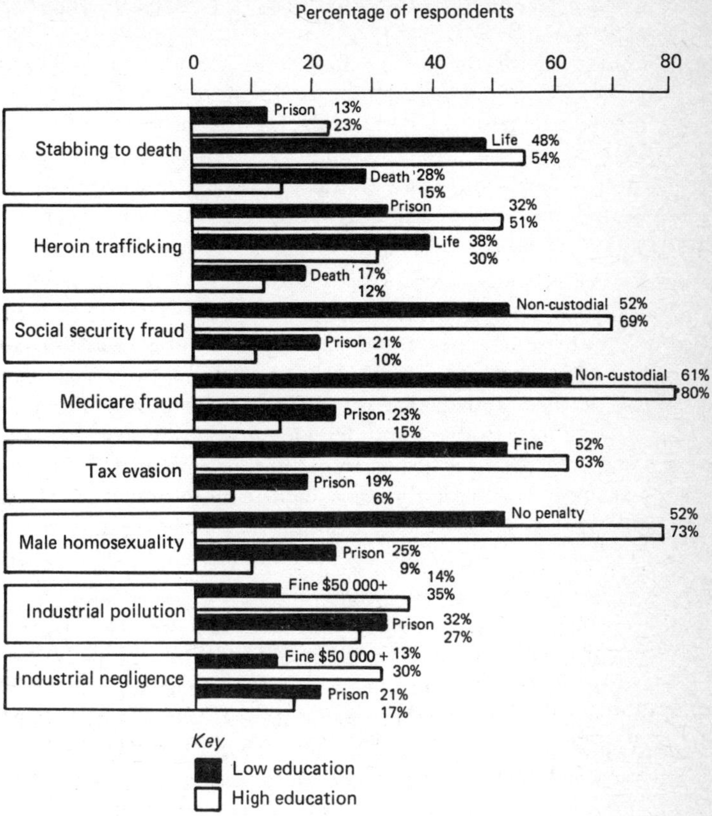

Figure 8.1 Significant sentencing preferences by education

there was a consistent trend in higher educational groups to impose fines, with a slightly lower propensity for imprisonment. For example, in the case of tax evasion, 19 per cent of the primary education group advocated imprisonment, but only 6 per cent of the graduates. A similar pattern was evident for factory pollution and employer negligence.

The offence which ranks next to last in seriousness — homosexuality — is the one which shows the greatest division of all between educational groups. The result for the primary education group was that 52 per cent advocated 'no penalty', while 25 per cent advocated imprisonment; of the graduates, however, 79 per cent advocated 'no penalty' and only 9 per cent advocated imprisonment.

Males usually more punitive than females

Males are more in favour of the death penalty than females, for both the stabbing and heroin trafficking offences. Males are also more punitive than females for the offences of burglary and male homosexuality. On the other hand, females are slightly more punitive than males for the offences of factory pollution, employer negligence and child beating. Surprisingly, males and females gave similar sentences for husbands guilty of wife beating. (See Figure 8.2.)

Complex differences between age groups

Older respondents were more likely to advocate the death penalty for heroin trafficking but no age differences emerged when sentences for the stabbing offence were analysed. The over-60s are the most punitive age group with respect to social security fraud, wife beating, tax evasion and homosexuality. They are also more likely to demand imprisonment for the fraudulent offences and to penalize homosexuals. Teenagers held similar views in relation to wife beating and tax evasion. (See Figure 8.3.)

Lower income groups more punitive

To some extent, income is positively correlated with education level, and the results confirm that generally the higher one's income the less likely it is for imprisonment to be advocated.

Political views

Virtually no differences exist between Australian Labour Party voters and Liberal voters. National Party voters were more punitive of heroin trafficking and homosexuality, but were less inclined to advocate prison terms for employer negligence. Democrat voters,

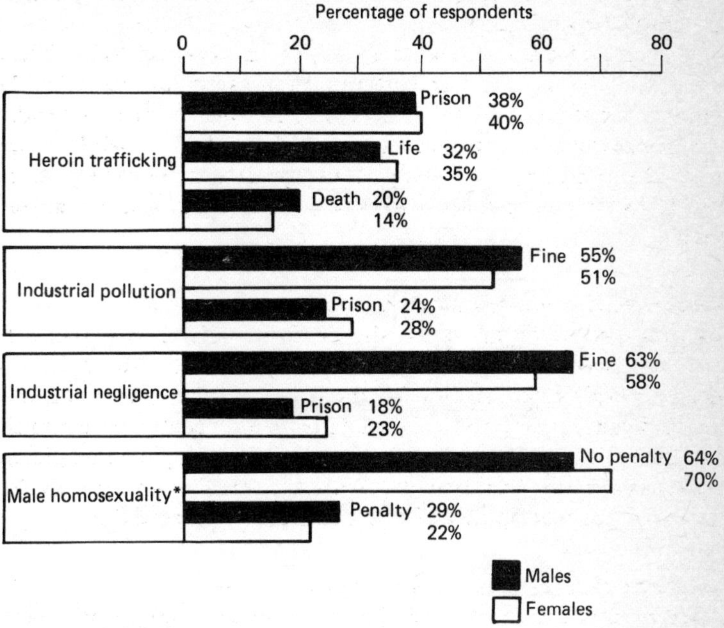

* Note that there was a significant non-response to this question. The percentages therefore do not add to 100%

Figure 8.2 Significant sentencing preferences by sex

while generally not advocating punitive sentences, were more inclined to advocate a prison term for employer negligence.

Church influence

Churchgoers were slightly less inclined than non-churchgoers to advocate the death penalty both for stabbing to death and for heroin trafficking. On the other hand, churchgoers were more inclined to impose penalties on homosexuals than were non-churchgoers.

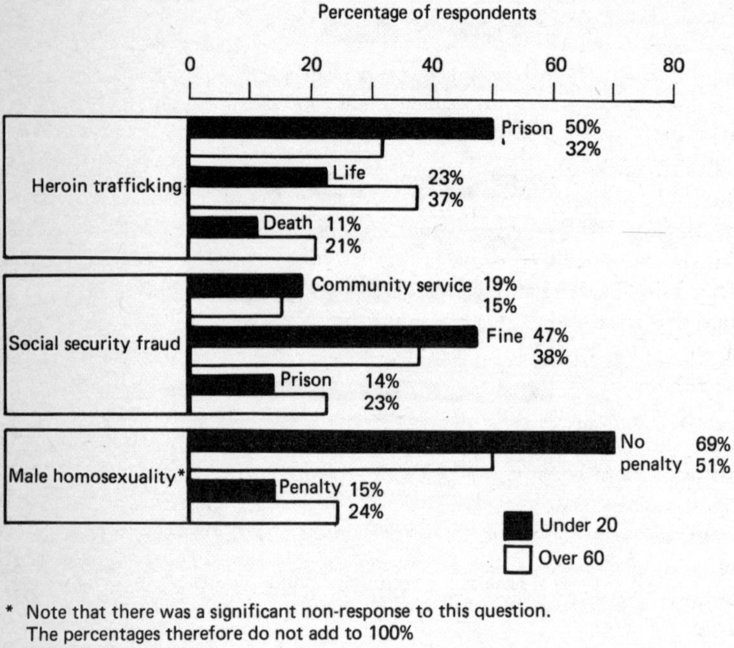

Figure 8.3 Significant sentencing preferences by age

Geographical variation

Rural residents tend to be more punitive than city dwellers for stabbing, child beating, heroin trafficking, shoplifting and homosexuality.

Summary and conclusions

What do these results tell us about the public's opinions of our courts' sentencing patterns? It is clear that there is no single set of views regarding punishment which is shared by all sections of the community. The better educated tend to be more lenient than those with lower levels of education. The elderly tend to be more punitive while males tend to be more punitive than females. The better-off tend to be more lenient than the less well-off.

Politically, voters from the two major parties — the Australian Labour Party and the Liberal Party — do not differ significantly in their views on sentencing. Political campaigns based on 'law and order' which have as their hallmark punitive sentencing policies will not affect supporters of either party in markedly different ways. But National Party supporters, generally more punitive than their Labour and Liberal colleagues, may be attracted by the rhetoric of punishment.

Punitiveness though, is not a characteristic of Australians. Though media headlines often suggest that Australians are harsh and uncompromising on issues relating to punishment — especially when violent crimes are committed — the data from this survey suggest otherwise. For example, even for the two most serious offences of stabbing to death and heroin importation, only a minority of the sample suggested that the appropriate penalty should be the death penalty.

The diversity of opinions regarding sentencing revealed in our study indicates an unexpected sophistication in public attitudes about crime and punishment. Significant numbers of Australians are willing to suggest non-custodial alternatives to imprisonment: fines, probation and community service orders. The complexity of the sentencing process, often unrecognized by thunderous editorials in tabloid newspapers, is apparently acknowledged by the public at large.

References

Braithwaite, J. B. and Grabosky, P. (1985), *Occupational Health and Safety Enforcement in Australia*, Canberra: Australian Institute of Criminology.

Grabosky, P. and Braithwaite, J. B. (1986), *Of Manners Gentle: Enforcement Strategies of Australian Business Regulatory Agencies*, Melbourne: Oxford University Press and Australian Institute of Criminology.

New South Wales, Bureau of Crime Statistics and Research (1983), *Court Statistics*, Appendices III and IV.

Potas, I. (1985), 'Sentencing for Break, Enter and Steal in New South Wales', S. K. Mukherjee and L. Jorgensen (eds), *Burglary: A Social Reality*, Canberra: Australian Institute of Criminology.

Potas, I. and Walker, J. (1986), *Capital Punishment*, Trends and Issues in Crime and Criminal Justice No. 3, Canberra: Australian Institute of Criminology.

Walker, J. and Biles, D. (1983–1987, annual), *Australian Prisoners*, Reports of the Annual National Prison Census, Canberra: Australian Institute of Criminology.

Wilson, P., Walker, J. and Mukherjee, S. (1986), *How the Public Sees Crime: an Australian Survey*, Trends and Issues in Crime and Criminal Justice No. 2, Canberra: Australian Institute of Criminology.

9 Minor offences and the fixed penalty system: a survey in England and Wales

Simon Orton and Julie Vennard

As is widely known, the contravention of a range of regulatory offences is dealt with in this country by way of mitigated or fixed penalties as an alternative to prosecution before the criminal courts. Such schemes are used, for instance, in respect of vehicle excise licence duty evasion, VAT and income tax offences. Minor traffic offences have been subject to a fixed penalty system for some time and since October 1986 the scheme has been extended to a wide range of more serious traffic offences. Similarly, so called 'penalty fare systems' — which may take the form of 'on-the-spot' fines — have been introduced in some parts of the country as an alternative to the prosecution of passengers found travelling on public transport without a valid ticket.

Such simplified procedures differ in approach. For example, fixed penalty systems operate at a flat rate whereas a mitigated penalty normally involves the addition of a fixed sum (the penal element) to the amount owing. Yet they have in common that the offender is offered an opportunity to pay the penalty within a specified period as an alternative to prosecution and the prospect of a criminal conviction. They also share the same over-riding objective — to relieve the criminal justice system of the more routine business which currently comes before the courts and save the time and expense entailed in enforcing regulatory offences. It is primarily with resource considerations in mind that an expansion of simplified penalty systems has been advocated in some quarters in recent years. Justice (1980), for example, expressed concern that the procedures and sanctions imposed for breach of regulatory offences were essentially on the same scale as for more serious crimes and seemed disproportionate to the gravity of the offence. An offence widely viewed as suitable for diversion from the courts by way of a fixed penalty system is the using of a television set without a valid licence, prosecutions for which were in the region of 120,000 at the time of the survey, and which increased to around 170,000 a year by the end of 1986.

Home Office interest in the possibility of developing simplified enforcement procedures prompted a small-scale study of the sentencing of TV licence evaders and alternative ways of dealing with this offence (Softley, 1984). More recently the Home Office commissioned the British Market Research Bureau (BMRB) to carry out a national survey of public knowledge about, and attitudes towards, TV licence evasion and the notion of a fixed penalty system. A key question addressed by the survey was whether a fixed penalty system could be devised which would represent an adequate deterrent while at the same time discouraging exercise of the option to go to court. At the time of the survey nearly 9 per cent of households requiring a licence did not have one, causing an annual revenue loss in the region of £90 million. Those prosecuted for evasion, however, accounted for only about 5 per cent of magistrates' court business and some 98 per cent pleaded guilty by post. A penalty high enough to deter potential evaders and thus avoid further loss of licence revenue runs the risk of encouraging those on low incomes to choose a court appearance; many such evaders would be likely to know that the court may take into account their means and may thus set the fine well below the maximum of £400 and allow payment by instalments. In short, is there evidence that payment of the licence fee is based on rational, economic considerations and would the same considerations apply to a fixed penalty option? Do people in fact know the current maximum fine for this offence and the levels of fine actually imposed by the courts? What would be the optimum level of a fixed penalty, balancing the risk of loss of deterrence against increased recourse to the criminal courts?

Beyond these core issues concerning TV licence evasion, the BMRB survey also had a wider interest in public attitudes towards a range of relatively minor offences, in knowledge of and views about enforcement procedures and sentencing practices. These issues have been explored in respect of offences at the more serious end of the spectrum, but not in relation to the sorts of offences which are already dealt with by administrative action or are potential candidates for diversion from the courts. Studies of the perceived seriousness of offences play an important part in the investigation of public attitudes to crime and, as Levi and Jones (1985) note, they have come to be seen as an important tool in the process of policy making. Surveys such as those by Sparks, Genn and Dodd, (1977) and Jones and Levi (1983) have understandably focused on offences of violence or dishonesty in which there is an identifiable victim or loser. The same focus on relatively serious offences is found in surveys of public attitudes to punishment, as for example in the 1984 *British Crime Survey* (Hough and Mayhew, 1985). Attitudes to regulatory offences have been touched upon in the course of such studies, but only tangentially.

The study reported in this chapter goes some way towards remedying this gap. Most of the offences selected entail breach of a regulation which may or may not result in financial loss to society at large. Typically, the definition of such offences is in terms of an omission (such as failure to obtain a TV licence) rather than a deliberate act of dishonesty. Public attitude surveys which have included these kinds of offence suggest that, despite the fact that the sums involved may be considerable (for example, in cases of income tax or VAT evasion), the public tend to rate them as far less serious than offences of violence or theft (see e.g. Walker, 1978; Levi and Jones, 1985). But how do the public perceive the relative seriousness of, say, not buying a road fund licence, speeding, or TV licence evasion? Are regulatory or 'victimless' offences regarded as prevalent and worth the risk of detection? Should they be fully enforced through the criminal courts and what do people consider the appropriate penalty for this type of offence? These wider questions provided an essential framework for more detailed enquiry into the perceived acceptability, advantages and disadvantages of a fixed penalty scheme for TV licence evasion.

Survey methodology

A random sample of 2,398 post-codes of unlicensed households was ACORN-coded[1] in advance, to generate a profile which might be used for sampling purposes. The profile included households without televisions and those without a valid licence. This yielded the data presented in Table 9.1.

On this basis, sampling points were purposely skewed to over-represent ACORN groups D, G, H, I and K to a level of 40 per cent compared with a 'natural' representation of 23 per cent in order to improve probabilities of finding current evaders for separate analysis. Of course, corrective weights were applied at the analysis stage to generate a nationally representative data set.

A random location (GRID) sample of 754 heads of household/housewives was then taken at 65 sampling points in England and Wales, skewed on the basis of the ACORN analysis. These points were enumeration districts (areas containing on average 150 households) selected from a listing stratified by ACORN within region, and issued to interviewers in the form of a street/house number list. Controls governed the spacing and timing of interviews as well as demographic factors relating to the probability of being 'at home'

Table 9.1 *ACORN profiles of unlicensed households and of the population*

ACORN group	Profile of unlicensed households (%)	Profile of England/Wales (%)
A	3.8	3.4
B	11.0	15.8
C	18.3	19.2
D	5.8	4.6
E	9.9	11.5
F	9.4	9.8
G	8.9	5.3
H	6.2	4.1
I	8.3	4.8
J	11.9	17.3
K	5.6	4.2
Unclassified	0.9	0
Total	100	100

and therefore available for interview. Other demographic factors were controlled, overall, by the sampling point selection process.

The questionnaire was piloted before full-scale operation in December 1985. It was carefully designed to begin with attitudes towards a broad base of relatively minor offences, both to set TV licence evasion in a relevant context, and to prepare the ground for more detailed and sensitive investigation of TV licence evasion. Respondents had been informed at the contact stage that the research was on behalf of the Home Office: therefore it was important to introduce questions of this nature with care.

As the depth of questioning was increased, so the range of offences covered was narrowed, 'funnelling down' towards a detailed assessment of TV licence evasion. At various points in the interview shuffle-packs (each card bearing a code number and one offence) were used so that responses could be given in code form, rather than verbalizing the offences concerned. Fifteen such offences were initially introduced, reduced to eight, then to three (speeding, fare evasion and TV licence evasion) before a thorough study of the fixed penalty option for TV licence evasion.

General attitudes

Before examining views on the relative seriousness of specified offences, a number of statements were offered for scaled agreement/disagreement across a five-point scale, to set a broad attitudinal framework in terms of the law, enforcement, penalties and practicalities versus principles. The results have been subjected only to simple cross-analysis, statement by statement, and there is scope for multivariate study, but the data shown in Table 9.2 offer some points of interest. Statements are tabulated in rank order of the level of agreement achieved.

The statements that 'a lot of court time is wasted on minor offences', and 'minor offences *should* be dealt with by a fixed fine', gained the highest levels of agreement. On the other hand, most respondents agreed that, in principle, all laws must be enforced equally and fully, however minor they are.

When it comes to issues like the deterrent effect of appearance in court *per se* or publication of offender's names, the population is much more divided. Views also differed as to whether 'fixed fines are unfair because they don't take all the circumstances into account'. About half agreed with this statement, thus qualifying the high level of support for the fixed penalty option noted above. While there may, therefore, be a strong rational appeal in fixed penalties for minor offences, the very offer of such an option may seem to demean the seriousness of an offence, and remove any social stigma attached to court appearances.

Also noteworthy is the finding that, at this early stage of questioning, one in ten respondents (the approximate level of known evasion) '*agree strongly*' with the proposition that 'not buying a TV licence isn't really breaking the law'. Though this sub-group is small, there is some evidence that those with children, in larger households, and those living in the Midlands and Wales are more likely to hold this view.

The 'seriousness' of offences, and beliefs about offence prevalence

In order to explore views on the relative seriousness of selected minor offences, 15 were offered for consideration on individual cards, using a four-point 'seriousness' scale in the form of a 'sorting-board' (Table 9.3). Scoring was from four for 'Very serious', to one for 'Not at all serious', the mid-point is 2.5, and the mean score actually achieved was 2.6. The offences are ranked overleaf in terms of mean score. 'Not buying a TV licence' appears fifth in relative seriousness overall. It was ranked lower, for example, than not buying a road fund licence and taking items from work.

Table 9.2 Attitudes towards minor offences

	Strength of agreement or disagreement*						
	5 %	4 %	3 %	2 %	1 %	DK %	Total
A lot of court time is wasted on minor offences like speeding	60	20	3	7	9	2	101
Minor offences should be dealt with by a mixed fine, rather than going to court	57	25	4	6	7	1	100
All laws must be enforced equally and fully, however minor they are	55	21	4	13	7	†	100
Most people have broken the law in some way or other	46	38	3	7	4	1	99
Some laws aren't as important as others	32	41	5	10	11	1	100
It is an important deterrent that minor offenders should have to appear in court	26	27	7	25	15	1	101
It is important that minor offenders' names should be made public, to embarrass them	22	14	8	23	32	1	100
Fixed fines are unfair because they don't take all the circumstances into account	19	29	11	23	14	3	99
If a lot of people break a law, it can't be enforced	12	18	10	23	32	6	101
If the penalty is just a fine, it can't be a serious offence	10	25	6	22	34	2	99
Not buying a TV licence isn't really breaking the law	10	9	2	16	62	1	100
If you can't catch *everyone* who commits an offence, it isn't fair to prosecute the few you do catch	9	9	3	17	60	2	100

Weighted data
Unweighted *n* = 754
Percentages may not total 100 due to rounding.
† = Less than 0.5 per cent, but not zero.
Question: 'First of all, I'd like to read out a number of statements that people have made about various offences and ways of dealing with them. I'd like you to tell me, from this card, how much you agree or disagree with each one. So firstly, how much do you agree or disagree with the statement . . . ?'

*Table headings = responses as follows:
5 = Agree strongly; 4 = Agree slightly; 3 = Neither agree nor disagree; 2 = Disagree slightly; 1 = Disagree strongly; DK = Don't know/no opinion

A variety of demographic differences emerged. Amongst women, 'Not wearing a seat-belt' rose to push TV licence evasion into *sixth* place, while for men, the rise of 'Deliberately travelling without a ticket', had the same effect. For those with children and for those aged under 34, TV licence evasion was depressed to *seventh* place by the rise of the 'seat-belt' offence and 'speeding'. For those of

Table 9.3 Seriousness ratings of offences

Offence	'Seriousness' Mean score; Range 4–1
*Not buying a Road Fund Licence for a vehicle as required	3.3
*Taking items from work without permission	3.2
Drunk and disorderly behaviour in the street	3.0
Not declaring income to the VAT or Tax Inspectors	3.0
*Not buying a TV licence as required	2.9
*Not wearing a seat-belt as required	2.8
*Deliberately travelling without a bus/tube/train ticket	2.8
*Speeding (but not driving dangerously)	2.7
Renting/buying a pirate video	2.4
*Not declaring *extra* duty-free goods to customs	2.3
Broadcasting illegally (e.g. pirate radio stations)	2.3
*Not buying a dog licence as required	2.2
Trespassing on private land (but not entering buildings)	2.2
Parking illegally (but not dangerously)	2.0
Copying a record or tape for your own use	1.7

Weighted data
Unweighted *n* = 754
Scaled data; Very serious = 4
Quite serious = 3
Not very serious = 2
Not at all serious = 1
'Don't knows' are excluded from the averaging process
Question: 'On each of these cards is a legal offence of the sorts I mentioned earlier. I'd like you to sort them under the headings on this board to show which ones you regard as more or less serious.'

Note: The asterisked offences were pursued in further questioning, and are discussed below.

social grade D (unskilled manual and casual workers), it fell to *eighth* because of the further intervention of 'Deliberately travelling without a ticket'. Analysis by region of the country and social grade showed little variation in seriousness rating, but mean scores for all offences tended to increase with age. This finding is consistent with Levi's (1985) study which indicated significantly higher average seriousness ratings among older people.

The eight offences *asterisked* above were investigated further. Amongst these eight, TV licence evasion was ranked third in 'seriousness'. At this stage, respondents were given a prompt card showing these eight offences, each allocated a number-code. Interviewers read out a series of statements and asked which of the offences each statement related to. Respondents could mention as many or as few as they wished, and identified them by number-code. This associative method provides data in a form which is open to various analyses. The statements offered (26 in all) were designed as opposites, allowing measures of '*character*' (i.e. the ratio of positive:negative associations) as well as the '*strength*' of association. Note that respondents were not forced to make any associations whatsoever.

To date only simple cross-tabulations have been performed on the results of this part of the survey, but some of the main points to emerge merit discussion. First, nearly half (46 per cent) of respondents felt that 'Not buying a dog licence' 'isn't serious enough to be worth enforcing', but for each other offence less than one in six (15 per cent) took this view. Endorsement of the opposite view ('the laws relating to this offence should be enforced fully') varied according to the offence; not buying a road fund licence and speeding secured the highest number of mentions (71 per cent and 66 per cent of the sample respectively) followed by TV licence evasion (53 per cent). Consistently with this finding, in the case of road fund licence evasion and speeding, few respondents (13 per cent and 5 per cent respectively) felt that 'this doesn't harm anyone else'. About a quarter of respondents considered that TV licence evasion does not cause harm to others. On the other hand, two-thirds endorsed the statement that evasion is 'unfair to others who don't break the law'. This level of concern about unfairness to others was exceeded only in relation to not buying a road fund licence.

Turning to views on the prevalence of these offences and the risk of being caught, the associative method indicated that speeding was thought by two-thirds of the sample to be a very common offence. Other offences were seen as less prevalent, though about half the sample considered TV licence evasion, taking items from work and not declaring excess duty-free goods to be very common. These offences were also seen as having a relatively low risk of detection with some two-thirds of respondents agreeing that 'a lot of people do this without getting caught'. Offered the statement 'I have done this', a third volunteered that they had broken the speed limit, and a fifth said they had not declared goods on which duty was owed or had taken items from work. Only 6 per cent admitted to TV licence evasion, even fewer to not buying a road fund licence (4 per cent) or fare evasion (5 per cent).

Some of the associative questions touched on the deterrent effect of the law in relation to the selected offences. Offered the statement 'doing this can be worth the risk of getting caught', in the case of speeding 16 per cent agreed. As many as 23 per cent thought that not declaring excess duty-free goods was worth the risk of detection but this figure dropped to 12 per cent for TV licence and fare evasion and taking items from work. With the exception of TV licence evasion, having to go to court and adverse publicity in the local papers were mentioned more often than the 'size of the fine'. The latter offence outstripped all others in the numbers of respondents (40 per cent) regarding the fine as the 'worst thing about being caught'. Evidently the fine for this offence is thought to exceed that for other offences in the survey, such as speeding.

In short, the associative analysis suggest that beliefs about the harm done to others, the chances of detection, and the social and financial costs of conviction all play a part in the assessment of whether an offence is worth the risk of being caught. Thus, not buying a road fund licence is seen by many as likely to result in detection, unfair to others who comply with the law, and not worth the cost in terms of court appearance and publicity in the local papers. Here, only 26 per cent mentioned the level of the fine. On the other hand, offences viewed as less likely to result in detection and relatively harmless to others — such as not declaring excess duty-free goods — seemed to many to be worth the risk of being caught.

Beliefs regarding enforcement

The questionnaire then presented three almost identical series of questions concerning *speeding*, *ticket evasion* and *TV licence evasion*. The aim was to explore in greater depth public beliefs about levels of offending, detection and prosecution. For each offence, respondents were asked to estimate how many out of 100 potential offenders (i.e. drivers, travellers and TV-owning households respectively) commit the offence in a year, whether they are caught or not. Subsequently, they were asked how many they thought were *caught*, and how many were simply 'let off with a warning'. The results are summarized in Table 9.4.

It must be borne in mind that speeding and ticket evasion differ from TV licence evasion in the sense that they are discrete, repeatable offences, while the latter is a continuous offence, the commencement of which may be difficult for the court to establish. Consistently with the response to the earlier associative questions, speeding was seen as by far the most common of the three offences, and the least often detected. As with ticket evasion, there is thought to be a good chance of being 'let off with a warning' though the majority are thought to be prosecuted. Figures for the actual rates of speeding and ticket evasion are not available, but it is clear that respondents exaggerated the extent of TV licence evasion. About a fifth of TV-owning householders are thought to be without a valid TV licence, roughly twice the actual rate. This tendency to overestimate crime

Table 9.4 Estimated levels of offence, detection, and prosecution, by offence

	Speeding (%)	Ticket evasion (%)	TV licence evasion (%)
Offenders per annum per 100 potential offenders			
0–20	2	59	60
21–50	16	29	33
More than 50	82	6	4
Don't know	1	6	3
Total	101	100	100
Mean	78	22	21
Percentage of offenders caught			
0–20	42	30	22
21–50	44	51	41
More than 50	12	17	36
Don't know	1	1	1
Total	99	99	100
Mean	30	38	53
Percentage of those caught who are warned			
0–20	27	40	70
21–50	42	24	11
More than 50	27	32	13
Don't know	3	3	5
Total	99	99	99
Mean	43	43	18

Weighted data
Unweighted $n = 754$
Percentages may not sum to 100 due to rounding.
Questions: After an introduction specifying the offence,
(a) '. . . out of every hundred (potential offenders), how many would you guess commit this offence in a year, whether they are caught or not?'
(b) 'And how many of these (number at (a)) would you guess are caught?'
(c) 'And how many of these (number at (b)) would you guess are let off with a warning?'

levels has been noted in relation to more serious crime. For example, the *British Crime Survey* generated an estimate for burglary which was almost five times the actual rate.

The estimated detection and prosecution rates reflect the perceived seriousness of the three offences, TV licence evasion being viewed as the most serious of the three and most likely to result in detection. This may also reflect the impact of the recent anti-evasion efforts of the Post Office, which have been widely publicized. Actual detection rates for speeding and fare evasion are not known but respondents overestimated the rate of detection for TV licence evasion. At the time of the survey some 1.8 million households were without valid licences and prosecutions were of the order of 120,000 per annum. Respondents, however, were correct in assuming that few evaders are let off with a warning, prosecution being the usual course. Nearly one in five respondents (18 per cent) incorrectly believed that people are offered the option of a fixed penalty for this offence, with slightly lower estimates for speeding and fare evasion. At the time of the survey, a fixed penalty for speeding had not been brought into effect but in some parts of the country penalty fare schemes were then in operation.

At this point, respondents were told of the current practice of bringing offenders before a magistrates' court, which decides upon an appropriate penalty. For each offence, respondents were then asked to estimate the maximum penalty allowed, and the average penalty actually used. These were 'open-ended' questions, and answers (given in respondents' own words) were coded *post hoc*, entailing multi-coding.

For *speeding*, small minorities mentioned disqualification, endorsement, or a formula related to excess speed; and one in four gave no answer. However, 60 per cent suggested a maximum fine which averaged £147 — only 7 per cent of the sample suggested a maximum fine of £300 or more. In fact, the maximum on conviction in a magistrates' court is £400, with a *recommendation* of £2 per mph over the limit, plus 'penalty points' and optional disqualification. The average penalty *actually* used was estimated at £57, or 39 per cent of the perceived maximum; in 1985 the average fine imposed by magistrates for speeding was £40, but only 14 per cent of our sample gave an estimate in the range £30–£49.

For *TV licence evasion*, about one in six respondents gave no answer, but 79 per cent of the sample suggested a maximum fine level which averaged £267. Only 23 per cent estimated a maximum fine of £300 or more, whereas the maximum fine is in fact £400. The average actual fine suggested was £143 (i.e. 54 per cent of the perceived maximum). Recent fines imposed (January–June, 1985) averaged just over £50, but only 20 per cent of respondents gave a figure in the range of £25–£74. The average fine of £50 imposed by magistrates may understate the level of fines at the time of the survey. The calculation is based on fines imposed in the period before the colour licence fee was increased to £58. Since that time fines may have increased in line with the higher licence fee. Second, it includes fines for monochrome licence evasion which are lower on the whole than for colour licence evasion.

The average fine also disguises wide variations in fine levels throughout the country, some magistrates imposing fines of £100 or more if the defendant is judged to have the means to pay (Softley, 1984). This said, respondents undoubtedly exaggerated the typical penalty imposed by magistrates for licence evasion while underestimating the maximum. In contrast, the results of the *British Crime Survey* suggest that, for the more serious offence of burglary, the leniency of the courts is overestimated (Hough and Mayhew, 1985).

For *ticket evasion*, nearly a third of respondents gave no answer, but 62 per cent suggested a maximum fine level which averaged £95, and an actual fine which averaged £41 (i.e. 43 per cent of the perceived maximum limit). Penalty schemes vary locally, so no easy comparisons can be made, and no published data are available on the actual penalties imposed.

Without correcting any of these beliefs, respondents were asked to rate the penalties used for each offence in terms of 'severity' and the appropriateness of perceived detection efforts. Table 9.5 summarizes these data.

Even though TV licence evasion is presumed to have the highest detection rate, and about half of all respondents thought detection efforts were 'about right', one in four feel that the time and effort committed to detection is inadequate. Also, though the prosecution rate is believed to be higher than for the other offences, as are the estimates of both the maximum and average fines imposed, nearly one in five (18 per cent) regard these penalties as 'not severe enough'. The majority (53 per cent) do regard their estimated levels of penalty as 'about right'; indeed, we should perhaps regard these estimates *not* as drawing on stored knowledge, but as a statement of a 'right and proper' level of penalty. The average estimated penalty for speeding was £57, roughly twice the new fixed penalty of £24 for the offence. It would seem that a sizeable minority of people may view the law as excessively lenient in the case of speeding.

When given the opportunity to recommend changes in penalty procedures, respondents made few suggestions, although 10 per cent recommended an 'on-the-spot fine' for speeding, broadly of the type now introduced. Only 8 per cent recommended heavier penalties for speeding whereas 28 per cent criticized penalties for this offence as being too lenient.

The fixed penalty option

For each of the three offences, the idea of a fixed penalty option was then introduced and a simple scaled reaction was gathered (see Table 9.6).

Table 9.5 Assessments of penalties imposed and detection efforts

	Speeding (%)	Ticket evasion (%)	TV licence evasion (%)
Penalties are:			
Too severe	8	4	16
About right	46	49	53
Not severe enough	28	14	18
Don't know	19	33	12
Total	101	100	99
Detection efforts are:			
Too much	24	9	13
About right	48	55	55
Not enough	22	20	25
Don't know	6	16	7
Total	100	100	100

Weighted data
Unweighted *n* = 754
Percentages may not total 100, due to rounding.
Question: In the section corresponding to each offence,
(a) 'In general, would you say that the penalties used for this offence are too severe, not severe enough or about right?'
(b) 'Would you say that the police and other authorities spend too much time and effort trying to catch people who . . . (commit offence) . . . not enough time and effort, or about the right amount?'

Although the concept seems *less* acceptable for TV licence evasion than for the other offences, the great majority do find it a good idea. Asked for their reasons, most respondents consider that a fixed penalty system would bring about savings of court and police time and paperwork. However, some feel that a fixed penalty 'would not take circumstances into account', and might allow a calculation of economic risk, if it is known in advance. Such a calculation is complex, involving beliefs about detection rates, in addition to the level of the fixed penalty imposed.

Up to this point, no factual information had been provided to respondents; their views had been based upon *their own beliefs* about the prevalence of evasion, the efficiency of detection, the procedures

Table 9.6 Acceptability of the fixed penalty option

	Speeding (%)	Ticket evasion (%)	TV licence evasion (%)
A very good idea	34	27	31
Quite a good idea	45	54	40
Not a very good idea	14	12	21
A very bad idea	4	3	5
Don't know	3	4	4
Total	100	100	100

Weighted data
Unweighted *n* = 754
(Percentages may not total 100, due to rounding).
Question: In the section corresponding to each offence, following an introduction relating to that offence, 'From this card, could you tell me what you think about that idea?'

followed, and the maximum and average fines imposed. In many respects these beliefs are *wrong*; evasion is overestimated by a factor of two and the likelihood of detection is overestimated (at 53 per cent of offenders). The average fine imposed is estimated at three times the actual recent level (though for reasons noted above the latter figure needs to be treated with caution), but the maximum fine available to magistrates is *under*estimated.

However, respondents do demonstrate reasonably accurate beliefs about current licence costs — the average estimated for a colour licence was £58, which was the actual fee. The level of accuracy may have been heightened by the fact that licence fees had recently risen from £46 to £58 per annum, amidst much public debate. Indeed, 81 per cent of our sample quoted a sum in the range of £40–£64.

At this stage, respondents were informed that the maximum fine for TV licence evasion was £400 (v. their average estimate of £267), but they were *never* disabused of their belief in the actual level of fines (a belief which averaged £143, in contrast to approximately £50 in actuality). True licence fees were also stated for all respondents.

Asked what they thought the fixed penalty should be for anyone failing to buy a *colour* licence, with the benefit of this new informa-

Table 9.7 Recommended fixed penalty for colour-licence evasion

	Total sample (%)
Less than £50	10
£50–£99	9
£100–£149	34
£150–£200	24
£201 or more	18
Don't know	5
Total	100

Weighted data
Unweighted *n* = 754
Question: 'In fact, the sums are now £18 for black and white, and £58 for a colour licence. What do you think the fixed fine should be for everyone failing to buy a *colour* TV licence?'

tion, respondents recommend *on average* a fixed penalty level of £166 — a marginal increase on their estimate of current actual fines (see Table 9.7).

Respondents were also asked to set upper limits designed to encourage take-up of the fixed penalty (rather than opting for court judgement), and lower limits designed to avoid increased evasion. The range provided, averaged across the entire sample, was £89 to £185. The income and social grade of respondents influences their perception of the appropriate penalty. The lowest average limit was £71 (suggested by those at the lowest levels of subsistence) and the highest average ceiling was £208 (by those earning £10,000 or more p.a.). Clearly, ability to pay is a relevant issue: if this is the fundamental reason for evasion of a £58 licence, it becomes a reason for failure to pay a *penalty* of such a scale and prompts the offender to seek court judgement. However, even those who later admitted 'ever' evading a TV licence payment (16 per cent of the sample) suggested a lower limit of £70, below which evasion might increase.

At this stage, respondents were asked a series of questions based on different penalty-level propositions. Half of the sample was asked about fines of £50, £100, £150 and £200, while the other half received these questions in reverse order. *For each penalty-level* suggested, respondents were asked to make two estimates:

Table 9.8 Anticipated evasion rates at alternative fixed-penalty levels

	Mean percentage estimates at:			
	£50 (%)	£100 (%)	£150 (%)	£200 (%)
Anticipated total evasion	56	31	23	18
— Expected to pay fixed penalty	52	26	16	11
— Expected to seek court judgement	4	5	7	7

Weighted data
Unweighted *n* = 754
Question:

(a) 'Thinking of every *hundred* households which *should* have a *colour* television licence, how many of them might *not* buy a licence if they knew that the fixed fine, if caught, would be £x?' If necessary say: 'Just a rough guess will do.'

(b) 'And if all of those . . . (number at (a)) . . . people were caught, how many of them would simply pay the fine of £x, rather than go to court?'

1 Of every 100 households which *should* have a colour licence, how many might not buy one?
2 If all of these were caught, how many would simply pay rather than go to court?

Of course this simple table disguises the range of answers offered; for example at a £50 fine level, 19 per cent of respondents felt that *everyone* would avoid, but at a £200 fine level, 15 per cent felt that *no-one* would avoid buying a TV licence.

Even so, the internal logic of these summary data is impressive, implying that as fine levels increase, evasion falls and the proportion of those caught likely to opt for court judgement increases. At the lowest fixed penalty level, the latter are perceived as a hard core of financial hardship cases unable to pay the penalty, while the more 'calculating' element (those who would pay the fixed penalty) dwindles rapidly as the penalty increases. However, these estimates are given in the context of current (mostly mistaken) beliefs, and to transfer the relationships between penalty levels and expected behaviours into the real world involves several questionable judgements; indeed, we might debate whether such a transfer is even necessary, if behaviour is founded on beliefs rather than fact.

Clearly caution is needed in interpreting these findings, not least because research questions encourage a rational response and a tendency to ignore other inhibiting factors. It is the calculating component of evasion which is thus likely to be exaggerated. Even so, a fixed penalty below the current perceived average fine of £143 seems likely to offer significant encouragement to evade on economic grounds, while a penalty set as high as £200 only marginally reduces expected evasion below current perceived levels. A penalty of this scale would tend to be viewed as out of proportion to the nature of the offence and would run the risk of increasing enforcement costs and imprisonment in default.

At various points, and in various ways, evasion amongst the sample was tested. The more oblique attitudinal tests tend to reveal minorities of a size which corresponds with known evasion (e.g. 10 per cent 'agree strongly' that 'Not buying a TV licence isn't really breaking the law'), but direct questioning, even towards the close of a reassuring interview, proved unsuccessful. Though 16 per cent then admitted to 'ever' evading (compared to 7 per cent in the broader context of the *British Crime Survey*), only 2 per cent admitted *current* evasion.

The profile of those admitting 'ever' evading (an unweighted sample of 131 downweighted to 188, which suggests that the intentional ACORN skew had marginally increased the representation of evaders) is distinctively male, young and at the lowest levels of subsistence compared to the total sample. Other analyses suggest that they are more likely to be council tenants, to live in a flat in a block, and to have occupied their home for a relatively short time.

Though evaders are difficult to identify directly by research questioning, it seems likely that multivariate analysis of the various approaches adopted might reveal a group with a high probability of being current evaders; on this issue, unlike many other offences, there is the distinct research advantage that the size of the target group can be estimated with a degree of accuracy.

The main task of this research was to assist in examining the viability of a 'fixed-penalty' scheme for TV licence evasion. Perhaps its main benefit was to reveal the level of public ignorance of the procedures and fine levels associated with this offence, and thus to stress the importance of public *beliefs* (as opposed to 'knowledge', which may be no more than a coincidently correct belief), as a control mechanism. The widespread *beliefs* about prosecution and fines imposed seem to suppress calculated evasion (though social factors under-recognized by research techniques must also contribute), allowing the courts latitude to deal sympathetically with genuine hardship cases while heavily penalizing those who have the means to pay.

However, the dangers indicated of a rise in calculated evasion (estimated at a cost in revenue of c.£10 million per percentage point increase), would be a very high risk compared to possible savings of court time on a current rate of 100,000 prosecutions per annum, 98 per cent of whom plead guilty by post. Even a relatively *high* fixed penalty would simplify the calculation of economic risk for those prepared to indulge in such a gamble, even if they are otherwise misinformed, and would certainly not reduce genuine hardship appeals to the court.

Note

1. ACORN: A Classification of Residential Neighbourhoods. This is a 38-cluster solution based on 40+ Census variables, identifying 11 'area types' (A–K) described briefly below:
   - A Agricultural area
   - B Modern family housing, with higher incomes
   - C Older housing of intermediate status
   - D Poor quality older terraced housing
   - E Better-off council estates
   - F Less well-off council estates
   - G Poorer council estates
   - H Multi-racial areas
   - I High-status, non-family areas
   - J High-status inter-war housing
   - K High-status retirement areas

References

Hough, M. and Mayhew, P. (1985), *Taking Account of Crime: Key findings from the 1984 British Crime Survey*, Home Office Research Study No. 85, London: HMSO.

Jones, S. and Levi, M. (1983), '*Police–Public Relationships*', unpublished research study, University College, Cardiff.

Justice (1980), *Breaking the Rules*, London: Justice.

Levi, M. and Jones, S. (1985), 'Public and police perceptions of crime seriousness in England and Wales', *British Journal of Criminology*, **25**, 234–250.

Softley, P. (1984), 'TV licence evasion', *Home Office Research and Planning Unit Bulletin*, **18**.

Sparks, R., Genn, H. and Dodd, D. (1977), *Surveying Victims*, London: John Wiley.

Walker, M. (1978), 'Measuring the Seriousness of Crimes', *British Journal of Criminology*, **18**, 348–364.

10 Tolerance of leniency and severity in England and Wales

Nigel Walker, Mike Hough and Helen Lewis

How punitive is the English public? Answers have varied, mainly because methods have varied, but also because the question is too simple. Is 'punitiveness' something that can be measured along a single parameter? The very diversity of the questions that have been cited as evidence suggests otherwise. They can be grouped according to their apparent objectives.

Choosing questions

Opinion polls concerned with sentencing have used many kinds of questions, with objectives which can be roughly classified into six groups:

A Ascertaining respondents' views about the main *aims* which sentencers should have: e.g.

> 'Do you think this is one of the things they (sc. sentencers) should be trying to do?' (Durant et al. (1972), offering seven choices but without 'Don't know'.)
>
> 'What should be the first concern of the Courts in sentencing a criminal?' (Gallup, 1982, 1986, offering three choices plus 'Don't know'.)

Durant et al., who very properly allowed their respondents to vote for more than one of the seven aims they offered, found that 97 per cent voted for (F) 'making criminals pay what they can for any loss of property or damage they have caused'; but that a very similar percentage voted also for (G) 'making criminals pay what they can for the suffering or loss of earnings they have caused when they injure people' (96 per cent), for (B) 'putting the criminal himself off committing crimes again' (95 per cent) and for (E) 'reforming criminals . . .' (94 per cent). Rather fewer voted for (A) 'showing other people what would happen to them if they broke the law' (84 per cent), for (D) 'making criminals suffer for what they have done' (78 per cent) and for (C) 'looking after people's property and safety by locking criminals away' (also 78 per cent). If 'punitive' is interpreted in the strict sense of 'wanting sentencers to achieve retribution' (or "just deserts") then three-quarters of the respondents were punitive. If it also includes 'wanting sentencers to inflict deterrent penalties', 95 per cent were punitive (96 per cent if G is included). But nearly all of them must also have voted for the reparative aim (F).[1]

The Gallup question was simpler and more clearly distinguished deterrence and retribution:

	1986	1982
	%	%
To punish him for what he has done to others	41	41
To do what they can to reclaim him as a good citizen	14	16
To punish him to stop others from following his example	41	38
Don't know	4	5

Both Durant's and Gallup's questions are open to the criticism that they make an assumption which is almost certainly false: that respondents' choices of aims would be the same whatever the type of offence. It seems more likely that their choices would depend on the seriousness with which they regarded the offence. They might also depend on what respondents are told about the offender. For example, respondents might be more likely to choose a reformative aim when the offender is young, or has been convicted for the first time. We know of no survey that has thoroughly explored this aspect.

B Ascertaining whether respondents are in favour of a *specified form of penalty*, e.g.

> 'Should we continue to do without the cat or should we bring it back?' (Gallup, 1982, 1986, offering two choices plus 'Don't know'.)
>
> 'So far as damage to property is concerned, do you think it would be best to make them (sc. criminals) pay in cash, or, where possible put them to work themselves on repairing the damage?' (Durant et al. (1972) offering five choices, plus 'Other' and 'Don't know'.)
>
> 'In a few areas fare evaders are offered the option of a fixed fine. From this card could you tell me what you think about that idea?' (British Market Research Bureau (1985), offering four choices, plus 'Don't know'.)

If 'punitive' means hankering for capital or corporal penalties, irrespective of the reason, Gallup polls suggest that a majority of respondents fall into this category.

C Ascertaining respondents' reactions to *their impressions of the courts' sentencing policy in general*, e.g.

> 'In your opinion, do the courts give out sentences that are too short or too long to persons convicted of committing crimes?' (Gallup, 1982, 1986, offering three choices plus 'Don't know'.)

The question seems to be confined to custodial sentences. In 1986 76 per cent of respondents replied 'too short' (67 per cent in 1982), only 3 per cent said 'too long' (5 per cent in 1982) and only a few more, 7 per cent, said 'about right' (11 per cent in 1982). Interestingly, a realistic 14 per cent (17 per cent in 1982) confessed that they didn't know.

D Assessing respondents' *confidence in the machinery of sentencing*, e.g.

> 'Do you think it is right or not that the magistrate or judge is the person who decides the sentence?' (Durant et al. (1972), offering four choices plus 'Other' and 'Don't know'.)

	(%)
Right	80
Not right	13
Right for judges but not magistrates	5
Right for magistrates but not judges	1

This indicates a fairly high level of acceptance of the sentencing system.

E Ascertaining what *sentence* (or more often type of sentence) *respondents would choose for a specified type of crime*. The degree of specificity varies greatly. Shaw (1982) for example, asked simply about 'burglary', 'shoplifting', 'vandalism' and 'confidence tricks' without describing the notional offender. The 1984 *British Crime Survey* (Hough and Mayhew, 1985) specified either a 17-year-old offender or a 25-year-old offender with previous convictions: some information of this sort is preferable, since even reports of sentences in news media usually provide such information. Few details, however, were given about the offences themselves: fewer than in most newspaper reports. Walker and Marsh (see Chapter 3) aimed at both specificity and realism by presenting information about offences in the form of faked newspaper cuttings, on the assumption that this would elicit more valid responses than would presenting the same information in short 'stories': an assumption which, though reasonable, needs testing (see our findings under 'Methodological lessons').

F Ascertaining respondents' reactions to *sentencers'* choices of sentences for particular offences. Since reading or hearing about sentences actually passed is the only real-life situation in which most members of the public have an opportunity to consider sentencing policy, it is remarkable how seldom questions of this type are included in surveys, even those expressly concerned with punitiveness. Durant et al. (1972) and Shaw (1982) for example, did not use them. In Canada, Doob and Roberts (Chapter 6) asked respondents whether a sentence passed on a case that had received some publicity was 'too harsh', 'about right' or 'too lenient' (with the interesting finding that respondents who saw only the newspaper report were much more likely to choose the 'punitive' phrase 'too lenient' than respondents who had been given more information about the offence and the offender than was provided in the newspaper). As we shall show, however, 'too harsh' or 'too lenient' are probably too crude: respondents should be offered at least two sub-divisions of each: 'much' or 'a little' too harsh (or too lenient).

The assumption underlying all such questions is that the answers have a message of some sort for sentencers or policy makers. This is not to overlook the possibility that designers of such questionnaires may also, or instead, be trying to satisfy a sociological or psychological curiosity about the sorts of people who give certain kinds of answer, or about the mental processes which lead to different kinds of answer. The purpose of this chapter, however, is to consider what sorts of questions are most likely, or ought to be most likely, to be considered relevant by those who pass sentences or have an influence on passers of sentences.

From this point of view, questions which ask people what sorts of sentence they would choose, whether for a loosely specified kind of offence or for a particular offence, seem likely to yield answers of only limited validity or value. They require respondents to arrive at a decision with which they have never been faced, unless they happen to be sentencers or probation officers, and to do so within an extremely short space of time, usually well under a minute. Even if they are supplied with a list of ready-made choices of a realistic kind, they are not usually supplied with as much information about the offence and the offender as sentencers are given. Yet even if they were given it, as they were in Doob's experiment, this would not put them in a more realistic situation: if anything it would be less like real life.

For in real life the great majority of respondents are faced with information about sentencing in a very special form. They do not see judicial statistics, Home Office circulars, practice directions or reports of cases decided in the Court of Appeal (Criminal Division). Nor do they study books on sentencing. What they see are newspapers, and what they read in them are reports of trials (or guilty pleas) and the resulting sentence. These contain varying amounts of detail about particular offences. They usually give the age of the offender, and if he has previous convictions this information may be included. It is only occasionally that the news media report statements about policy, as when in February 1986 the Lord Chief Justice proposed a tougher tariff for rapists, followed a few weeks later, by the Home Secretary's White Paper proposing higher maxima for certain types of violent crime (Home Office, 1986).

This suggests that, for policy makers, questions which put respondents in artificial situations are less likely to yield valid answers than questions about what they are in the habit of seeing in the news media. If there are such things as public attitudes to sentencing they must be attitudes towards what they are told about sentencing; and what tells them is usually the typical newspaper, television or radio report of a particular case.

Finally, how much weight should policy makers or sentencers themselves attach to respondents who choose sentences which are less or more severe than the courts', or who rate courts' sentences as too severe or too lenient? Should such expressions of disagreement be interpreted as serious disapproval, or merely as mildly critical armchair views? Is it sensible to attempt the 'fine-tuning' of sentences so as to accord with the views of the public? These were some of the issues which our survey set out to explore, along with the other methodological points we have raised. (Other aspects of public reactions to crime were also studied in the survey, but are the subject of the next chapter.)

The survey

The survey was financed by the Home Office, designed by the authors and carried out by the professional staff of NOP Market Research Limited[2] in 81 constituencies of England and Wales, during late February and early March, 1986.

The sampling frame used was adapted from NOP's Random Omnibus Surveys, whose 180 constituencies are selected with a probability proportional to size from a list of all constituencies stratified by region, urban mix and social class; half of the selected constituencies in England and Wales were used. The sample size was 1,249 adults drawn from the Electoral Registers, with 21 names selected for each sampling point (23 names in the GLC area, to adjust for the greater non-response rate there); where the named elector had moved, a substitute was selected using a Kish grid. A pilot survey was carried out in February 1986; and face-to-face briefings were arranged for all interviewers. The response rate was 75 per cent. Numbers and percentages have been weighted to correct for differences in the chances of selection between original and substitute respondents, in those cases where the named elector had moved.

By an unforeseeable mischance the fieldwork coincided with an unusual amount of media attention to sexual crimes and sentences for them. Two days before fieldwork began, the Lord Chief Justice issued guidelines for the tougher sentencing of rapists, which received considerable publicity. While the interviews were in progress, several sexual attacks achieved notoriety. A vicar's daughter was raped and her family beaten up in their home. A man charged with the sexual murder of Leonie Darnley was acquitted but sentenced to life imprisonment for other serious sexual offences. Towards the end of the interview period, statistics were published showing marked increases in the countrywide incidence of rape, and especially in London. It was of course impossible to assess the extent to which these events influenced the replies of our respondents, but in what follows we have not overlooked this problem.

Crime as a topic of discussion

The survey was introduced to potential respondents not as being about 'crime' but as being about 'social issues'. We were therefore surprised to find that the most frequently discussed topics were 'the level of crime' and 'sentencing criminals' (see Table 10.1).

No less than two-thirds of our respondents said that they discussed 'the level of crime' very or fairly often, and well over half claimed to discuss 'sentencing criminals' with similar frequency. 'Inflation' and the 'National Health Service' were rather poor seconds. 'Strikes and industrial relations' came in fourth with 'road accidents' not far behind. 'Nuclear energy' was 'rarely' or 'never' discussed by nearly two-thirds (we wonder what the frequencies for it would have been if the survey have been conducted a few months later after the Chernobyl disaster). No doubt the frequencies for 'the level of crime' and 'sentencing criminals' would have been lower if the Lord Chief Justice's pronouncement and the other events described had not been publicized at the time. Yet the findings are consistent with those of Gallup about the salience of crime as a social problem, described in this book's introduction. Seventy per cent of our respondents said that crime had come up as a conversation with family or friends within the last week, and there can be no

Table 10.1 Frequency of discussion of various topics

	'Very often' (%)	'Fairly often' (%)	'Occasionally' (%)	'Rarely' (%)	'Never' (%)	Total (%)
Nuclear energy	3	10	27	34	27	100
Inflation	20	29	27	16	8	100
The level of crime	31	36	23	7	3	100
Strikes and industrial relations	18	31	32	12	7	100
Sentencing criminals	26	28	29	14	4	100
Road accidents	10	25	39	21	6	100
The NHS	20	25	31	17	7	100

Weighted data
Percentages do not sum to 100, due to rounding
Question: 'I am going to read out a list of topics. Please tell me, using a phrase from this card, how often you discuss each topic with your friends or family. Could you tell me how often you discuss . . . ?'

doubt that nowadays crime and sentencing are problems in the forefront of most people's minds.

Attention to media reports

Was this concern associated with the impression made by media reports of particular cases? Respondents were asked, a few questions later, 'Can you remember any court cases about crimes you have heard or read about recently?' and if they said 'Yes' were asked what the case was about, whether it was a local one, and how long ago the trial had taken place. Finally they were asked what the sentence was. Only half (54 per cent) could recall a recent case. The percentage was larger (61 per cent) among those who had told us that they discussed sentencing 'very' or 'fairly' often, and lower (45 per cent) among those who discussed it less often. Of those who could recall a recent case, only three-quarters could recall its outcome, whether this had been an acquittal (14 per cent), a sentence (46 per cent) or the fact that a verdict or a sentence was still pending

(14 per cent). When asked whether they had been shocked or surprised by a recent sentence only 46 per cent had been either 'shocked' (28 per cent) or 'surprised' (18 per cent). Most (80 per cent) of these respondents gave the leniency of the sentence as the reason: only 12 per cent gave severity as the explanation. A few others referred to such matters as inadequate compensation orders, disparate sentences for co-defendants or the avoidance of punishment by pleas of insanity (which in actuality are very rare).

The main aims of sentencing

Next we asked 'What do you think should be the main aims of the courts when sentencing someone?' Mindful of the criticisms we have made of Durant's and Gallup's questions, we specified sentencing for 'a crime like burglary or robbery'[3] and drafted the choices offered in terms which distinguished as clearly but colloquially as possible between aims such as deterrence, general or individual, retribution, reparation and — since symbolic theories have been resurrected recently — expression of public disapproval. We placed no limit on the number of choices which each respondent could make.

As Table 10.2 shows, the most popular choice was just deserts. The 44 per cent who chose it is much closer to Gallup's 41 per cent than to Durant's 78 per cent, although it must be remembered that her sample was interviewed 20 years ago. Deterring the offender came next, but with compensation, reform and incapacitation very close behind. Symbolic theory was not popular. Least popular was 'making the victim happier', perhaps because it overlapped in respondents' minds with compensation or just deserts; but that is speculation.

General knowledge and beliefs about sentencing policy

Another group of questions was concerned with respondents' beliefs about sentencers and sentencing. They were asked how much attention judges and magistrates should pay to what the public thinks when making up their minds about sentences. 'A lot' said half (47 per cent); 'some' said a third (34 per cent); but a fifth (19 per cent) said 'very little' or 'none'. Yet those who thought sentencers were 'in touch with what ordinary people think' were in the minority (35 per cent).

Not many, however, were well informed about sentencing practice. The majority underestimated the percentage of adult burglars who are sent to prison: two-thirds thought that only a third were, although the true fraction is a half. Again, though courts imprison about a half of drivers who cause death by reckless driving, three-quarters

Table 10.2 Respondents' choices of the main aims of sentencing for crimes like burglary or robbery

Choices in showcard order	(%)
'To scare offender so he won't do it again'	33
'To scare other people so they won't do the same thing'	17
'To reform the offender'	28
'To give the offender what he deserves'	44
'To show that the public disapproves of what was done'	17
'To compensate the victim'	31
'To make the victim feel happier'	6
'To put the offender where he can't do any harm'	29
'For some other reason (Please state)'*	7
(Don't know)†	2

Weighted data
Question: 'What do you think should be the main aims of the courts when sentencing someone for a crime like burglary or robbery?'

*For example 'to find out why he did it'. But a few respondents had clearly failed to understand the question.
†This option was not listed on the showcard.

of our respondents put the fraction at a third or less; and most of the three-quarters said 'very few'. What is interesting is not their ignorance, since only those who know their way around the supplementary volumes of *Criminal Statistics* are in a position to know the right answers. More to the point is the fact that most respondents underestimated the courts' use of imprisonment. As for what a prison sentence really means in terms of time spent inside, most respondents seemed well-informed about remission: 41 per cent knew that this reduced the time by one third, and another 30 per cent gave only slight underestimates. In strong contrast, however, was respondents' ignorance about parole. Fully 42 per cent did not think that a prisoner given a six-year sentence could be released before serving four years; 23 per cent 'didn't know'; and only 11 per cent gave roughly correct answers. Whether it is desirable that the public should be better informed about the effect of parole is an interesting question, but beyond the scope of this chapter.

Impressions of courts' policies

Before presenting respondents with 'cases' we asked them what they

Table 10.3 Views on the adequacy of court sentences for selected crimes

	Rape (%)	Mugging (%)	Burglary (%)	Shoplifting (%)
Too soft	90	87	54	17
About right	6	7	34	50
Too tough	1	1	1	15
No opinion either way	2	3	7	12
Don't know	1	2	4	6
	100	100	100	100

Weighted data
Question: '... can you tell me using one of the phrases from this card what you think of the sentences that courts generally give for [crime]?'

thought of the sentences that courts generally give for burglary, rape, shoplifting and mugging, offering them five choices of reply, with the results shown in Table 10.3.

Where the two crimes of violence — rape and mugging — were concerned, overwhelming majorities thought courts were too soft (although again it is possible that the recent pronouncements by the Lord Chief Justice and the Home Secretary had temporarily inflated the majorities). In the case of burglary there was a majority for 'too soft', though a narrow one. Only in the case of shoplifting did more than a negligible number think courts 'too tough'; and just as many thought them 'too soft'.

Reactions to examples of sentencing

We then presented respondents with specific sentences for particular offences of these — and other — kinds. They were given six stories, based loosely on cases reported in the press in recent years, but with important details tailored to fit the experiment. All the offenders were said to be adult males, of ages varying from 22 to 26, and in all cases a similar previous conviction was mentioned. In four-fifths of the interviews the story was presented in the form of a faked newspaper cutting (see Figure 10.1). The sentence which the offender was said to have received was systematically varied on a Latin square design, so that each story was presented with four different sentences to four sub-samples of interviewees, and in a

SHOPLIFTER QUEUED ALL NIGHT FOR SALE

SO KEEN was Peter Simpson (26) to get an overcoat at Lewis' sale that he was at the head of an all-night queue. Store detectives told the court that in the confusion of the opening minutes he was seen to put the coat on and walk out while the end of the queue was still pouring in.

Simpson, who had a previous conviction for shoplifting, was sent to prison for 6 months at Marylebone Court yesterday.

Tattoo gives rapist away

A GIRL'S NAME tattooed on his hand identified Evan Pritchard (25) as the man who raped a young housewife at knife-point in the garden of her house as she was returning from shopping.

Pritchard, who had a previous conviction for attempted rape, was put on probation for 2 years at the Crown Court yesterday.

Traffic Warden catches phone vandal

A TRAFFIC WARDEN waiting to use a phone box saw Nicholas Thompson (22) smashing the receiver inside.

Thompson, with a previous conviction for criminal damage, was ordered to pay £263 compensation.

Bag-Snatcher breaks Woman's arm

A woman's arm was fractured in two places when she was knocked down and robbed of her handbag in a well-lit car-park at Sainsbury's Supermarket.

Clive Skelton (26), with a previous conviction for attempted robbery, was sent to prison for 4 years at the Crown Court today.

JOY-RIDER RAN OUT OF PETROL

Though he knew how to start a Metro without the ignition key, Barry Wright (23) did not notice that the one he had 'borrowed' to get him home was almost out of petrol. The police found him stranded at 2am near Wicken.

The magistrates were told that this was Wright's second offence of taking a car without the owner's consent, and sent him to prison for 6 months.

Burglar heard in attic

Ray Fairbrother (22) had reached the attic of the house he was burgling when the owner returned unexpectedly.

Hearing noises overhead she telephoned the police, who were waiting for him at the foot of the stairs.

Fairbrother, who was convicted of another burglary two years ago, was ordered to do 40 hours' community service by the Crown Court last week.

Figure 10.1 Facsimiles of the 'newspaper cuttings'[4]

different order. (For the way in which a fifth sub-sample was used, see 'Methodological lessons'.) The sentences were chosen from what seemed, according to the *Criminal Statistics, England and Wales,* to be more lenient or severe than the most common sentences for the types of offence concerned. Thus each of the stories was presented to one or other of the sub-samples with a sentence which was, by the courts' standards, very severe, mildly severe, or lenient in one of two ways which we shall discuss. They can be studied in one of the four versions in Figure 10.1, and the way in which they were varied for the four main sub-samples can be studied in Table 10.5.

The lenient sentences

Choosing the severe sentences gave us less difficulty than choosing the lenient ones. Obviously the former had to be terms of imprisonment, and their lengths could be determined by looking at the tables in the *Criminal Statistics, England and Wales* which showed the terms used by the Crown Court or magistrates' courts, as the case might be. The lenient sentences presented more problems. For four of the offences — shoplifting, joy-riding, burglary and vandalism — non-custodial disposals seemed to be indicated. We chose fines of £50 for the shoplifting and £75 for the joy-riding (fairly common sums), and a compensation order of £263 for the vandalized public telephone, and a short community service order for the burglary (a common disposal for a petty, unaggravated burglary). We also decided to use a two-year probation order (a common length) for all six offences, in order to see how our respondents reacted to probation. It was not unrealistic to present a rapist or bag-snatcher as being put on probation: it is the one non-custodial disposal which is regularly, though not frequently, used for such offences.

Ranking penalties

What we could not be sure of was that a probation order would be regarded by all respondents as more *lenient* than, say, a fine or a community service order. We knew from the Walker–Marsh survey (1984) that when respondents are asked to rank common penalties in order of severity they vary greatly when they come to probation, community service and suspended sentences. This was confirmed when we asked our respondents to rank the same list of penalties.[5] The variety of rankings was even more striking than in the Walker–Marsh survey, perhaps because some of our respondents were younger. 1,215 respondents found 203 ways of ranking the seven penalties. As always, some of the rankings were careless, as when a £50 fine was ranked as more severe than a £100 one. Excluding rankings used by very few respondents reduced the variation to some extent:

Excluding	*Number of remaining rankings*
Rankings used by not more than 1 R	86
Rankings used by not more than 2 Rs	65
Rankings used by not more than 3 Rs	49
Rankings used by not more than 4 Rs	39
Rankings used by not more than 5, 6, 7, Rs	30
Rankings used by not more than 8–13 Rs	20
Rankings used by not more than 14–20 Rs	14
Rankings used by not more than 21–33 Rs	11

We are not implying that all the excluded rankings were merely irrational or unthinking. Even the 11 respondents who ranked a suspended sentence as more severe than 12 months' imprisonment may have been making a deliberate point: that they would prefer undergoing the sentence to having it hanging over them. But in Table 10.4 we have presented only the eleven rankings chosen by at least 40 respondents, omitting all those rankings used by 33 or fewer.

The 11 rankings shown in Table 10.4 account for 51 per cent of the 1,215 respondents whose responses were complete. It is clear from the tables that the main reason for the great variety of rankings is respondents' differing evaluations of suspended sentences, probation and community service. If all of these are omitted, the eleven rankings are reduced to a single one. Otherwise, the only important difference between groups of the rankings in Table 10.4 is that six of them placed fines last, whilst in the other five the suspended sentence, probation or community service were ranked below one or both fines. Omitting probation reduces the rankings to 5, and the effect of omitting the suspended sentence is the same. Leaving out community service is even more effective, since it reduces the rankings to 4, with very large groupings of respondents who differ only in their ordering of probation and suspended sentence. An analysis of this kind underlines Walker and Marsh's point about the superficiality of the practice of calculating mean rankings, which merely serve to disguise complexity, and may even present a ranking order which was actually used by few or even none of the respondents. Methodology apart, our analysis emphasizes that while probation and the other non-custodial sentences used in our stories are of course more lenient than imprisonment in the eyes of sentencers and most respondents, not all respondents regarded probation

Table 10.4 'Toughness' rankings chosen by at least 40 respondents

Penalty	Rank order chosen										
Prison for 12 months	1	1	1	1	1	1	1	1	1	1	1
Prison for 6 months	2	2	2	2	2	2	2	2	2	2	2
Suspended prison sentence	3	4	5	4	3	5	4	7	3	7	7
Probation for 2 years	4	3	4	5	5	3	3	3	4	6	6
Community service for 120 hours	5	5	3	3	4	4	7	4	7	3	5
Fine of £100	6	6	6	6	6	6	5	5	5	4	3
Fine of £50	7	7	7	7	7	7	6	6	6	5	4
Numbers choosing rank order	96	88	55	55	52	40	41	45	51	48	53
As % of total *n* of 1,215	7.9	7.2	4.5	4.5	4.3	3.3	3.4	3.7	4.2	4.0	4.4

Weighted data
Question: 'I would now like to ask you what you think about different sentences people might get for committing a crime. On these cards are seven sentences. Can you sort them into order, with the one that you personally think is the toughest sentence first and the one that you think is the mildest sentence last, and of course the others in between?'

as more lenient than fines or community service.

The point of this is that while it is possible to design an experiment such as ours on the assumption that for the great majority of respondents a longer prison sentence is 'tougher' than a shorter one, no safe assumptions can be made about the relative toughness of non-custodial measures in respondents' eyes. *Each respondent must be categorized according to his or her rating of a sentence as 'tough' or 'soft'*. So after asking the respondents whether anything in particular about the case struck them[6] we asked 'Do you think the sentence (in the story) was too tough, too soft or about right?'. (Answers of 'don't know' or 'not enough information' were accepted, but accounted for a negligible 1 per cent of responses). If the response was 'too tough' or 'too soft' the respondent was asked whether he or she meant 'much' or 'a little' too tough or soft. The results are shown in Table 10.5.

Not unexpectedly, probation was rated much or a little too soft by most respondents for most of the six offences.[7] Only for the shoplifter was there a majority which considered it 'about right' (55 per cent) or 'too tough' (9 per cent). For the joy-rider there was a bare 50 per cent which rated it about right, and 49 per cent

Table 10.5 Respondents' ratings of the varied sentences in the newspaper cuttings

	Rapist	Shoplifter	Burglar	Bag-snatcher	Joy-rider	Phone vandal
Respondents' choices	probation (%)	probation (%)	probation (%)	probation (%)	probation (%)	probation (%)
'much too tough'	2	1	—	—	—	½
'a little too tough'	—	8	1	½	1	4
'*about right*'	*4*	*55*	*31*	*10*	*50*	*35*
'a little too soft'	6	28	31	22	27	38
'much too soft'	89	9	37	68	22	23
	prison, 1 yr	fine, £50	com.ser. 40hrs	prison, 1 yr	fine, £75	compens., £263
'much too tough'	1	—	—	1	½	1
'a little too tough'	—	1	½	1	1	2
'*about right*'	*4*	*61*	*20*	*34*	*41*	*57*
'a little too soft'	12	26	35	33	33	25
'much too soft'	83	12	45	31	24	15
	prison, 6 yrs	prison, 3 mths	prison, 2 yrs	prison, 4 yrs	prison, 3 mths	prison, 3 mths
'much too tough'	—	5	2	2	—	2
'a little too tough'	½	13	16	14	7	10
'*about right*'	*55*	*56*	*70*	*74*	*57*	*53*
'a little too soft'	16	15	9	6	27	17
'much too soft'	29	11	3	4	10	18
	prison, 9 yrs	prison, 6 mths	prison, 3 yrs	prison, 6 yrs	prison, 6 mths	prison, 6 mths
'much too tough'	½	6	3	9	2	2
'a little too tough'	4	17	17	29	11	7
'*about right*'	*63*	*64*	*71*	*54*	*71*	*57*
'a little too soft'	17	7	5	4	11	19
'much too soft'	16	5	4	4	5	16
Weighted no	1001	991	985	996	996	988

Question: 'Do you think the sentence given (in the newspaper story) was too tough, too soft or about right?' (If the respondent said 'too tough' or 'too soft' he or she was asked 'Is that much too (tough) or a little too (tough)?')

rated it 'too soft'. For the other four offenders, majorities ranging from 61 per cent to 95 per cent rated it too soft. Nor did the other lenient disposals command a lot of support in most of the cases. The shoplifter's £50 fine and the phone vandal's £263 compensation order were approved (or in a few cases rated too tough) by about 60 per cent. Forty hours' community service for the burglar was acceptable to 20 per cent; but 80 per cent considered it too soft. The joy-rider's fine of £75 was approved by 41 per cent, but 57 per cent would have liked something tougher. For the rapist and the bag-snatcher a one-year prison sentence seemed too soft to considerable majorities (95 per cent and 64 per cent). In contrast, all sentences which we had taken from the severe half of the spectrum commanded majorities. Even so, six years' imprisonment for the rapist seemed too soft to 45 per cent, and nine years was not tough enough for 33 per cent. (We could not tell, of course, whether these percentages would have been quite as large without the Lord Chief Justice's published views.) Even for the bag-snatcher prison sentences of four and six years had majority votes.

No doubt there are members of the public who accept sentences as 'about right' because they regard sentencers as the people best qualified to determine them. It will be recalled that we had earlier asked our respondents how much attention judges and magistrates should pay to what the public thinks when making up their minds about sentences; and that about one in five (19 per cent) had said 'very little' or 'none'. We wondered whether this minority was more likely than the rest to accept sentences as 'about right'; but when tested on our cuttings they showed no such tendency. If there are members of the public who feel that sentencers know best, the feeling is not connected with the view that sentencers should pay no attention to what the public thinks.

A demand for action?

Having thus distinguished the respondents who rated the sentence 'about right', from those who expressed some degree of disapproval of it, we asked the latter 'Do you think anything should be done about the sentence in this case, or does nothing need to be done about it?' Not by any means all of the respondents who had disapproved of the sentence thought that something should be done about it:

	Percentage thinking something should be done
'much too tough'	89
'a little too tough'	57
'a little too soft'	56
'much too soft'	93

In short, there was a marked difference between the 'much' and 'a little' responses. Slightly more than half of those who felt that the sentence was 'a little too soft' or 'a little too tough' felt that something should be done; but almost all of those who thought the sentence 'much too tough' or 'much too soft' wanted something done — 89 per cent and 93 per cent respectively.

Drastic action?

But how drastic were the things that respondents who wanted 'something done' had in mind? We had constructed, and piloted, a list of seven possibilities, ranging from the mild suggestion that 'a higher court should be able to correct the sentence' to the drastic proposal that 'the judge or magistrate should be forced to resign'. As a final question about each cutting, the items on this list were read out to the respondent by the interviewer; in each case, the choice was offered of replying 'definitely', 'possibly', 'no' or 'don't know'. The question did not prove hard for many respondents: small percentages, ranging from 1 to 5 per cent 'didn't know'. Larger percentages, ranging from 11 to 30 per cent chose 'possibly'; but for the sake of clarity Table 10.6 shows only those who chose 'definitely', which in any case was what we really wanted to quantify ('possibly' is more akin to 'don't know' than to a firm desire for action).

A 'tolerance measure'

This question proved a very satisfactory discriminator, in two ways. Not only was there a marked, and more or less linear, slope in the frequencies with which the seven 'things' were chosen; the frequencies also differentiated sharply between respondents[8] who used 'much' and 'a little' to qualify 'too tough' or 'too soft'. The 'muchers' were at least twice as likely as the 'littlers' to choose any item. The question thus seems to have proved a useful measure of what might be called public 'tolerance' of leniency and severity in sentencing cases. It is particularly satisfactory at the extreme end, where the percentages choosing Item 7, the forced resignation of the sentencer, were so small that a still more drastic item would probably not have been chosen by more than one or two respondents.

Regarding it then as a satisfactory measure of tolerance, we can detect a difference between the ratings of respondents who thought sentences too tough and those who thought them too soft. 'Too-softers' chose items more often that did 'too-toughers': in our terms they showed less tolerance of the sentences. Not surprisingly it was the sentences for rape which elicited the largest numbers of intolerant responses at the upper end of our scale. Yet even so only 15 per

Table 10.6 Respondents' preferences for 'things that might be done about the sentence'

Order of presentation	Order of preference	Too tough: much	Too tough: a little	Too soft: a little	Too soft: much
		Percentage of respondents thinking an option should 'definitely' be done			
5	'A higher court should be able to correct the sentence'	53	30	34	69
2	'It should be made impossible to give that kind of sentence for this sort of crime'	28	13	23	60
1	'The judge or magistrate should get more training'	37	18	22	39
3	'The judge or magistrate should be told off'	26	10	17	41
4	'An MP should take the matter up in Parliament'	23	5	11	32
6	'The judge or magistrate should be taken off cases of this type'	9	4	8	24
7	'The judge or magistrate should be forced to resign'	2	1	3	10

Respondents' ratings of sentences

Weighted data
Question: 'I am going to go through each of the things that might be done about the sentence, in turn. For each one can you tell me if you think it should definitely be done, possibly be done or definitely not be done?' (The items were then read out by the interviewer.)

cent of the much-too-softers demanded the judge's resignation (interestingly, this was the one case which produced almost as many demands for his resignation from the much-too-toughers: 13 per cent). The idea that he should be 'taken off cases of this type' was more popular with both much-too-softers (34 per cent) and much-too-toughers (25 per cent). The other offence of violence — the bag-snatching — elicited fewer responses at this level of intolerance: evidently probation for it shocked fewer respondents to the same extent. The shoplifting produced the fewest intolerant responses: only half of the 'muchers' thought an appeal should be allowed.

Two-way appeals

An interesting by-product of these findings was the substantial number of too-softers who thought that 'a higher court should be able to correct the sentence'. Over the last two decades there have been tentative proposals — for example by Walker (1969) and Thomas (1972) — that instead of a one-way system which allows appeals against sentence only on the grounds that they are too severe[9] we should, like some other common-law jurisdictions, have one which allows appeals on the grounds of excessive severity *or* leniency. The Donovan Committee (1965) rejected this for the rather simple reason that it would be 'a complete departure from our tradition . . .'; and in 1983 the Home Secretary proposed a compromise: that the Attorney General should be able to refer over-lenient sentences to the Court of Appeal for a pronouncement as to the appropriate sentence, but without alteration of the sentence itself. Even this was rejected by Parliament; and a compromise proposed in the 1986 White Paper *Criminal Justice* (Cmnd 9658) had to be dropped from the 1987 Criminal Justice Bill in order to expedite its passage before the sudden dissolution of Parliament. As Table 10.6 shows, a majority of respondents who thought sentences much too soft were in favour of allowing a higher court to correct them; and if those whose response to this item was 'possibly' are added the majority is even larger.

Statutory minimum sentences

Amongst much-too-softers, however, the most popular course of action seemed to be 'making it impossible to give that kind of sentence for this sort of crime'. This would presumably involve statutory minimum sentences on the lines of penal codes adopted in some US and Continental jurisdictions. It was not very popular however with little-too-softers.

Respondents' views about suitable sentences

One further question enabled us to look at tolerance from a slightly different perspective — respondents' views on what would have been suitable sentences. Those who had rated sentences as too soft or too tough, whether 'much' or 'a little', were asked 'what sentence do you personally think the man should have got?' and they were offered 11 choices, ranging from a 'court warning' to 'prison for over 10 years'. This question was not put to respondents who rated sentences as 'about right'; but if one makes the working assumption that they would have *selected* the sentence to which they *acquiesced*, it is possible to compute views about suitable sentences for each crime story across the whole sample. Table 10.7 summarizes the results of this, showing the percentage of responses in favour of

Table 10.7 Respondents' views on the suitability of custodial sentences, by type of sentence in cutting

	Percentage favouring prison sentence Sentence described in cutting	
	Custodial	Non-custodial
	(%)	(%)
Crime		
Shoplifting	79	21
Burglary	95	66
Vandalism	66	49
Joy-riding	67	54
Bag-snatching	97	89
Rape	100	97

Weighted data
Question: 'What sentence do you personally think the man should have got?' (accompanied by showcard of options).

Note: The question was not asked of respondents who thought that the sentence described in the cutting was 'about right'. These have been counted in the table as favouring the sentence in the cutting.

custodial sentences, according to whether the cutting displayed a custodial or non-custodial sentence.

Table 10.7 demonstrates the degree to which respondents' judgements are shaped by the sentence relayed to them. The effect is most marked for burglary and shoplifting, where 95 per cent and 79 per cent respectively viewed imprisonment as suitable where the cutting described a custodial sentence, in contrast to 66 per cent and 21 per cent for cuttings with non-custodial sentences. Differences were smaller but still marked for the car thief and vandal; for the rapist and the bag-snatcher, however, the stated sentence had little influence on respondents, the great majority of whom chose substantial prison sentences.

We have not dealt in this chapter with the variations in response-distributions which were associated with demographic variables such as age, sex and socio-economic status, or with the type of newspaper read. These are discussed in our next chapter. Already, however, we are in a position to make a number of methodological points, and to sum up some useful findings.

Methodological lessons

The methodological lessons seem to be as follows.

Multi-dimensional nature of attitudes to punishment
A single question, however well designed to elicit respondents' views of sentencing policy, is likely to yield an oversimplified impression: groups of questions are likely to reveal interesting complexities.

Levels of knowledge
Respondents are so ill-informed about sentencing policy that such questions should include specific examples of sentencing for particular types of offence, described in the sort of detail usually provided in newspapers. (To give details of the kind only found in social enquiry reports or similar documents would be unrealistic.) Realism can be maximized by faking newspaper cuttings; but a finding we have not mentioned so far is that this does not seem to be essential. The fifth sub-sample of our respondents were simply told the main features of each story in our cuttings: for example 'a man of 25 stole an overcoat from a shop at the start of their sale. He had a previous conviction for shoplifting. He was sent to prison for 6 months.' The sentences presented were identical with those in the cuttings shown to one of the other sub-samples. Comparison of the two sub-samples' responses to the crucial question 'Do you think the sentence given was too tough, too soft or about right?' showed only slight differences. There seemed to be a tendency for respondents who had been shown cuttings to choose 'about right' a little more often: but if there was such a tendency it was too faint to matter. In short, perfectionists would use newspaper cuttings in preference to an oral story because that is how most members of the public learn about sentences; but they would not get a different picture from the distribution of responses.

Strength of disagreement
It is not enough merely to ask respondents whether they think a sentence 'about right', 'too tough', or 'too soft'. 'Too toughers' and 'too softers' must at the very least be asked whether they mean 'much' or 'a little too tough (or soft)', and preferably also whether they think that anything should be done about the sentence; for by no means all will turn out to think this.

Those who do think that something should be done ought to be questioned further to find out how drastic are the measures that they favour. The quasi-operational[10] scale we used discriminated well between mild and drastic measures, and between 'muchers' and 'littlers', although no doubt it is capable of improvement. Perhaps, for example, we should have included a measure which would have taken the function of sentencing away from judges and magistrates altogether, impracticable as this would be.

Penalty rankings

Asking members of the public to rank even common penalties in order of 'toughness' yields a variety of rankings so great that the statistic called 'mean ranking' is dangerously misleading. When respondents are asked to rank non-custodial measures, a much more complex analysis is necessary.

Substantive findings

Our substantive findings were:

- that the level of crime and the sentencing of offenders are subjects frequently discussed by most of our sample. Whether the frequency was raised by the unforeseeable intervention of the Lord Chief Justice's statement about sentences for rape and the Home Secretary's White Paper, only re-interviewing would tell us;
- yet only about half of the sample could recall a recently reported court case, and less than half had been surprised (18 per cent) or shocked (28 per cent) by a sentence;
- as in most other surveys, respondents underestimated the frequency of prison sentences for burglary (and causing death by reckless driving). Most had a good idea of the extent to which a prison sentence would be shortened by remission, but were ignorant of the effect of parole;
- only a minority — but a fairly substantial one of 19 per cent — thought that sentencers should pay little or no attention to what the public thinks; but only a third thought that sentencers were in touch with what the public thinks;
- when asked about the sentences 'generally given' for rape, burglary, mugging and shoplifting, most respondents said 'too soft'; only in the case of shoplifting did half say 'about right'. Very few indeed said 'too tough'.

The findings of most interest, however, concerned respondents' reactions to the sentences in the six newspaper cuttings:

- even the sentences which had been chosen by us from the severe end of the scale were rated 'about right' by majorities ranging from 53 to 74 per cent;

- sentences chosen from the lenient end of the scale were less likely to be rated 'about right'; this was especially true for the rapist's and bag-snatcher's probation sentences, for the rapist's one-year prison sentence and for the burglar's community service order;
- when respondents thought the sentence too tough or too soft they did not always think that something should be done about it;
- overall, respondents felt that something should be done in less than two-fifths of the cases presented to them;
- when respondents did opt for specific remedies for leniency or severity, the most popular options were an appeal to a higher court and (especially in cases of leniency) making such a sentence impossible. More drastic options, such as the forced resignation of the sentencer, were markedly less popular;
- respondents who thought sentences too soft were more likely to choose any of the offered remedies than respondents who thought sentences too tough.
- those who thought sentences *much* too soft were roughly twice as likely to opt for one of the remedies as those who thought them a little too soft.

Since the sentences in our six cuttings were deliberately chosen as examples not of typical or modal sentences but of leniency or severity, our respondents' fairly high degree of tolerance of them suggests that policy could move some distance *in either direction* without any increase in public intolerance. At the same time, it seems to be leniency which provokes the greater degree of intolerance, and a move in that direction would be more likely to stimulate demands for drastic remedies.

We hope we have demonstrated that estimating the public's *tolerance* of leniency and severity in sentencing is not merely easier but also more realistic than attempting the *fine-tuning* of sentences so as to accord with what an ill-informed majority feel to be the 'right' sentence. Our most interesting findings were: first, that when presented with sentences *deliberately chosen so as to be more severe or lenient than the norm*, very substantial percentages of our respondents accepted them as 'about right'. Second, that tolerance for our lenient sentences was less than for our severe ones — markedly so for the rapist's and bag-snatcher's probation sentences, for the rapist's one-year prison sentence and for the burglar's community service order. Third, that even when a respondent did regard the sentence as too severe or lenient, he or she did not necessarily feel strongly enough to want 'something done about it'. Fourth, that sentences seen as too lenient were more often associated with a desire for something to be done than were those seen as too severe. These findings support the belief that *within limits* substantial percentages of the sentences for common crimes are acceptable to the English public. What we call 'tolerance limits' are not merely a sounder methodological concept than 'fine-tuning' but also of more practical relevance for policy makers.

Notes

1 Shaw (1982) elicited a very different set of responses; but they are not comparable with Durant's, since he asked for the 'main' purpose, allowed only one choice, added 'of sending people to prison' and used 'punish' without distinguishing retribution and deterrence. Not surprisingly, 'to punish' was by far the most popular response.

2 To whom we should like to record our gratitude, not only for the care taken in carrying it out, but also for valuable suggestions for improving the wording and coding of questions.

3 It would have been better still if we had also specified less serious offences for a random sub-sample, to see how this affected the distribution of choices.

4 The versions shown are those presented to one of the sub-samples; but the versions presented to the others differed only in respect of the sentences: see Table 10.5 and the text.

5 We altered it in minor respects, increasing the fine of £40 to £50, and inserting 'for 120 hours' after 'community service'.

6 Fifty-two per cent mentioned the sentence: but the percentage was as high as 88 per cent for respondents who were told that the rapist had been put on probation, and as low as 17 per cent for those who were told that the burglar had been sentenced to 3 years' imprisonment.

7 We should note in passing the small number of respondents who rated probation as 'much too tough'. In the case of the bag-snatcher and the phone vandal only one respondent did so; but in the case of rape eight did so. Half were women. It is possible that they had in some way misunderstood the question, or were being frivolous.

8 Although we have here referred to respondents as 'muchers' and 'littlers', their *responses* did of course vary from one cutting to another. A respondent might reply 'much' in one case and 'a little' in another.

9 Or of course *ultra vires*.

10 A genuinely 'operational' measure would have involved respondents in *doing* something. We could, of course, only ask them what *should* be done — hence 'quasi-operational'.

References

British Market Research Bureau (1985), unpublished questionnaire.

Durant, M., Thomas, M. and Willcock, H. (1972), *Crime, Criminals and the Law: a study of public attitudes and knowledge, carried out for the Home Office*, London: Office of Population Censuses and Surveys.

Gallup (1982, 1986), unpublished questionnaires.

Home Office (annually), *Criminal Statistics, England and Wales*, London: HMSO.

Home Office (1986), *Criminal Justice: Plans for Legislation* (Cmnd 9658), London: HMSO.

Hough, M. and Mayhew, P. (1985), *Taking Account of Crime*, Home Office Research Study No. 85, London: HMSO.

Hough, M. and Lewis, H. (1986), 'Penal Hawks and Penal Doves: Attitudes to Punishment in the British Crime Survey', *Home Office Research Bulletin No 22*, London: Home Office.

Shaw, S. (1982), *The People's Justice: a Major Poll of Attitudes on Crime and Punishment*, London: Prison Reform Trust.

Thomas, D. A. (1972), 'Increasing Sentences on Appeal', *Criminal Law Review*, 288ff.

Walker, N. (1969), *Sentencing in a Rational Society*, London: Allen Lane, the Penguin Press.

11 Factors associated with 'punitiveness' in England and Wales

Mike Hough, Helen Lewis and Nigel Walker

Opinion polls have generally indicated that the public would welcome tougher sentences (e.g. Gallup, 1981, 1982; Marplan, 1983; AMSO, 1986) — a theme developed with some enthusiasm by the tabloid press; the more academic surveys in this book have also shown considerable dissatisfaction — in response to questions pitched at a general level — though more concrete questions about specific cases suggest that public opinion and sentencing practice may be less out of step (see Chapters 6, 7 and 8 in particular). Wherever the 'centre of gravity' of attitudes may lie, however, it is self-evident that some people favour much tougher court sentences than most, and others much more lenient ones. The aim of this chapter is to describe some of the factors which differentiate between these two groups and the rest of the public. The results presented here are from a survey carried out in early 1986 with a sample of 1,249 people aged 18 or over in England and Wales. The survey's aim was to assess people's tolerance for sentences of varying severity, and, where people disagreed with court sentences described to them, to measure the strength of feeling behind this disagreement. The main findings, together with details of methodology, are to be found in the previous chapter. But the survey also collected a great deal of information on factors associated with attitudes to punishment, and it is these findings which are the focus of this chapter.

Explaining punitiveness

This chapter equates punitiveness with a belief that court sentences are too soft. In other words, the term is used simply as a shorthand to indicate a preference for heavy sentences — whether for retributive, vindictive, deterrent or incapacitative reasons. Why are some people punitive, while others are lenient towards those who have committed crimes? Several types of explanations can be offered, including those which:

- locate punitiveness towards criminals within broader constellations of attitudes, e.g. arguing that punitiveness is a natural concomitant of a disciplinarian outlook;

- draw attention to demographic correlates, pointing out that members of a particular social or demographic group tend to be punitive;
- make reference to differences in experience and knowledge of crime and criminals; or
- explain punitiveness in terms of emotional responses to crime (such as fear, anxiety, and sense of threat), and in terms of other attitudes towards crime.

The first sort of explanation — locating attitudes to punishment in a broader attitudinal set or ideology — appeals to the idea that our attitudes on different topics are coherently interrelated; and that this consistency can be explained either by psychological theories about personality or sub-cultural theories grounded in sociology. Theories about the 'authoritarian personality' are probably the best known of personality theories which might explain punitiveness (see, e.g. Adorno et al., 1950) — though it should be said that after 40 years of research, there is still no firm agreement amongst psychologists that such a phenomenon exists. There is also a large body of work attempting to chart the existence and correlates of 'conservatism', 'liberalism', 'dogmatism' and similar constructs. Explanations which draw attention to demographic correlates inevitably orientate us to the sociological dimension of attitude formation — and to sub-cultural theories about variations between classes, for example, or generations.

Psychological theories about personality and sociological ones about sub-culture share the assumption that attitudes to punishment can be shaped by factors less directly connected with crime; attitudes to punishment are seen as a reflection of personality, on the one hand, or group membership on the other. But one would also expect people's experience of, knowledge about, and general orientation toward crime and criminals to exercise an effect on attitudes to punishment. And these factors in turn are likely to depend on people's exposure to information about crime, for example via the mass media. For those who have to maintain popular confidence in the criminal justice system, it is of more than passing value to have some feel for the relative explanatory power of these different sorts of factor. Dissatisfaction grounded in experience, for example, demands a quite different response to that stemming from ignorance or misinformation.

Our survey enabled us to put many such explanations to the test. In presenting the results, we look first at simple or 'first order' relationships between punitiveness and explanatory factors of the

Table 11.1 *Attitudes to sentencing, by scores on a discipline scale*

	Punitive (%)	Average (%)	Lenient (%)	Total sample (%)
Discipline Scores				
High	41	33	16	31
Average	44	40	41	40
Low	16	27	43	29
	100	100	100	100

Discipline scale derived from three items ('strongly agree' to 'strongly disagree', 5-point scale);

'A good employer should be strict with his employees'
'School children should be given plenty of discipline'
'Soldiers should refuse to obey orders which they feel are morally wrong'

sort listed above, including the impact of the mass media. At the end of the chapter, we describe the results of multivariate analysis which summarizes these findings and allows some assessment of the relative importance of the different explanatory factors.

Most of the analysis depends on a scale of punitiveness derived from answers to four questions about the adequacy of sentences for four types of crime: burglary, rape, shoplifting and mugging.[1] The individual responses to these questions are shown in Chapter 10 (Table 10.3). The pattern of responses varied considerably by crime. Almost everyone thought that the courts were too soft on rapists and muggers, and just over half felt that they were too soft on burglars. For shoplifting, however, half thought sentences were about right, and only 17 per cent thought they were too soft.

Punitiveness as part of a broad attitudinal set

Time did not allow us to include any of the scales which measures traits such as authoritarianism (such as the F scale); but we included a few items on attitudes to social issues unrelated to crime; three of these concerned the need for discipline — in the workplace, at school and in the army. An additive scale derived from these items correlated positively with the punitiveness scale ($r = .24, p < .01$), and the relationship is shown in Table 11.1.[2]

The table shows that a very small percentage (16 per cent) of punitive respondents showed libertarian sentiments about schooling, work or the military; and an equally small percentage of lenient respondents emerged as disciplinarians. It is not surprising that there should be *some* relationship between attitudes towards discipline in varying social contexts; what is of interest is that of all the variables we examined, the discipline scale turned out to be the *best* predictor of punitiveness — a point to which we shall return later.

Social and demographic correlates

Table 11.2 shows that age and gender are both related to attitudes to punishment. Though age was clearly associated with punitiveness in our sample ($r = .22$, $p < .01$.), we could not tell the extent to which the differences should be attributed to 'aging' or to an 'era effect'. Were the older people simply expressing the unchanged views of earlier generations, or did their greater punitiveness reflect factors which increase with age? Aging may well be associated with a tendency to impatience, to simplification of issues, to pessimism. Certainly it is associated with longer experience, whether of victimization or of learning at secondhand about the victimization of others, or of the success or failure (real or reported) of different approaches to crime. It is also known to be associated with a stronger feeling of vulnerability to crime, whether realistic or not (though Pease, 1988, in the context of judgements of crime seriousness, has also found evidence of an 'era effect'). The results also partially confirm the idea that men are more punitive than women, but, interestingly, the difference between the sexes disappears in middle age.

The bottom part of Table 11.2 shows that punitive attitudes are related to social class and extent of education. Those in social class C who left school at the minimum school-leaving age have the highest proportion of punitive respondents; while the educated ABs have the most lenient.

Knowledge and experience of crime

Victimization

It would be a reasonable guess that direct experience of crime as a victim would amplify punitive attitudes. Surprisingly, neither previous research (e.g. Shapland et al., 1981; Maguire, 1982; Hough, 1985) nor the present survey offers support for this. In fact 9 per cent of victims fell into our 'punitive' category, as against 13 per cent of our non-victims (defined here as someone who said that a crime had been committed against themselves or their household in the previous year); and controlling for education and class, there

Table 11.2 Attitudes to sentencing, by age and sex, and by class and education

		Punitive (%)	Average (%)	Lenient (%)	Total (%)
Age 18–34	Male	6	71	22	100
	Female	2	72	26	100
Age 35–54	Male	15	66	19	100
	Female	5	74	21	100
Age 55+	Male	19	68	13	100
	Female	19	67	14	100
Basic education	Class AB	8	79	13	100
	Class C	14	69	17	100
	Class DE	12	71	17	100
Further education	Class AB	7	58	35	100
	Class C	5	75	20	100
	Class DE	12	63	24	100
Total sample		11	70	19	100

was no discernible difference in punitiveness between victims and non-victims.

One explanation for this finding could be that people with little experience as victims imagine the worst: burglars always ransack and desecrate homes, muggers inflict gratuitous violence, car thieves smash up victims' vehicles, and so on. If this is the case, being a victim would for most people serve to underline the more mundane reality of most crime. Certainly, they might well adjust upwards their estimates of the risks they run — and worry about further incidents — but they may no longer see as appropriate the kinds of tough sentences they might have advocated previously to deal with the offence and offender of their imagination (cf. Chapter 7). Being a victim may thus exercise a moderating influence on attitudes to punishment for the majority of victims; it seems less likely that the same would be true of those rarer crimes which are deeply distressing for their victims — an issue which our survey cannot address (but see Shapland et al., 1981).

Knowledge of sentencing levels

If experience of crime seems unrelated to punitiveness, ignorance

Table 11.3 Attitudes to sentencing, by knowledge of sentencing practices and estimates of crime rates

	Punitive	Average	Lenient	Total sample
% underestimating severity of sentencing for burglary	84	67	53	66
% underestimating severity of sentencing for causing death by reckless driving	86	78	71	77
% thinking more than 10% of households in their area are burgled per year*	48	45	41	44
% thinking more than 20% of crimes are violent*	77	77	75	77

*Respondents offering extremely high estimates of burglary rates and of the proportion of violent crime have been excluded from analysis, on the grounds that they had probably misunderstood the question.

of sentencing practice certainly does play a part. We asked respondents to say what proportion of convicted burglars and those convicted of causing death by reckless driving were sent to prison. Two-thirds of the sample underestimated the severity of sentences for burglars; they guessed that a third or fewer of such defendants go to prison, when the true figure is a half (cf. Chapter 10). As for causing death by reckless driving, 58 per cent thought 'very few' (i.e. well under a third) of those convicted would be sent to prison. Only 11 per cent of the sample chose the correct answer — 'around half' — and a further 12 per cent opted for higher levels. As one might expect, those who underestimated the severity of the courts tended in general to feel that court sentences were not tough enough. Table 11.3 (top two rows) shows that people with punitive attitudes are much more likely than others to underestimate court severity. The offences in these two questions were selected partly for technical reasons: we chose offences where the right answer was around half, so that those who guessed at random had equal chances of overestimating and underestimating. It would be interesting — but more difficult — to chart beliefs about sentencing levels for crimes such as rape and robbery, where the vast majority of offenders receive custodial sentences.

Awareness of particular cases

Asked if they could remember a recent criminal case, 54 per cent of respondents could do so — much in line with Walker and Marsh's finding (see Chapter 3) that 58 per cent could remember 'details about a local or national court case'. Those cases which were mentioned most frequently tended to involve extreme acts of violence, particularly against children and women. (Forty-two per cent mentioned child murders, 11 per cent rapes and 10 per cent incidents of non-sexual child abuse. In contrast only 5 per cent mentioned burglaries.) However, in a large proportion of these cases, it seemed to be factors other than the sentence which were memorable, and indeed 40 per cent of those who said they could remember a recent case could not recollect the sentence passed by the court. We found no evidence that awareness of particular cases was related to punitiveness: a smaller proportion (43 per cent) of the lenient group could relate details of cases than of those in the punitive group (53 per cent); but those occupying the middle ground seemed better informed than both outlying groups, 56 per cent being able to provide details of recent cases.

Awareness of crime risks

Table 11.3 also shows how perceived risk of crime is related to punitiveness. Respondents were asked to estimate the burglary rate in their area: 'Out of every hundred homes around here, how many do you think were burgled last year?' Overall, as was found in the *British Crime Survey (BCS)* (see Hough and Mayhew, 1985), the sample considerably overestimated rates: 47 per cent thinking that more than 10 in 100 houses were burgled and 30 per cent thinking the rate was more than 20 per 100. In reality, the national average is under 3 per cent — approaching 5 per cent if attempts are included — and rates in areas of highest risk, such as the ACORN category of 'poorest council estates' are three or four times higher (Hough and Mayhew, 1985).

As Table 11.3 shows, a greater proportion of punitive respondents gave high estimates of the burglary rate in their area. We cannot say with any certainty whether this relationship reflects *misperceptions* or differences in *objective* level of risk.

Respondents were also asked to estimate the proportion of all crimes which involved violence, 'for example where the victim was beaten up, mugged, raped, etc.'. The average figure was 47 per cent, which only drops 5 percentage points to 42 per cent if analysis excludes the 142 respondents who offered (possibly confused or frivolous) estimates in excess of 75 per cent. This contrasts sharply with crime figures: both *Criminal Statistics* and the *BCS* show that only 5 per cent of offences are crimes of violence, and even on a broader definition which includes common assaults (involving no injury), the *BCS* shows that only 17 per cent of all offences involved violence of this nature. To an extent, the average over-estimation made by our respondents must simply reflect innumeracy; but the findings imply very considerable misperceptions about crime risks. However, we found no evidence that overestimating the proportion of violent crime was associated with punitiveness (see Table 11.3).

Contacts with the criminal justice system

In contrast to victims, one might expect people whose friends or acquaintances include offenders to have a more relaxed attitude towards punishment. Conversely, one might expect those who work within the criminal justice system, and their acquaintances, to be more tough-minded. Our data fail to confirm either hypothesis.

Several things could explain this. With the benefit of hindsight, it is clear that we should have distinguished between offenders and their close friends, on the one hand, and their casual acquaintances on the other, and similarly for people working within the criminal justice system. Nor is it implausible that some law-breakers have split minds about offending, or at least differentiate sharply between their own 'minor' or 'technical' transgressions and those of 'real criminals'. As for the range of attitudes of criminal justice employees, this is far broader than some stereotypes would allow.

Other attitudes to crime and punishment

The final type of explanation for punitiveness discussed at the start of the chapter related punitiveness not to knowledge and experience of crime, but to people's emotional responses to crime and to the value-judgements they make about dealing with the problem. We collected information about people's fear of crime, and also asked them what they thought should be the main aims of sentencing.

Fear of crime

People who are anxious about being victimized are more likely than others to call for stiffer sentences. This is not just because anxiety about crime and punitiveness are both related to age: the relationship still holds when this is taken into account. Table 11.4 shows that

Table 11.4 Attitudes to sentencing, by worry about burglary

		Punitive (%)	Average (%)	Lenient (%)	Total (%)
Aged under 45	Very worried	8	73	19	100
	Average	4	72	24	100
	Unworried	3	68	29	100
Aged 45+	Very worried	19	73	9	100
	Average	18	67	16	100
	Unworried	13	65	22	100
Total		11	70	19	100

regardless of age, punitiveness increases with concern about being burgled; similar findings emerge for a measure where respondents were asked how safe they felt walking alone at night in their area, though the correlation was less marked amongst younger respondents.

Sentencing aims

We asked respondents what they thought should be 'the main aims of the courts when sentencing someone for a crime like burglary or robbery'. Some people's views on the adequacy of sentencing clearly derive from an underlying philosophy about the aims of sentencing; others will offer aims as a justification or rationalization or reaffirmation of their position about the adequacy of sentences. Our survey was obviously unable to resolve this 'chicken and egg' problem. However, the two sets of attitudes were clearly interrelated.

As Table 11.5 shows, retribution and incapacitation were favoured by punitive respondents, while the more lenient stressed the need to reform offenders. In other words, the former tended to favour tariff sentencing, where the punishment fits the crime, whilst the latter were more likely to prefer individualized, rehabilitative sentences. It is worth noting that all groups rated deterrence, both general and specific, as important.

The impact of the media

The findings in the previous two sections have shown that people's views on the adequacy of sentencing are shaped amongst other things by experience and knowledge about crime, and by emotional responses to, and value-judgements about, crime. What part do the mass media play as a source of information?

Table 11.5 Attitudes to sentencing, by views of the main aims of sentencing

	Punitive (%)	Average (%)	Lenient (%)	Total sample (%)
Deterrence	35	40	40	40
Retribution	52	47	27	44
Incapacitation	36	30	23	29
Rehabilitation	13	27	43	28

Note: more than one response permitted per respondent
Question: 'What do you think should be the main aims of the courts when sentencing someone for a crime like burglary or robbery?'

It is notoriously hard for research to disentangle the impact of the media on public opinion. Correlations can quite readily be found between exposure to media and attitudes. But factors related to attitudes about punishment — age and level of education, for example, and social class in particular — are also related to media consumption, and these may explain both attitudes and media consumption. And even where there seems to be a causal relationship, the direction of causality is a problem. It is a truism that people prefer to read those things which confirm their prejudices; and in large part, the prime concern of the media is to maintain readership or audience levels — especially where advertising revenue is at stake. But at the same time, some sectors of the media, and the national press in particular, are not simply commercial enterprises, but set out to shape opinion.

Certainly, our survey showed that for most people, the media were an importance source of information about crime. When asked about their main source of information about crime, 48 per cent mentioned newspapers or magazines, and 43 per cent television or radio. In contrast only 1 per cent mentioned their own experience as one of their main sources. There is a high level of exposure to such sources: 78 per cent of our sample read a daily newspaper five or six times a week, and 82 per cent watched the television news daily.

Our analysis of the media focused on differences in newspaper readership. People who read the quality press, which we defined as *The Times*, the *Daily Telegraph* and the *Guardian*,[3] were slightly

Table 11.6 Attitudes to sentencing, by readership of daily papers and age

		Punitive (%)	Average (%)	Lenient (%)	Total (%)
Aged under 45	Tabloid and/ or local	5	73	22	100
	Quality press	6	63	31	100
	None	6	64	29	100
45 or older	Tabloid and/ or local	19	70	11	100
	Quality press	7	64	29	100
	None	16	68	16	100
Total		11	70	19	100

more likely to remember recent cases than those who read tabloid or local papers, but both groups were more aware of recent cases than the minority who never read a daily paper; of these, only 40 per cent could remember a case, compared with 62 per cent of quality press readers.

The data suggested that there is a relationship between media consumption and punitiveness. In essence, readers of the quality press were more likely than others to have lenient views; those who read tabloid and/or local papers were likely to be more punitive, and those who did not read papers fell in between. As will be seen below, this relationship remained even when other factors such as age, sex and class were taken into account. (It could be argued, however, that our media variable simply measured class, or perhaps educational attainment, rather better than the variables intended to measure these.) Table 11.6 shows the relationship taking age into account; the effect is more marked for people over 45.

Our survey cannot say how much attitudes determined choice of newspaper, and *vice versa*. However, findings on the extent of exposure to papers are suggestive. We asked respondents whether they had been surprised or shocked by recent court sentences. Table 11.7 presents the percentage of respondents saying they had been shocked, broken down both by newspaper preference and by levels of readership. The table shows that avid newspaper readers — especially those who read tabloids — are more likely to be shocked than less frequent readers.

Table 11.7 Respondents' shock at a recent court sentence, by type and frequency of newspaper readership

Type of paper	Percentage shocked	
	Frequent reader	Less frequent reader
Local and tabloid	38	10
Tabloid only	35	29
Local only	32	22
Quality	25	24
No daily paper	21	

Note: Frequent readers are those reading daily papers 5–6 times/week.
Question: 'Have you been surprised or shocked by a court sentence you have heard or read about recently?'

Multivariate analysis and discussion

How much weight should be attached to each of these explanatory factors? To answer this, we carried out a stepwise regression analysis, the results of which are presented in Table 11.8. Given a dependent variable and a number of independent or predictor variables, stepwise regression identifies at the first step the independent variable which best predicts the dependent variable; at step 2 it selects the next-best predictor, taking into account the contribution already made by the first; at step 3 it selects the third most predictive variable, taking into account the contribution of the first two, and so on until it can find no more variables which make a statistically significant improvement to the prediction. In other words, some idea of the comparative explanatory power of different variables can be derived from the *order* in which variables are selected by the stepwise regression. Some caveats should be stated, however. Measurement error, especially in attitudinal research, can reduce the apparent explanatory power of a variable (where a factor is highly explanatory but badly measured). And where two independent variables are intercorrelated, only one is likely to make a significant contribution to prediction, so that the causal significance of a variable may be masked by the predictive power of an intercorrelated — but causally trivial — variable.

The first variable identified by the regression was the discipline scale, derived from items measuring attitudes about the need for

Table 11.8 Results of stepwise regression analysis

Dependent variable: Scale of punitiveness				
Mutiple R	0.42	All variables included in the equation make a statistically significant contribution ($p < .05$)		
Adjusted R squared	0.17			
Variable	Order of entry into equation	Standardized Beta value	Standard error of B	F value
Discipline scale (Higher scores = punitive)	1	.16	.016	35.3
Estimate of imprisonment rate for burglars (Underestimates = punitive)	2	.15	.022	28.0
Age (Older = punitive)	3	.14	.019	23.6
Newspaper reading (Quality = lenient)	4	.13	.112	21.4
Penal philosophy (Retributive = punitive)	5	.10	.059	12.7
Anxiety about burglary (High anxiety = punitive)	6	.08	.032	9.9
Gender (Male = punitive)	7	.07	.058	6.9
Estimate of impris. rate for causing death by dangerous driving (Underestimate = punitive)	8	.06	.021	5.2
Educational level (Basic education = punitive)	9	.05	.023	2.7
Estimate of local burglary rate (High = punitive)	10	.04	.002	2.3

discipline in schools, the armed forces and the workplace. This suggests that first and foremost, attitudes to the punishment of criminals can be explained by reference to broader attitudinal sets, or people's ideologies. In other words, punitiveness (or leniency) tends to be just one expression of a more general disciplinarian (or libertarian) outlook, and will be shaped by the same factors. One implication of this, of course, is that some people's attitudes to punishment will be resistant to any changes which fall within the control of criminal justice administrators.

However, the variable making the second largest contribution to prediction of punitiveness was a measure of ignorance of sentencing: people who underestimated most the imprisonment rate for burglars were most punitive. The analysis also selected the variable measuring the perceived imprisonment rate for causing death by dangerous driving — but later in the stepping process. Within limits, public knowledge on such issues can be improved, and if the need for confidence in the criminal justice system is taken as axiomatic, there is an obvious and pressing need to improve levels of awareness about sentencing practice, and thus reduce the dissatisfactions grounded in ignorance and misinformation.

Of the other factors identified in the regression analysis, it is noteworthy that newspaper choice was selected early (at step 4). As discussed earlier, this does not necessarily mean that newspapers shape attitudes to punishment — though newspaper proprietors and editors might regard as naive the suggestion that they are without impact. Whether newspapers create or simply reflect opinion, a more tractable question here is whether journalists and their masters mount their campaigns about sentencing on the basis of a well-rounded knowledge about court practice, or whether their perceptions *too* are coloured by the notable and newsworthy exceptions.

Anxiety about crime and perceptions of risk, selected by the regression at steps 6 and 10, seem to fuel punitiveness. In so far as anxieties are misplaced and risks exaggerated, these findings lend added weight to calls for fuller and more accurate information not just about sentencing, but about the extent and nature of crime. But it must be recognized that in some parts of the country, particularly in parts of conurbations, risks are indeed substantial; and here, anxieties are unlikely to be allayed in this way.

Notes

1 The punitiveness scale was simple and additive: scores for all four crimes were coded ('too tough' = 3, 'about right'/'no opinion' = 2, 'too soft' = 1), and summed. Where respondents have been assigned to 'punitive', 'average' and 'lenient' categories on the basis of their score on the scale, this has been done in such a way that 11 per cent of the sample fell into the 'punitive' category, and 19 per cent into the 'lenient'. (The aim was to achieve two roughly equal size groups with extreme views, each accounting for about 15 per cent of the sample.)

2 The discipline scale, like the punitiveness scale, was simple and additive. Respondents were offered the following options to the questions shown in Table 11.1: 'Agree strongly', 'Agree', 'Neither', 'Disagree', 'Strongly disagree' — coded 1–5. 'Don't know' was also offered, but in constructing the scale, this was recoded as 'Neither'. Scores for the question about military discipline were reversed, so that agreement scored 5 rather than 1. Scores on the three items were then summed. In Table 11.1, respondents have been grouped into one of three categories on the basis of their discipline score, so that about 20 per cent fall in each of the outlying categories.

3 At the time of fieldwork, *The Independent* had not been launched. A variable including readership of Sunday papers showed no greater discrimination than that which was restricted to dailies.

References

Adorno, T. W., Frenkel-Brunswick, E. M., Levinson, D. J. and Sanford, R. N. (1950), *The Authoritarian Personality*, New York: Harper.

AMSO (1986), *Crime in Britain*, London: Association of Market Survey Organisations.

Gallup (1981), *Gallup Political Index, No. 252, August 1981*, London: Social Surveys (Gallup Poll) Ltd.

Gallup (1982), *Gallup Political Index, No. 260, April 1982*, London: Social Surveys (Gallup Poll) Ltd.

Hough, M. (1985), 'The impact of victimisation: findings from the British Crime Survey', *Victimology*, **10**, 488–497.

Hough, M. and Lewis, H. (1986), 'Penal Hawks and Penal Doves: attitudes to punishment in the British Crime Survey', *RPU Bulletin No. 21*, London: Home Office Research and Planning Unit.

Hough, M. and Mayhew, P. (1985), *Taking Account of Crime: key findings from the 1984 British Crime Survey*, Home Office Research Study No. 85, London: HMSO.

Maguire, M. (1982), *Burglary in a Dwelling*, London: Heinemann.

Marplan (1983), Survey carried out for BBC Broadcasting Research Department, 22–24 August, 1983.

Pease, K. (1988), *Judgements of Crime Seriousness: evidence from the 1984 British Crime Survey*, Home Office Research and Planning Unit Paper, London: HMSO.

Shapland, J. with Willmore, J. and Duff, P. (1981), *The Victim in the Criminal Justice System*, Oxford: Centre for Criminological Research.

Postscript

Nigel Walker and Mike Hough

This collection of surveys from the 1980s emphasizes the multiplicity of angles from which public attitudes to sentencing policy can be studied. Meaningful questions can be put, and sensible answers obtained, about the views of the man or woman[1] in the street on the subject of sentencers and their aims, their practices and the extent to which they are 'in touch' with the public's views; about the budgetary policies of governments and the adequacy of the custodial and non-custodial service they provide; about the meaning of such things as remission and parole; about the effect of sentences on moral disapproval of offences; and about the acceptability of lenient or severe sentences.

Nor is it only 'crimes' about which people can usefully be questioned. Orton and Vennard's chapter (9) demonstrates the good sense of asking about penalties for regulatory offences, which, unlike most crime, arouse no fears and little disapproval. Indeed it is at the other end of the scale that surveys yield less interesting results. Where homicide and rape are in question respondents' views are consistently severe, and it is not easy to find much difference between sub-groups.

At the same time, we may have succeeded in demonstrating some of the complexities underlying the apparently simple question of whether the public wants tougher sentences. People's views on punishment are multi-faceted, and not always internally consistent; there is no shortage of conceptual confusion over terms such as 'punitive'; and these problems are compounded by the technical difficulty of measuring attitudes which tend to be neither well-informed nor well-articulated. Thus, the sentences which people think appropriate vary according to the options offered them: if they are provided with a 'menu' of sentences, responses are more varied (and less weighted towards imprisonment) than if they are left to think of sentences for themselves. Second, as our own survey has shown, preferences seem labile: if respondents are told what sentence the case attracted, their own choice will gravitate towards that sentence. Finally, and most important, choices seem dependent on the amount of information provided about the case. The general rule would seem to be that the more information respondents are given about the offender and the nature of the offence, the more likely they are to select a sentence in line with the courts', or to concur with sentences handed out by the courts; certainly this is suggested by the experiment by Doob and Roberts reported in Chapter 6.

Bearing these points in mind, and at considerable risk of over-simplification, the findings on public punitiveness in the countries covered in this book can be distilled into a number of propositions:

1 Questioned about the *aims* of sentencing, people are not markedly punitive in the sense of 'retributive'; but most support sentencing aims which point toward severity.
2 General questions asking whether sentences are long enough or tough enough consistently show large majorities in favour of greater severity.
3 Respondents generally answer these questions with dangerous, violent and 'professional' criminals in mind.
4 Respondents generally answer these questions in ignorance of current sentencing practice, and tend to underestimate the percentage of offenders sent to prison.
5 Questions about suitable sentences for specified offences and offenders generally show a convergence of public opinion and court practice over the *category* of sentence which offenders deserve.
6 The exception to 5 is murder (and some categories of rape), where majorities are likely to favour capital punishment — at least in the context of questions about the death penalty.
7 Where people advocate prison sentences, they generally suggest sentence lengths longer than those currently served.
8 Where people assess sentences passed in specific cases, the probability of agreeing with the sentence increases with the amount of information provided about the case.

These results illustrate what we have called 'the fine-tuning fallacy': the implication that sentencers should try to adjust their sentences so as to accord as closely as possible with responses elicited in a few seconds of an interview from respondents who are ill-informed and who in some cases may have been induced to express what we have called 'pseudo-views'. We have argued that it would be more realistic, and of more practical interest to sentencers and policy makers, to find out what people will *tolerate* by way of leniency or severity for this or that example of law-breaking, given what they are told about it by the news media; and we have shown how this can be done in such a way as to distinguish genuine intolerance from slight disapproval.

When asking questions about the adequacy of sentences, how specific and detailed *should* the descriptions of offences be? When, for instance, is it sufficient to ask simply about 'burglary'? The answer depends on what one is trying to measure. If all one is trying to do is measure respondents' cynicism about the sentencing of burglars, a general question along these lines will do service. But if one wants to find out whether opinion and sentencing practice are in step, or, as we tried to do, to assess the limits of public tolerance for sentences, respondents must be given a lot more information about the case.

But how much more? If a survey is intended to gauge public confidence in sentencing, there is a case for limiting details to the sort of information which ordinary members of the public get from newspapers, radio or television. To give respondents any more is to put them in a position in which they will not find themselves in real life, where they form their opinions on sentencing. This stricture, however, obviously does not apply when the intention is to assess the 'mechanics' of opinion formation, as in experiments of the kind carried out by Doob and Roberts.

Whatever degree of specificity is aimed at, methodologists are bound to interest themselves in the sensitive technique used by Rossi et al. for varying the contents of offence descriptions (see Chapter 1 under 'specificity'). It seems to be a solution to the problem which confronts the researcher who wants to experiment with the effects of ringing the changes with information about the offender, the type of offence, the harm done and the sentence. The larger the number of variables to be varied the more numerous and smaller must be the sub-samples into which respondents must be divided. Rossi's multivariate approach makes it possible for each individual respondent to be given a unique set of offence descriptions.

On the correlates of attitudes to sentencing, we should sound a note of caution about extrapolating from one country to another. It cannot be assumed that the findings of a survey in country *X* are applicable to the populations of other countries, even if, like the countries represented in this book, their cultures and criminal justice systems have many features in common. For one thing, popular beliefs about sentencing tariffs may differ. For another, what is regarded as severe in country *X* may not be in country *Y*. And one survey hardly ever words its questions in exactly the same way as another (and even where they do, the nuances of language do not travel across geographical boundaries).

One would expect, for example, that differences between the

'punitiveness' of the sexes — more precisely the percentages who opt for the more severe kinds of penalty — would appear consistently in different countries. Yet this does not seem to be so. Brillon, like Stinchcombe in the USA, found no such difference (p. 97). Rossi et al. in Boston found men more 'punitive' than women. John Walker et al. in Australia found the same (p. 156), with the exception that the difference was in the other direction where certain offences were concerned (factory pollution, employer negligence and child-beating). In England and Wales as well, Hough et al. (Chapter 11) found men more punitive than women, with the interesting qualification that the gap closes as people grow older. Worth noting too, was the finding that the sexes were equally punitive where rape was the example in question, a finding which endorses our earlier point that there are a few crimes about which nearly everyone feels so strongly that differences between sub-groups are not discernible. The explanation of these different findings may lie in the types of crime chosen as examples or in the methods of measurement.

Severe attitudes to sentencing seem more consistently associated with increasing age (e.g. Hough et al., Brillon, van Dijk and Steinmetz). But even so, in Boston Rossi et al. found only an association so weak as not be significant, and in Australia John Walker et al. found that age differences did not extend to all offences (stabbing was an exception: p. 156). We can only speculate at present about possible explanations. Brillon suggests that people become more severe in their later years

> because, it seems, the increase in violent criminality has made their image of the delinquent correspond more to that of the dangerous criminal. (p. 98).

Hough et al. found it impossible to be sure whether aging really had such an effect or whether older people have simply acquired their attitudes in earlier and more punitive decades; but they concede that:

> . . . certainly [aging] is associated with longer experience, whether of victimization or of learning at second hand about the victimization of others, or of the success or failure (real or reported) of different approaches to crime . . . (p. 206).

Whatever the explanation, however, aging is not something policy makers or penal reformers can influence.

Education is. The earlier the age at which a man or woman's full-time education ceased, the more likely he or she is to want severity (John Walker et al. p. 154; Hough et al., Table 11.5; Brillon, p. 99). But we do not yet know why the better-educated are less likely to favour severity. It cannot be that they are deliberately taught facts or theories about crime and punishment. Penology is not a popular option, even for sentencers. It is more likely that as a result of their superior education their spare-time reading and selective use of radio and television introduces them to relevant facts (or at least propaganda). Consistent with this possibility is the finding (both in Canada by Doob and Roberts (p. 125) and in England and Wales by Hough et al. (p. 212)) that the news media are the main sources of people's information about crime; and that, in England and Wales at least (Hough et al., Table 11.8) the quality of the newspapers which respondents read regularly is associated with their attitudes to penal severity.

One very consistent finding — and one which common sense would not predict — concerns the direct experience of crime. Being a victim does not seem to make more people want severe penalties (Brillon, p. 109; Hough and Moxon, p. 144; van Dijk and Steinmetz, Table 4.1; Rossi et al.). Why this should be so has not been investigated. A possible explanation is that relatively few respondents have suffered crimes which had grave and lasting effects on them, and that most victims have realized, from personal experience, that most crimes do not inflict great harm, whereas respondents who have not had this experience exaggerate the consequences in their imaginations.

Certainly, ignorance of the nature of crime and of the sentences typically meted out by the courts seems to play a part in shaping attitudes. Chapters 6 and 11 suggest a consistency in popular misconceptions about crime in Canada and England and Wales. People tend to overestimate the proportion of crimes involving (for example) violence, to overestimate the prevalence of crime, and to overestimate the leniency of the courts; and as one might expect, those most prone to such overestimates tend to be punitive in their attitudes.

Where 'fear of crime' is concerned, apparent discrepancies are almost certainly the result of asking different questions. Hough et al. in England and Wales found that high anxiety about burglary is associated with a desire for severity; but Brillon in Canada and van Dijk and Steinmetz in the Netherlands seem at first sight to find no such association. Brillon, however, seems to have had death sentences for homicide in mind; and many respondents are opposed to capital punishment however fearful they are. Van Dijk and Steinmetz were asking respondents about their perceptions about the probability of becoming victims, which is not the same thing as Hough et al.'s 'worry' about being burgled. One may worry about a danger even when one knows the risk is low.

More influential, however, than any of these factors, seems to be one that is less easily named and defined. In Brillon's Canadian samples it was an 'ideology' or 'world view' which favours authoritarian government and believes that women with children should stay at home to look after them, that people today have no respect for anything, and so forth (p. 101). In the Netherlands van Dijk and Steinmetz's data suggest that preferences for preventive or repressive methods of crime control depend more on basic political or ideological preferences than on personal experience of crime (p. 82). In England Hough et al.'s analysis pointed to people's views about discipline and allied topics as the most powerful predictor of their 'punitiveness'.

Adorno would have said that all these measures are diagnostic of the 'authoritarian personality'; and indeed some of them are derived from his measurement scale. We hesitate to use the term 'personality', because it implies that the attitudes in question are immutable, or at least very hard to alter. So far as sentences are concerned this has still to be proved. It is conceivable — perhaps more than conceivable — that they are formed by the ways in which sentencing is reported and commented on by the news media. That would not be inconsistent with the fact that people's ideologies play an important part in their selection of newspapers and periodicals: attitudes can be either reinforced or undermined by the selectiveness of reporting. Nor are we implying that a certain degree of 'cynicism' about the leniency (or severity) of the criminal justice system is necessarily misguided. We are concerned only to describe, explain and suggest improvements in the techniques of surveying.

Note

1 And also, probably, the views of adolescents, but this interesting area has been entered by only a few pioneers.

Name index

Subject index